LEARNING NOT TO BE FIRST
THE LIFE OF
CHRISTINA ROSSETTI

Not to be first: how hard to learn
That lifelong lesson of the past;
Line graven on line and stroke on stroke,
But, thank God, learned at last.

CHRISTINA ROSSETTI
'The Lowest Room'
30 September 1856

BY THE SAME AUTHOR

A Glorious Fame

LEARNING NOT TO BE FIRST
THE LIFE OF
CHRISTINA ROSSETTI

KATHLEEN JONES

OXFORD UNIVERSITY PRESS

1992

Oxford University Press, Walton Street, Oxford OX2 6DP

Oxford New York Toronto
Delhi Bombay Calcutta Madras Karachi
Petaling Jaya Singapore Hong Kong Tokyo
Nairobi Dar es Salaam Cape Town
Melbourne Auckland

and associated companies in
Berlin Ibadan

Oxford is a trade mark of Oxford University Press

First published 1991 by The Windrush Press
First issued as an Oxford University Press paperback 1992

British Library Cataloguing in Publication Data
Data available
ISBN 0–19–282902–5

Printed in Great Britain by
Biddles Ltd.
Guildford and King's Lynn

To David, Peta, Meredith, Sarah and Chris
With love

CONTENTS

PART FOUR : *Tenacious Obscurity*

ACKNOWLEDGEMENTS

Many individuals and organisations have given assistance to the author, granted permission to quote from manuscripts and books, or to reproduce illustrations, and the author gratefully acknowledges their help. Particular thanks must go to Cathy Henderson at the Harry Ransom Humanities Research Center, University of Texas at Austin, George Brandak at the University of British Columbia, David Burnett at the University of Durham, staff at the Bodleian Library, Oxford, the British Library, London, and Clifton Library, Bristol; to Macmillan Publishers Ltd for permission to quote from the Rossetti-Macmillan correspondence; to Carcanet Press, the Hulton Picture Library, the Mary Evans Picture Library, the National Portrait Gallery, and the Tate Gallery. Also to the family of Dora Greenwell, the Trustees of the Trevelyan Family Papers, Sir Rupert Hart-Davis, Jan Marsh, Mrs Gwynneth Hatton, Mr and Mrs R.A. O'Connor, Victoria Huxley and Frances Kelly.

Emily Dickinson's poems (nos. 512, 414 and 642) are reprinted by permission of the publishers and the Trustees of Amherst College from *The Poems of Emily Dickinson*, edited by Thomas H. Johnson, Cambridge, Massachusetts: The Belknap Press of Harvard University Press, Copyright © 1951, 1955, 1979, 1983 by the President and Fellows of Harvard College. Quotations from poems nos. 430, 646, 590, and 642 from *The Complete Poems of Emily Dickinson* edited by Thomas H. Johnson, Copyright © 1929, 1935 by Martha Dickinson Bianchi; Copyright © renewed 1957, 1963 by Mary L. Hampson, reproduced by permission of Little, Brown and Company.

Every effort has been made by the author to contact the copyright holders of manuscript material. In some cases no replies were ever received to communications sent. The author therefore apologises to anyone whose name has been omitted due to inadequate or out of date information.

INTRODUCTION

Christina Rossetti fascinates because she is an enigmatic figure, in life and in literature. She is often remembered chiefly as Dante Gabriel's sister – an austere Victorian lady of formidable piety, dressed invariably in black, who wrote children's poetry and religious verses. One of her poems, set to music by Gustav Holst, has become one of the most popular Christmas carols, though many people sing 'In the Bleak Midwinter' without giving a thought to its author. It was typical of Christina that she chose to write, not of mangers and pretty Christmas-card scenes, but of the bleakness of winter cold. This bleakness also epitomised her religious creed and appealed to something ascetic and astringent deep inside a spirit that otherwise yearned for sunshine and the warmth of human relationships.

The quality Raymond Williams (writing on the Brontës) called 'an emphasis of want' was the essence of Christina Rossetti's poetry. Her brother Dante Gabriel would have preferred her to write of the beauties of nature – that was, after all, what a woman was expected to write about. But she chose instead to deal with the realities of life as she experienced them, including loneliness, betrayal, despair, sickness and death. Her poetry was not always sad. There was also joy, both the joy found in human love and the spiritual ecstasy of the soul, the two often indistinguishably fused together in the poems, because she saw in one a reflection or extension of the other. In her 'Monna Innominata' sonnet sequence she wrote about her love for God and for Charles Cayley

> I cannot love you if I love not Him,
> I cannot love Him if I love not you.

Although Christina was surrounded all her life by either the unconventional characters of the Italian émigré community, or the extraordinary relationships of the Pre-Raphaelites and their friends, she herself chose to be sternly conventional like her mother and her sister. But inside that conventional exterior was a passionate, angry woman who refused to dress according to the fashion and wrote poetry whose sensuality occasionally embarrassed her brothers.

'Finding' Christina as a person is not an easy task for the biographer. Not only did she herself destroy large quantities of personal material, but she also asked her friends and relatives to do the same. Some of them complied with her request, burning letters and deleting journal entries which referred to Christina. They did this, not to hide a family skeleton, but to protect the saintly image that had been constructed in the public mind. Dante Gabriel's portrayal of her as the meek virgin in his painting *The Girlhood of Mary Virgin*, MacKenzie Bell's careful hagiography, Katharine Tynan Hinkson's *Santa Christina* and William Rossetti's own respectful memoir, all foster the image of Christina as a dutiful daughter, sister and friend, unbelievably patient and repulsively pious. Christina would have been appalled. She once wrote to her brother Gabriel that she did not want to be seen as 'too dreamily sweet'.

William Rossetti was a good publicist and his carefully laundered account of his sister's life persisted for a long time, hardly challenged by the selection of letters and papers he passed on to posterity. There is no way of knowing how many of these he destroyed or edited. Though he was an essentially truthful man, he would not have considered it wrong to conceal material he thought might be harmful to Christina's reputation, or that he found too personal.

All that is left of the 'real' Christina are her letters, prose pieces and poetry. That this poetry was 'very subjective' she freely admitted, and the fact that after her death she had over three hundred unpublished poems – many of them judged too personal for publication, confirms her statement. She wrote to a family friend that her poems were not only the 'fruits of effort', but also the 'record of sensation, fancy etc', and her manuscript notebooks often read like an emotional diary, charting her moods, her fears and her dreams.

However, it would be a great mistake to regard her poetry as autobiography without corroborative evidence and, even then, the process by which a poet converts personal experience into art takes the finished result into the public rather than the private domain and involves alteration or selection of the facts. A biographer must be careful not to fall into the autobiographical trap and, conversely, must not use the life to explain the work too neatly.

Lona Mosk Packer, whose *Christina Rossetti* was published in 1963, constructed her otherwise excellent biography around the hypothesis that Christina had a secret, lifelong love affair with a married man, W.B. Scott. The spectre she created from what she admitted was a 'tentative hypothesis', has haunted all subsequent biographers. Professor W. Fredeman, the leading Rossetti scholar, dismissed her theory as being derived from 'circumstantial evidence' culled from the poetry, for which there is not 'a single scrap of positive and direct proof'. What evidence there is on Christina's relationship with the Scotts actually supports Professor Fredeman rather than L.M. Packer.

Her reason for putting forward this theory was the conviction that the circumstances of Christina's life and her existing love affairs were inadequate to account for the impassioned poetry she wrote. L.M. Packer's extraordinary conclusion is completely unsubstantiated. She herself writes 'I have not considered it necessary to qualify every statement made in the course of my narrative, or to supply documentary "proof" for every speculation hazarded'. She also assumes too readily that the date of composition of a poem is contiguous with the event which inspired it. Where a link between an event and a poem can be tentatively established, there is often a long period of gestation before Christina puts pen to paper. Nor does L.M. Packer take sufficiently into account the capacity of what Christina called the 'Poet Mind' to create 'unknown quantities'. Christina's imagination, particularly at the beginning of her career, was very acute, fed by gothic novels, romantic poetry and the Bible.

I have tried in this account of Christina's life to strip away some of the literary accumulations of the past years since her death in 1894 and, by studying the manuscript material and first hand recollections, and by a close analysis of her work, to put forward a picture that is, I hope, as close to the truth as Christina herself would have desired it to be.

PART ONE

Pricked to a Pattern

We call it love and pain,
The passion of her strain;
And yet we little understand or know:
Why should it not be rather joy that so
Throbs in each throbbing vein?

CHRISTINA ROSSETTI
'Twilight Calm'
7 February 1850

CHAPTER ONE

When Christina Rossetti was born on 5 December 1830, Elizabeth Barrett was twenty-four, already a published poet, and Emily Brontë, immersed in the imaginary world of Gondal at Haworth, was twelve. Five days after Christina's birth Emily Dickinson was born in Amherst on the other side of the Atlantic.

These four women, the most frequently anthologised of nineteenth-century women writers, shared more than mere historical proximity. They shared the 'double mischief' of the female poet, struggling for credibility in a century when even a gifted author like Willa Cather could write that it was 'a very grave question whether women have any place in poetry at all'.[1] Although they never met, they read each other's work and influenced each other more than has been previously acknowledged. They belonged to a wider community of female poets which included Jean Ingelow, Felicia Hemans, Laetitia Landon, Dora Greenwell and Augusta Webster, now unknown, but all celebrated at the time. They were all connected together by a complex web of references and borrowings that demonstrate a shared experience of female poetic art.

They were not, in Emily Dickinson's vivid phrase, to be 'shut up in prose'. They inherited a shared literary tradition and there are striking parallels, both literary and personal, in their work. The poetry of one illuminates the poetry of the others, and to read them all is to be conscious of how much they had in common. And when they subvert the masculine literary tradition for their own purposes it is an exhilarating experience. Ellen Moers, in her book *Literary Women* writes that reading the love poetry of Christina Rossetti, Emily Brontë, Elizabeth Barrett and Emily Dickinson together is like 'uncorking a bottle of rare wine'.

Elizabeth Barrett Browning was the oldest of the group and held in such high regard that she was considered for the post of poet laureate when Wordsworth died. Her reputation could not be overlooked by the younger women. Elizabeth's art transcended her sex and situation. Her poetry exhibits the muscularity of a sinuous intellect and the fruits of a determined programme of self education. Her long poem *Aurora Leigh* casts light on the creative rage burning inside her contemporaries and, in particular, Christina Rossetti. The rage that divided Christina between the modesty demanded by her religion and her sex and her need to write and be recognised.

Like Elizabeth Barrett Browning's passionate heroine Aurora Leigh, Christina was both Italian and English. Christina's father Gabriele Rossetti was a political refugee who had come to England via Malta in 1824 after a dramatic escape from Naples disguised as an English sailor. He kept his Neopolitan nationality until he died. For Gabriele politics and patriotism were the 'permanent platform of life'. When he married in 1826 he was forty-three, eighteen years older than his wife Frances.

She was half-English, the daughter of Gaetano Polidori – another Italian exile – and his English wife Anna. Frances Polidori had been brought up in England, baptised as a Protestant and educated to earn her living as a governess. She was the epitome of the good Victorian wife – hard working, self effacing and modest to a fault, but it was dearly bought. Her son Gabriel told a friend that Frances Rossetti 'must have become an important figure in literature' if her remarkable intellectual gifts had not been stifled 'in some great degree . . . by the exercise of an entire self-abnegation on behalf of her family.'[2]

There was a strong literary tradition within the family. Gaetano Polidori had been secretary to the Italian dramatist Alfieri and was himself an author. Frances' favourite brother, John, had been Byron's travelling physician and under the influence of Byron and Mary Shelley had written a gothic novel called *The Vampyre*. Gabriele Rossetti was famous in Italy for his patriotic verses, some of which were still being sung at the time of the First World War. He had also published controversial articles and books on Dante and Petrarch, all of which were banned in his native country as being anti-church and in some cases anti-Christian.

The newly-married Rossettis lived in London at No. 38 Charlotte Street, now renamed Hallam Street, a dingy cul-de-sac near Portland Place. It was a cramped terraced house in a rather run-down neighbourhood. Occasionally the more respectable inhabitants would make an effort to evict some of the dubious characters who lodged there, but without much success. The barber's shop, run by a 'local Figaro', was a source of much complaint, partly because of the indecent posters displayed in the window. But the street was cheap, and the Rossettis had very little money.

Gabriele held the post of Professor of Italian at King's College, London. From this and private teaching he earned only two or three hundred pounds a year. They were only able to afford one servant, though this was supplemented by a nursemaid when the children were small, and much of the housework and childcare fell on Frances, who was rarely seen during the day without what she called a 'pincloth' tied around her waist.

In the first four years of her married life Frances had four children. Maria Francesca in 1827, followed at yearly intervals by Gabriel Charles Dante, William Michael, and finally in 1830 Christina Georgina. They were all delivered by Dr William Locock, afterwards accoucheur to Queen Victoria. Gabriele insisted on the best possible attention for his wife, but, in spite of it, Frances Rossetti apparently had a 'fearful time' giving birth to Christina, which may explain why there were no more pregnancies.

All the children were baptised into the Protestant faith. Christina's godmother, whose name she was given, was a niece of the great Napoleon, Princess Christina Bonaparte, who was living in England at the time, and had married an Englishman. The Bonaparte family, including Louis – the former Napoleon III – were occasional visitors to the Rossetti household, bringing a little glamour to the dingy neighbourhood.

Other wealthy connections helped out with money from time to time. A friend of Coleridge, the Rt Hon John Hookham Frere, who lived in Malta and had helped Gabriele escape to England, sometimes sent fifty or a hundred pounds, and Charles Lyall, a Dante enthusiast living in Scotland, financed Gabriele's publications.

Apart from financial anxieties the marriage of Gabriele and Frances seems to have been happy: the only thing their children remembered them arguing about was religion. Gabriele was a lapsed Catholic, who although believing in the teachings of Christ did not believe in the 'supernatural and legendary elements' of the Christian faith. He was very free with his criticism of the scriptures and fervently anti-Catholic. William Rossetti remembered him holding forth on the story of Abraham, when he was ordered by God to sacrifice his beloved only son as a mark of his faith. Gabriele declared that if he'd been asked to do the same he would have replied, 'You aren't God, you are the Devil'.[3]

He loved his children, spoiling them with lollipops and sweets prohibited by Frances as 'trash'. He also wrote poems to them. One to Maria and Christina describes them as violets and roses, and beautiful 'turtle doves in the nest of love'. His main fault was what his son William described as that habit of self opinion 'which involves self applause'.[4] The children sadly preferred their mother or their maternal grandfather Gaetano.

Frances, much stricter with the children than her husband, was very devout, and her husband's unorthodox views must have caused her some pain. Though her brothers were Catholic, she and her sisters had been brought up in the Protestant evangelical tradition of their English mother. They were later attracted by the High Church 'Tractarian' or 'Oxford' movement as it was sometimes called, based on the teachings of John Keble and Thomas Pusey. This movement saw the Anglican Church as a true branch of the Holy Catholic Church. Conversions to Rome rocked the movement to its foundations from time to time and engendered a deep distrust of Catholicism, particularly of its cult of the Virgin Mary. Family differences about religion and the continual divisions between Catholic and Anglican made a very deep impression on Christina as a child.

The family was otherwise a lively, unconventional and very Italian household. Although the children talked English to their mother, Italian was always spoken in the presence of their father and grandfather. William, the family historian, later recalled the house full of 'exiles, patriots, politicans, literary men, musicians . . . fleshy good natured Neopolitans, keen Tuscans, emphatic Romans'.[5] They crowded into the small sitting room in the evenings, arguing and gesticulating. One of the more colourful characters who came to the house, a sculptor called Sangiovanni, was a bigamist and had apparently assassinated a man in Calabria. He made a paperweight for Christina which she kept until she died. Another friend from Italy brought her a locket of the Virgin and infant Christ set in mother-of-pearl.

The children were rarely asked to leave the room, whatever conspiracy was under discussion. They played on the hearth rug or under the table and were never segregated from the adults as other English middle class children were. None of the children grew up to be even vaguely interested in politics.

There was hardly any contact with other English families at all. The only children who came to the house were the offspring of Cipriano Potter, a friend of Gabriele's who was the Principal of the Royal Academy of Music. He was married to a pianist who moved in very fashionable circles and could have given Frances Rossetti an entrée into society if she had wished it. Their two sons and two daughters were of a similar age to the Rossetti children, but they had little in common. They also played occasionally with the children of another musician, Signor Rovedino, who gave Maria singing lessons, but these occasions were rare. Like the Brontë children, the young Rossettis were dependent upon themselves for occupation and amusement, only one of the 'many points of resemblance' which contemporaries observed between the two families. The closeness of the children, their non-English heritage, their literary activities and the parallels between Branwell and Dante Gabriel can all bear comparison.

There was the usual sibling rivalry between the Rossetti children as their personalities began to develop. Maria, who could read Italian and English fluently by the age of five, was the eldest and most intellectually precocious of the four. She was also the least imaginative and was inclined to be jealous, particularly of Christina who was prettier and livelier than she was. Maria had a strong personality, a rich impressive voice and an imposing physical presence. She was dark complexioned, Italian looking – apparently taking after Gabriele's mother – and was considered to be extremely plain, even by her family. Christina nicknamed her Moon, or Moony, because of her round face and contemplative habit. Maria was very devout, even as a child, and shortly after her confirmation at the age of thirteen seems to have felt the call of a vocation. Religion became the chief concern of her life, her days revolving around prayer and little acts of service to others. Her brother William viewed Maria's influence on Christina with misgiving – feelings shared later by others. Maria's 'hard, convinced mind' and narrow outlook worked on Christina's sensitive and imaginative disposition in a restrictive way.

The eldest son Gabriel, who later chose to be known as Dante, was an engaging, spirited little boy who became the dominant member of the family, hot tempered and proud of his precocious artistic talent. His first sketches were made before he was five and the family decided that he should be trained to be an artist. He often teased Christina to the point where she was forced to call on William to defend her.

Gabriel and Christina were known as the 'two storms', inheriting their volatile Italian temperaments from their father. Christina was the more fractious of the two, passionate and given to terrible tantrums. But even as a child she had a special quality that caused adults to single her out. It was not just her fascination with and precocious use of words. In later life people who met her referred to her 'elusive fascination'. She was 'thoughtful, watchful, melancholy, wistful'. But none of the words used were adequate to describe the haunting quality she possessed, which her brother Gabriel tried to capture in his portraits of her as the Virgin Mary, the quality sought by Holman Hunt when he used her expression for the face of Christ in *The Light of the World*. Christina's grandfather Gaetano Polidori predicted that she would be the most brilliant of the four children – *'avra piu spirito di tutto'*. Christina herself had no such expectations. She wrote in a letter to Edmund Gosse that 'I in particular beheld far ahead of myself the clever sister and two clever brothers who were a little (though but a little) my seniors. And as to acquirements, I lagged out of all proportion behind them, and have never overtaken them to this day'.[6]

William, only a year older, had a much more gentle disposition than Maria and was less volatile than either Gabriel or Christina. By nature affectionate and dependable, he also inherited his mother's modest demeanour and her capacity for hard work and self sacrifice. It was William and not Dante Gabriel who came to be regarded as the head of the family as their father's health declined. The effect of this premature responsibility was to make him more serious and pedantic than he might otherwise have been.

The Rossetti children invented fantastic stories – though nothing so exceptional as the Brontës' Gondal or Angria, and produced a family magazine called the *Hodge Podge*. They were also adept at a verse game called bouts-rimés where the contestants have to produce a sonnet using given rhymes. Christina and Gabriel vied with each other to win these contests and both developed a high standard of technical skill very early on. Christina was also a keen contributor to their other literary activities, composing her first poem before she could write, and later prose tales such as *The Dervise* and *Retribution*. They got many of their ideas from the stories and poems that Frances Rossetti read to them from her commonplace book, stimulating their love of literature long before they were old enough to read the texts for themselves.

The *Hodge Podge* and its successor, the *Illustrated Magazine*, were regular productions containing stories, poems and illustrations by the children. They wrote verses quite naturally. William could not remember a time 'when, knowing what a verse was, we did not also know and feel what a *correct* verse was'.[7] His own published poetry, admired at the time, is now completely neglected.

Until Christina was nine, family holidays were spent in their grandparents' house near Little Missenden in Buckinghamshire. The journey by stage coach took six hours and became a major event to look forward to. At Holmer Green they had the freedom of the countryside and were allowed out for limited excursions unsupervised. Christina loved to wander alone in the garden, inspecting the small creatures who lived there. She told Edmund Gosse that

> If any one thing schooled me in the direction of poetry, it was perhaps the delightful idle liberty to prowl all alone about my grandfather's cottage grounds . . . quite small, and on the simplest scale – but in those days to me they were vast, varied, worth exploring.[8]

Their grandmother Anna Polidori was a permanent invalid, confined to bed by one of those unspecified female afflictions that seem to litter the pages of Victorian novels. There was a son Philip still at home and described as 'weak-minded and rather odd'; a daughter Margaret, who appears to have suffered from nervous illness, and they were all looked after by the youngest daughter Eliza – an outspoken and unconventional woman who wore coal-scuttle bonnets twenty years after they had gone out of fashion and whose greatest comfort was that a day only lasted twenty-four hours.

Another brother, Henry, was an unsuccessful solicitor in London, despite having anglicised his name to Polydore. Frances' favourite sister Charlotte – the family nicknamed them 'Shadow and Substance' because of their respective sizes – was often away from home in Somerset working as a governess to the Marchioness Dowager of Bath.

Gaetano Polidori was more often in London than at Holmer Green. He rented two rooms near Oxford Street so that he could earn his living teaching Italian. He was a genuine eccentric, much loved by his grandchildren, who could be found translating Milton into Italian before lunch and indulging his passion for carpentry in the afternoon. He had apparently been present at the fall of the Bastille and had been rather disgusted by the proceedings. When given a sword by a Frenchman to dispatch any aristocrats he might happen to meet, he gave it away on the next street corner to the first unarmed Frenchman he came upon.

In 1839 Gaetano rented a house in Park Village East, Regents Park and moved his family there. This put a stop to the children's visits to Holmer Green and from then on they rarely left the city. Christina described herself as being 'pent up in London' and wrote of the 'delight reawakened' by the sight of primroses in a railway cutting at the age of fourteen – her first trip out of London since then.

The only compensation was the frequent visiting between the two families. Gaetano bought a printing press and set it up in a shed in the back garden where he employed a Sicilian compositor who fascinated the children by collecting snails from the banks of the canal to make into soup. The press provided the children with their first opportunities for publication. In 1841 Gaetano printed a translation of an Italian poem by Maria, followed in 1843 by Gabriel's ballad *Sir Hugh the Heron* and in 1847 an edition of Christina's *Verses*. All three are now collector's items.

In 1839 the Rossetti family moved into a slightly bigger house at the other end of Charlotte Street. No. 50 was much more expensive than No. 38 and still not really large enough. For £60 a year they had five floors with two rooms on each floor. It had no garden and faced a public house and a hackney carriage stand. There was the usual basement kitchen opening onto a backyard, a family dining room and sitting room on the ground floor, a drawing room and bedroom on the first floor and five or six bedrooms on the second and third floors, one of which was occupied by the maid. One of the smallest of the rooms, used at first by Gabriele as a dressing room, was gradually given over to William and Gabriel as a 'den'.

It was here in this house that Christina completed the painful metamorphosis from a vivacious, hot-tempered, passionate child to a shy, over-restrained, over-scrupulous adult. This change, which took place between 1842 and 1847, is one of the most complex problems confronting a biographer, because it is so poorly documented. However, it seems to have been as mysterious to those around her. Her brother William, who was also her closest friend, wrote that

> In innate character she was vivacious and open to pleasurable impressions; and during her girlhood, one might readily have supposed that she would develop into a woman of expansive heart, fond of society and diversions, and taking a part in them of more than average brilliancy.

What happened next was quite the opposite. William explained it as a combination of circumstances. Not only the desperate financial anxieties that beset the family but 'ill health and an early blight to the affections told for much; for much also an exceeding sensitiveness of conscience, acted upon by the strictest conceptions in religion.' The result was that 'Her temperament and character, naturally warm and free, became "a fountain sealed" . . . Impulse and elan were checked, both in act and in writing.'[9]

CHAPTER TWO

The process by which Victorian girls were educated for life was partially responsible for the spiritual and emotional maiming of Christina, brought up as she was by her mother in the English evangelical tradition. The manner of her education, being taught exclusively by her mother at home, meant that as a young girl she was never exposed to outside influences at all.

In *Aurora Leigh*, Elizabeth Barrett Browning describes the effect of an English education on the Italian temperament as being 'pricked to a pattern with a pin', the metaphor aptly conveying the pain of the process as well as one of the methods used to train young women to obedience. In his painting *The Girlhood of Mary Virgin* Dante Gabriel portrays Christina dutifully stitching an altar cloth under her mother's instruction, but in real life Christina hated needlework and avoided it wherever possible, just as in poetry she avoided using female domestic metaphors.

In later life, after *Aurora Leigh* had been published, Christina wrote about the process of education, comparing the upbringing of her Italian friend Enrica with her English counterpart.

> We Englishwomen, trim, correct,
>   All minted in the selfsame mould,
>   Warm-hearted but of semblance cold,
> All-courteous out of self-respect.
>
> She, woman in her natural grace,
>   Less trammelled she by lore of school,
>   Courteous by nature not by rule,
> Warm-hearted and of cordial face.[1]

Christina was by nature rebellious, passionate and spontaneous, and these qualities did not fit very well with Victorian notions of feminine meekness and submission. Christina strove to emulate her more phlegmatic mother, applying her strength of will to curb her passionate temper. She told her nieces Helen and Olive that she had not always been 'calm and sedate', and explained that she had learned to control herself, for her mother's sake, urging them to do the same. She told them that she had once, when reproved for a fault, taken a pair of scissors and ripped her arm with them in a fit of passion. Christina's feelings for her mother were very strong. In April 1842, while only eleven, she wrote elegant verses to accompany the flowers she gave to her on her birthday.

> Today's your natal day;
>   Sweet flowers I bring:
> Mother, accept I pray
>   My offering.
>
> And may you happy live,
>   And long us bless;
> Receiving as you give
>   Great happiness.[2]

Elizabeth Barrett Browning wrote *Aurora Leigh* while living in Italy, before Christina published her first book, yet her choice of situation for her heroine was close to Christina's own and by a remarkable coincidence gives us an insight into her disposition and her problems. There are several parallels: Italian by birth and temperament but educated to be English; a poet who is also a woman at a time when women's gifts were undervalued; the rejection of love and marriage for a higher ideal. And it was in *Aurora Leigh* that Elizabeth Barrett Browning, at the height of her powers, used the analogy of a bird in a cage to describe the life of the middle class Englishwoman.

> . . . She had lived
> A sort of cage bird life, born in a cage
> Accounting that to leap from perch to perch
> Was act and joy enough for any bird.
>
> . . . I, alas
> A wild bird scarcely fledged, was brought to her cage,
> And she was there to meet me. Very kind.
> Bring the clean water, give out the fresh seed.[3]

Christina used the same analogy in her poem 'A Royal Princess' written in 1861.

> Two and two my guards behind, two and two before
> Two and two on either hand, they guard me evermore,
> Me, poor dove that must not coo – eagle that must not soar.

Women were not the only ones to make the comparison. Walter Deverell, one of the Pre-Raphaelite circle, painted *The Pet*, a picture of a girl feeding a bird in a cage. She is just as much a captive as her pet, contrasted with the wild creatures in the garden beyond the door.

Only the soul of the poet could escape the cage – imagination soaring like Elizabeth Barrett's lark 'Behind the wall of sense, as safe from harm . . . In vortices of glory and blue air'.[4]

Christina's poetry was inward looking, using images of closed rooms and locked gardens. She portrays the endless introspection and reflection, self on self, the search for perfection.

> All my walls are lost in mirrors, whereupon I trace,
> Self to right hand, self to left hand, self in every place,
> Self-same solitary figure, self-same seeking face.[5]

Emily Brontë had the wild moors of Haworth to keep her in touch with her feelings, and she fought her way to a religious philosophy that has sometimes been characterised as pagan, in the effort to retain her individuality and mental freedom. But most women were confined to the interior world of the Lady of Shalott, only permitted to view reality through a mirror.

The repressed passion showed itself occasionally in violence; Christina cutting her arm with a pair of scissors when reproved by her mother; Emily Brontë beating her dog Keeper with her bare fists. It emerged in the symbolism of the novel – Charlotte Brontë's Red Room in *Jane Eyre*, and George Eliot's Red Deeps in *The Mill on the Floss*. The nineteenth-century poet Alice Meynell in one of her essays wrote that 'Red is not the colour of life, it is the colour of violence,' but a concealed violence – 'the colour of blood under the skin . . . In the case of women, it is of the living and unpublished blood that the violent world has professed to be delicate and ashamed'.[6] Emily Brontë projected her own interior violence into *Wuthering Heights*, Christina repressed it, crushing it far down into her psyche and only occasionally does it well up into passionate, terrible poetry.

> For all night long I dreamed of you:
> I woke and prayed against my will,
> Then slept to dream of you again.
> At length I rose and knelt and prayed.
> I cannot write the words I said,
> My words were slow, my tears were few;
> But through the dark my silence spoke
> Like thunder. When this morning broke,
> My face was pinched, my hair was grey,
> And frozen blood was on the sill
> Where stifling in my struggle I lay.[7]

It would not have been surprising if, like Aurora Leigh, Christina had 'read a score of books on Womanhood'. However, the young Rossettis hated 'improving' books and moral tales, though the nineteenth-century novels they read as they grew older were only slightly less didactic. Maria liked the High Anglican novels of Charlotte M. Yonge, which are only thinly disguised conduct books. Christina preferred Mrs Gaskell. Their novels describe for us the process by which rebellious independent girls became demure, dutiful wives and daughters. It was nothing less than the killing of the self. When Mrs Gaskell's heroine Molly is abjured in *Wives and Daughters* to think of others and put their interests before her own in order to achieve happiness she replies

> It will be very dull when I shall have killed myself, as it were, and live in trying to do, and to be, as other people like. I don't see any end to it. I might as well never have lived. And as for the happiness you speak of, I shall never be happy again.[8]

The education of the children was left to Frances Rossetti, though the boys were sent to school at the age of seven. It was not an easy task, despite her training as a governess. Maria was a docile pupil, acquiring knowledge easily, and William was not far behind her, but Gabriel and Christina were quite different. Neither had the patience to apply themselves to subjects they disliked. Christina resisted formal education and would only read books she enjoyed. She 'picked up' knowledge in a haphazard kind of way.

The Rossetti children had the freedom of Gaetano Polidori's library and fed their minds with a wide range of literature – favourites were Sir Walter Scott, the gothic novels of Mrs Radcliffe, 'Monk' Lewis and Maturin, the poetry of Keats, Shelley and Byron, and Italian poetry by Petrarch, Tasso and Metastasio. Dante's poetry, their father's life's work which he pursued with obsessive enthusiasm, initially produced feelings of revulsion. William wrote that 'Dante Alighieri was a sort of banshee in the Charlotte St. houses; his shriek audible even to familiarity, but the message of it not scrutinised.'[9]

In Christina's early poetry, the fairy tale, the gothic, the romantic and the biblical jostle happily with the Italian to create an effect that William described as 'somewhat devious from the British tradition and the insular mind.'[10]

Physical recreation was provided by excursions to Regent's Park where Christina often explored the zoological gardens with Gabriel. She was fascinated by the strange animals and birds she saw there, but distressed by the caged conditions in which they lived. The birds in particular upset her, despite Gabriel's attempts to cheer her up by inventing comic biographies for them. One night she dreamed vividly that all the canaries in London left their cages as soon as darkness fell, returning at dawn to sweep from the trees 'in a wave of yellow light'.

When William was seven and Gabriel eight they were sent to a day school run by the Rev. Dr Paul in Portland Place and from there to King's College, where their father was professor of Italian. Neither of the boys was happy there. Their upbringing had been too different from that of the other English children who came mostly from professional backgrounds. They had also had no acquaintance with the sporting activities which were the pivot of the male educational system. Gabriel, after a turbulent interlude, left in 1842 at the age of thirteen to study painting. William doggedly persevered with his studies.

In 1842, Gabriele's health began to decline suddenly. His sight faded and through the winter he developed severe bronchitis. Bronchial diseases were endemic during the winter months in industrialised areas, exacerbated by the lethal mixture of cold, damp English air and fossil fuel pollution that produced thick winter smog.

On medical advice Gabriele went to Paris, accompanied by Frances, and after a few months was declared well enough to return. But the improvement was shortlived and his eyesight and general health continued to deteriorate. He woke up one morning completely blind in one eye and with only partial sight in the other. For a time it was feared that he would be totally blind. His illness made it virtually impossible for him to write or teach. He was forced to give up his post at King's College and kept only one or two private pupils – among them Charles Cayley, a young scholar, extremely shy, who became a family friend. The Rossettis' financial situation became desperate.

In 1844 Frances Rossetti advertised for pupils to teach and was forced to ask her family for loans against her maternal grandfather's estate, under which she stood to inherit £2,000 when her mother died. The advances were freely given but the Polidoris were comfortable rather than wealthy and it was humiliating to have to ask. There was considerable disappointment in 1849 when Frances Rossetti's aunt Harriet died. The old lady had left her substantial fortune to Frances, but then it was discovered that the will had not been properly witnessed and she got only the small share due to her as the relative of an intestate.

Maria at seventeen, recommended by Aunt Charlotte, went as governess to the Rev. Lord and Lady Charles Thynne, brother-in-law of the Marchioness Dowager of Bath. She remained away from home until 1848.

In 1845 William left school to work in the Excise Office (now the Inland Revenue), a job he obtained through one of his father's old pupils. He hated it, and would have preferred to study medicine, but there was no money to pay for his training. The job at the Excise Office brought in £80 a year.

Dante Gabriel was studying painting, first at Sass's Academy in Bloomsbury, and then in the Antique School of the Royal Academy. As the elder brother, with a recognised talent, he had the first call on the family finances. Gabriele pinned all his hopes on him but he was no happier at the Royal Academy than he had been at King's College. He chafed under the method of instruction, complained continually, and was careless of the sacrifices that were being made to keep him there.

Christina was too young to contribute anything to the family finances, but she was very sensitive to her parents' sufferings, particularly the burden laid upon her mother. In between looking after her father and helping her mother with domestic chores she experimented with verse, copying her poems out into narrow notebooks – rather like a rent book in shape and size.

Her early poetry charts her reading with poems about characters in the gothic novels she enjoyed – Isadora, Zara, Eva, Immalee. The poems are full of adolescent morbidity, but the sentiments are trite and lack the conviction of personal experience. 'Present and Future' is typical.

> Earthly joys are very fleeting,
> Earthly sorrows very long;
> Parting ever follows meeting,
> Night succeeds to evensong.

Some of the poems foreshadow future themes – none more than 'The

Solitary Rose', perfumed only by its own fragrance, blooming alone.
Christina used the rose as her own symbol.

> What though for thee no nightingales are singing?
>   They chant one eve, but hush them in the morning.
> Near thee no little moths and bees are winging
>   To steal thy honey when the day is dawning;
> Thou keep'st thy sweetness till the twilight's close,
>   O happy rose.

Christina was beginning to feel the 'difference', not only of the creative
artist, but also of gender as well as the isolation of a different culture. Her
poems reveal a natural sensuality, influenced by Keats and Tennyson.
She often used water as a metaphor for 'oceanic feelings' – consciously
or unconsciously using it to represent powerful, often sexual emotion, as
well as the exercise of personal freedom and the creative imagination.
'The Water Spirit's Song' was written in 1844 and was not included in
any of the later collected editions of Christina's work.

> When murmurs thro' the forest trees
> The cool refreshing evening breeze;
> When the nightingale's wild melody
> Is waking herb and flower and tree
> From their perfumed and soft repose
> To list the praises of the rose;
> When the ocean sleeps deceitfully;
> When the waves are resting quietly;
> I spread my bright wings, and fly far away
> To my beautiful sister's mansion gay:
> I leave behind me rock and mountain,
> I leave behind me rill and fountain,
> And I dive far down in the murmuring sea
> Where my fair sister welcomes me joyously;
> For she's Queen of Ocean for ever and ever
> And I of each fountain and still lake and river.[11]

Christina's earliest biographer, MacKenzie Bell, detected the influence
of Felicia Hemans and Laetitia Landon in her work, and there are
similar themes and sentiments in Christina's juvenile poems, in
particular the cultivation of melancholy and a longing for death. The
Rossetti family possessed copies of Laetitia Landon's volumes *The
Improvatrice*, *The Golden Violet* and *The Venetian Bracelet*. *The Improvatrice*
depicts a young poet 'entirely Italian, – a young female with all the

loveliness, vivid feeling and genius of her own impassioned land'. It includes poems inspired by the poetry of Sappho, and some of Christina's early verses also include poems to Sappho, whose fate seems to have fascinated her. One of them is titled 'What Sappho would have said, had her leap cured instead of killing her', and is a lament for lost love. Laetitia Landon's Sappho bids farewell to her lute, Christina's longs for death – sighing through the empty days.

> Eased from my weight of heaviness,
> Forgetful of forgetfulness,
> Resting from pain and care and sorrow
> Through the long night that knows no morrow;
> Living unloved, to die unknown,
> Unwept, untended and alone.[12]

Felicia Hemans and Laetitia Landon were, with Elizabeth Barrett Browning and the scandal-haunted Caroline Norton,[13] the dominant female influences of the early nineteenth century. They were all referred to at one time or another as the 'female Byron of our time'. Eliza Cook was also very much in demand, but her popular style and domestic subject matter were denigrated by the critics. Felicia Hemans (now remembered chiefly for *The Boy Stood on the Burning Deck*) died in 1835 and Laetitia Landon three years later, after short and rather tragic lives. Christina seems to have identified with both women at difficult periods in her own life – particularly with Laetitia, or L.E.L. as she is usually referred to.

In 1844 Elizabeth Barrett (as she was then) published a volume of collected poems, dedicated to her father, whose increasing tyranny had still not completely extinguished the deep affection she felt for him. William and Gabriel were keen followers of Elizabeth Barrett and her poems were eagerly read. Their admiration was shared by Christina, who thought her far greater than any other living woman poet. This opinion was not shared by the critics, who claimed that Elizabeth's experiments with rhyme, particularly half rhyme, spoiled the poems.

Christina was fascinated by metrical innovations, the use of half rhymes and end rhyme, and these became a feature of her own poetry. Two poems written in 1845 show her pairing *pure* with *store*, *heaven* with *even*, and perhaps with less felicity *blossom* and *bosom*, *daisies* and *raises*. She also experimented with the ballad form that Elizabeth Barrett used so successfully and the same themes. The uncertainty of earthly love compared to heavenly love appears in 'The Dead Bride' and 'The Dying Man to His Betrothed'.

One of the most remarkable of her poems 'The Dead City' has its roots in the gothic, and the tales of the Arabian Nights which Christina had read with such delight as a child. Many of the images come from Zobeide's tale and their rich sensuality prefigures 'Goblin Market'. A wanderer lost in a strange wood is drawn towards a 'fair city of white stone', empty and silent. In the garden of the King's palace is a tent containing a luscious feast, spread before guests who have been turned to stone.

> All the vessels were of gold,
> Set with gems of worth untold.
>   In the midst a fountain rose
>   Of pure milk, whose rippling flows
> In a silver bason rolled.
>
> In green emerald baskets were
> Sun-red apples, streaked and fair;
>   Here the nectarines and peach
>   And ripe plum lay, and on each
> The bloom rested everywhere.
>
> Grapes were hanging overhead,
> Purple, pale, and ruby-red;
>   And in panniers all round
>   Yellow melons shone, fresh found,
> With the dew upon them spread.
>
> And the apricot and pear
> And the pulpy fig were there,
>   Cherries and dark mulberries,
>   Bunchy currants, strawberries
> And the lemon wan and fair.

The vision vanishes as mysteriously as it appeared leaving the wanderer, the 'I' of the poem, awed and afraid.

Not all the poems are so serious. Christina had a playful witty side to her nature which reveals itself in short epigrammatic verses. 'On Albina' was written when she was thirteen.

> The roses lingered in her cheeks
> When fair Albina fainted;
> O gentle reader, could it be
> That fair Albina painted?

Christina's first verses compare very favourably with Dante Gabriel's early productions. Here, an extract from *Sir Hugh The Heron* describes the hero in battle

> And the shrieks of the flying, the groans of the dying
> And the battle's deafening yell,
> And the armour which clanked as the warrior rose,
> And rattled as he fell.

Between the ages of thirteen and eighteen Christina was alone at home for the first time without Maria. The stress of family circumstances, the dread of having to earn her own living as a governess as soon as she was old enough, worries about her father's health, the onset of puberty and an adolescent religious crisis all seem to have combined upon a sensitive, volatile temperament to produce a crisis of health.

It is difficult to discover exactly what happened. A friend of her biographer MacKenzie Bell reported that it had been 'religious mania bordering on insanity'. That she 'fell in love with Christ' as many young people do at this age seems very likely, but there seems to be little evidence of excessive religious zeal. Her poetic output is less religious at this period of her life than at any other.

Originally the family had worshipped at Trinity Church, Marylebone Road, until Mrs Rossetti had been bullied by the rector about her pew rent. But by the time Christina was thirteen they were attending Christ Church, Albany Street, where Margaret and Eliza Polidori worshipped. The incumbent was a Rev. William Dodsworth, one of the leading figures in the High Anglican movement, who shortly afterwards joined the Church of Rome. His teachings had a profound effect on Christina, and her outlook became increasingly Anglican, with its emphasis on the minute examination of motives and conduct, self denial, humility and the suppression of vanity.

The novels of Charlotte Yonge exemplify this process more than any others. Christina mentions only one book by Miss Yonge specifically, so it is difficult to prove which of the novels she read, and the sentiments are so in keeping with her own feelings as expressed in her poetry that the poems often run as a kind of counterpoint to the prose. A discussion in *The Daisy Chain* about ambition and the necessity to desire only the lowest place, centred around the text 'the last shall be first', is followed a few months later by Christina's poem 'The Lowest Room' based on the same text and putting forward the same arguments.

In Miss Yonge's novels women give up love and independence to be useful to their families, they give up studying so that they don't threaten the egos of less academic brothers, they resign themselves to a life of partial vision because fathers dislike seeing them in glasses. Duty to parents had to be paramount, even if it led to a life 'spoilt and made joyless'. Characters subject themselves to a kind of moral flagellation. Personal ambition and achievement was sinful unless motives could be absolutely pure. This was the religious faith Christina embraced, one which denied the pursuit of excellence, except for its own sake and if it was dedicated to Christ.

Christina seems to have been also deeply affected by the death of Lady Isabella Howard, an old pupil of Charlotte Polidori's, who went into a decline and died at the age of eighteen. Apparently Christina 'entertained an ardent admiration for the loveliness of character and person' of Lady Isabella. Her manuscript notebooks contain poem after poem on her death. Some of the poems are in Maria's handwriting, others in her mother's; according to William she was at times too weak to copy out her poems herself, although she was able to compose them.

The onset of puberty also caused complications, with its hormone changes and violent mood swings, and the change of lifestyle caused by menstruation. Primitive methods of coping hygienically with the menstrual flow, and the necessity for chaperoning an adolescent girl, meant an inevitable loss of personal freedom. One of the doctors treating Christina noted that she was suffering from anaemia. She also exhibited all the symptoms of angina pectoris – breathlessness, palpitations, and chest pain. These symptoms are also associated with anaemia and acute anxiety, but without modern diagnostic techniques it would have been difficult to be sure. There was also bronchitis, always a worry because it damaged the lungs and could eventually lead to tuberculosis, or chronic emphysema.

Christina was seen by several doctors, one of them a gynaecologist, who do not seem to have agreed on a diagnosis. Almost inevitably the word hysteria was mentioned. That her illness was partly psychosomatic – a physical manifestation of an emotional and nervous disorder, cannot be overlooked. One of her symptoms was a 'suffocating sensation' which sounds very similar to a panic attack. The word hysteria has its roots in the greek *hystera* meaning womb. Nervous illness was thought to originate in the womb; so too was literary output in women. The two ideas were so strongly linked that it was thought by many eminent physicians until the beginning of the twentieth century that writing and studying could make girls either sterile, or mad, or both. Until the First World War, when it was renamed neurasthenia, hysteria was thought to be an exclusively female affliction.

There were however several Victorian psychiatrists who made the connection between social repression and nervous illness in women. Charles Mercier in *Sanity and Insanity* stated that few women passed through adolescence without some form of hysteria caused by lack of an outlet for their developing emotional and sexual forces. Freud, on the other hand, largely ignored the social pressures on women, although he had the evidence in front of him. Freud and Breuer in *Studies on Hysteria* observed that 'Adolescents who are later to become hysterical are for the most part lively, gifted and full of intellectual interests before they fall ill,' though they did also state that 'repetitious domestic routines could be the cause of hysteria in very intelligent women'. The novels of Charlotte Brontë chart the process, the walk 'from breakfast to madness'. In *Jane Eyre* and *Villette* repression of feeling, particularly sexual feeling, leads to breakdown and sometimes madness – Jane Eyre, Bertha Mason and Lucy Snowe are all victims. And *Villette* is one of the most vivid accounts of mental breakdown ever written.[14]

The incidence of psychosomatic illness among nineteenth-century women is startling. Elizabeth Barrett suffered a breakdown of health as a young teenager which kept her an invalid until 1845 when she was rescued by Robert Browning. Emily Brontë was physically ill every time she left Haworth. Florence Nightingale suffered a similar sort of breakdown, which she described in *Cassandra*, when her hopes and ambitions for a career in nursing were thwarted by her parents.

One of the problems for Christina was her family history. She had an uncle who was mentally retarded and a neurasthenic aunt. Her uncle John Polidori had also been mentally unstable and had committed suicide in 1821 after incurring huge gambling debts he was unable to pay. The family history probably contributed to the way she was treated. Christina was very highly strung and the effect of auto suggestion by diagnosis on her personality would have been strong. The young Elizabeth Barrett was confirmed in invalidity by the doctor who wrote to her parents that he could find no evidence of a diseased spine, but that she should be treated as if there were. Elizabeth, restless, ambitious, and apparently suffering from post-viral depression was encouraged, like Christina, to believe herself ill.

The convenience of hysteria was not lost on Victorian psychiatrists either. It sometimes allowed the sufferer, otherwise powerless, to manipulate those around her. Christina's friend, Dora Greenwell, regarded her ill health as a respite – a 'little cave to run into', which had 'many social immunities' which she intended to take full advantage of. Elizabeth Barrett became the centre of her family's attention and her illness left her free from irksome domestic and social duties in order to write. Emily Brontë was able to remain quietly at Haworth rather than have to earn her living as a governess or teacher like her sisters. Christina's frail health helped her to escape a similar fate and curtailed her education, leaving her free to occupy her mind as she pleased. She later told Swinburne that she felt like an 'escaped governess ... wherefore I ought to feel for my "sisters-who-should-have-been"'.[15]

Her time was increasingly deployed in writing poetry. In 1847 her grandfather Gaetano Polidori published a small volume of Christina's verses, judged by the family to be good enough to print. Gaetano hinted at future possibilities in his foreword

> ... though I am ready to acknowledge that the well-known partial affection of a grandparent may perhaps lead me to overrate the merit of her youthful strains, I am still confident that the lovers of poetry will not wholly attribute my judgement to partiality.[16]

Copies of her *Verses* were given to family and friends and were warmly received by most – though there were exceptions. In July Dante Gabriel wrote to his mother

> As to the nonsense about Christina's *Verses*, I should advise her to console herself with the inward sense of superiority (assuring her moreover that she will not be the first who has been driven time after time to the same alternative) and to consign the fool Mr L. [Lyall?] and his folly to that utter mental oblivion to the which, I doubt not, she has long ago consigned all those who have been too much honoured by the gift of her book.[17]

As Christina's health improved her life began to open out again. Maria returned from Somerset (the Rev. Lord Charles Thynne had become a Catholic convert) and was living with the Read family at Finsbury Pavement. Christina was invited to the house to meet their daughter Elizabeth, known as Bessie. They became friends, though never close, and Christina wrote her an elegant poem and sent her postage stamps for her collection.

Dante Gabriel and William had begun a small poetry reading circle with some friends in the small study/dressing room at the top of the backstairs. Here they shared not only their own work but the latest publications. *Wuthering Heights*, *Agnes Grey* and *Jane Eyre* were all published in 1847 and the Rossettis, like everyone else, argued their merits. *Jane Eyre* found a permanent place in Pre-Raphaelite art.

Wuthering Heights was more difficult. Dante thought it 'a fiend of a book. The action is laid in hell.' Christina was urged to join them. Characteristically she refused, partly from shyness and partly because she was afraid of anything that might have been called 'display' according to the strict precepts of her religion. She wouldn't even allow her brothers to read her poems for her.

Gabriel had been finding the Royal Academy increasingly irksome, and in March 1848 he left to receive private tuition from the painter Ford Madox Brown. This step led to the formation of the Pre-Raphaelite Brotherhood, which was one of the most important events of Christina's life.

CHAPTER THREE

Dante Gabriel's time at the Royal Academy had brought him into contact with people with similar interests and ideas. Less shy and self-effacing than William or Christina he happily made himself known to people he particularly admired. In 1847 he wrote an extravagant letter to William Bell Scott, a painter who taught art in Newcastle upon Tyne, and also wrote poetry. Gabriel described how he had sought out Scott's volume of poetry the *Year of the World*, and fallen upon it like a vulture, devouring it at a single sitting. Scott responded and was invited to call when he came to London.

Scott, intrigued by Gabriel's manner of address, and the verses he had sent him, called at the house when he came to London just before Christmas, at a time when only Gabriele and Christina were at home. When he was ushered into the room by the maid, Gabriele was sitting in his usual chair beside the fire with a manuscript book open in front of him and a large box of snuff.

> By the window was a high, narrow reading desk, at which stood writing a slight girl with a serious, regular profile, dark against the pallid wintry light without. This, most interesting to me of the two inmates turned on my entrance, made the most formal and graceful curtsey, and resumed her writing . . .[1]

Scott was a handsome and highly impressive looking man, with cold blue eyes. Very attractive to women and fond of their company, he had many affairs. Although the Rossettis were not aware of it until later, he was married – one of those strange, sexless nineteenth-century marriages. Christina's biographer L. M. Packer has constructed, from this brief meeting, their subsequent friendship, and isolated poems, a love affair between Scott and Christina based almost entirely on her poetry and unsupported by hard evidence. The fact that, between 1847 and 1851, Christina's affections were fixed on another Pre-Raphaelite acquaintance, James Collinson, (a fact which L.M. Packer discounts) makes the possibility extremely remote.

Gabriel also made himself known to Ford Madox Brown, a painter, aged twenty seven, whose wife had died a year or so earlier leaving him with a small daughter, Lucy. Gabriel wrote to him praising his work and asking whether he could become Ford's pupil, in terms so enthusiastic that Ford was uncertain whether to take it seriously. He called somewhat suspiciously at 50 Charlotte Street brandishing the letter and asking 'What do you mean by it?' He, too, quickly fell under the spell of Gabriel's fascination and soon Gabriel, ·tired of the Royal Academy's methods of instruction, was installed in Ford's studio practising still life techniques by painting groups of pickle jars and antique bottles.

Christina, herself a talented artist, also took lessons, attending a small art class run by Madox Brown for artisans in Camden Town.

An acquaintanceship with Holman Hunt and John Millais at the Academy became the basis of the Pre-Raphaelite Brotherhood. There is still confusion about how it actually began and who was responsible for what. William Rossetti became the unofficial historian of the group and his views are often disputed as being biased, on the grounds that he tended to see his brother as the most important member of the group and the driving force behind the Pre-Raphaelite ideal.

Holman Hunt went to great lengths in his own book on the Pre-Raphaelites to set the record straight. According to him, he was the main influence on Dante Gabriel and not Madox Brown. Gabriel had only stayed for a few months there, but had worked under Hunt's direction for a considerable time. He regarded Gabriel as a protegé taken up by himself and Millais and seemed to believe quite sincerely that they had taught him his technique.

The details of the actual formation of the Pre-Raphaelite Brotherhood as given by Hunt seem reasonably accurate. He met Millais at the Royal Academy school where the young painter, predicted to have a brilliant future, was collecting all the prizes. They shared a dislike for the conservative art establishment which they considered had turned the Royal Academy into a mutual admiration society, deeply suspicious of anything innovatory. The Academy taught by encouraging pupils to copy old masters, and they looked back at a golden age of art – particularly Raphael – which set a standard by which they measured their own.

Millais and Hunt condemned Raphael for 'grandiose disregard of the simplicity of truth' and thought his figures guilty 'of pompous posturing' and 'attitudinising'. They read Ruskin's *Modern Painting* which admired Turner and expounded Truth to Nature as the way forward. They also discovered Keats, whose poetry was not well known at the time. Hunt found a small volume of his poems in millboard covers in a book bin labelled 'this lot 4d'. They were particularly struck by 'The Eve of St Agnes', which Hunt thought illustrated 'the sacredness of honest responsible love and the weakness of proud intemperance.'[2]

This was the beginning of the Pre-Raphaelite close association with poetry. They created a synthesis of poetry and painting that has rarely been equalled. Hunt painted the *Eve of St Agnes*, and this led to an introduction to Dante Gabriel, who saw the painting and forcefully expressed his admiration to the painter. They discovered mutual aims and ideals and soon Gabriel – who was dissatisfied with painting old bottles at Madox Brown's – was installed as Hunt's pupil, though they were of a similar age. Gabriel was twenty and Hunt twenty-one.

Hunt was both attracted and repelled by Gabriel, describing him as a 'young man of decidedly southern breed and respect, about 5 feet 7 inches in height with long brown hair, touching his shoulders, not caring to walk erect, but rolling carelessly as he slouched along, pouting with parted lips, searching with dreaming eyes.'[3] Hunt himself was dubbed The Maniac, partly because of his appearance and also because of his singlemindedness which bordered on fanaticism.

Hunt and Millais were invited to the Rossetti family home and there they met Christina. She had grown into a young woman of less than average height, with a well-formed figure. Her face was longer than was consistent with beauty and her best features were her eyes which were large and expressive. She had previously worn her hair in ringlets round her face but in 1848 she adopted a more severe style and the ringlets were wound into 'earphones' on either side of her head. She dressed plainly like her mother, with a complete disregard for fashion, in sober colours relieved by a scrap of lace or ribbon tied at the neck. She appeared to Hunt, who knew nothing then of her gifts, as a 'pure and docile hearted damsel'. He never penetrated the madonna-like exterior at all.

They were lively evenings. Mrs Rossetti presided gently from the dining table, while Maria – probably the most sociable member of the family – acted the part of hostess 'overflowing with attention to all, expressing interest in each individually'. The fireside, where Gabriele sat, very frail and almost blind, was the place for 'tragic passions'.[4] All the talk was of Italian politics and revolution, everyone gesticulating and arguing and jumping from their seats to declaim their opinions on the hearth rug. Millais and Hunt had never experienced anything like it.

When supper was served the exiles, knowing the stringency of the Rossettis' economy, either left to eat at their own houses or remained at the fireside declaring that they had already dined. Hunt, on his first visit was served macaroni and invited to play dominoes and chess afterwards.

Christina liked chess and played in a highly competitive spirit. She exulted when she won and was furious when she didn't. This brought her into conflict with her Christian principles. It was part of the sin of pride and eventually she forced herself to give up the game as an exercise in self denial. 'If thy right eye offend thee, pluck it out' was the text she applied. Similarly she gave up going to the theatre because actors and actresses tended to be immoral and she would not, however remotely, encourage immorality. William described her as a puritan, and her attitude certainly owed much to Mrs Rossetti's evangelical zeal, strengthened and refined by the Anglican creed. In *Letter and Spirit*, which she published in 1883, Christina explained and justified this kind of self-denial.

> . . . all our lives long we shall be bound to refrain our soul and keep it low; but what then? For the books we now forbear to read, we shall one day be endued with wisdom and knowledge. For the music we will not listen to, we shall join in the song of the redeemed . . . For the companionship we shun, we shall be welcomed into angelic society . . . For the amusements we avoid, we shall keep the supreme Jubilee. For the pleasure we miss, we shall abide, and for evermore abide, in the rapture of heaven.

Hunt, Millais and Gabriel had begun to talk through their beliefs about art, and found that they all admired the 'naïve traits of frank expression and unaffected grace' of early Italian painting. They thought that it showed the principles of Truth to Nature which they themselves sought. They travelled miles to find the right landscape. Hunt sat up night after night in an orchard to get the exact effect of moonlight on the trees. Money was spent on clothes and items of jewellery for the paintings. But they were far from being realists – Hunt wrote that 'a man's work must be the reflex of a living image in his own mind, and not the icy double of the facts themselves.' Carlyle unkindly remarked that the Pre-Raphaelites were 'said to copy the thing as it is, or invent it as they believe it must have been.'[5]

They were all romantically inclined and deeply attracted to the Arthurian myths. Gabriel particularly liked painting 'knights rescuing ladies, lovers in medieval dress' and 'stirring incidents of romantic poets', especially Tennyson. Sometimes poem and painting became part of a whole, with the text attached to the frame. Gabriel wrote that 'Picture and poem must bear the same relation to each other as beauty in man and woman; the point of meeting where the two are most identical is the supreme perfection.'[6] Courtly love and chivalry, the beatification of women and the sadness of early death were recurring themes.

Christina's poetry began to reflect the Pre-Raphaelite ideals, so much so that she was afterwards referred to as 'the High Priestess of Pre-Raphaelitism.' Her simplicity and lack of sentiment, the use of emblems, the gold thread of embroidered detail like a medieval tapestry, and her themes of renunciation, loss and longing are all in keeping with the preoccupations of her brother and his friends. Like them she was influenced initially by Keats and Tennyson, but she brought to her poetry not only the Italian heritage, but also a thorough knowledge of the Bible, particularly the incomparable prose/poetry of the King James' translation, creating an effect that is thoroughly individual.

Her Pre-Raphaelitism reached its highest point in the second verse of 'A Birthday', which reads like a description of one of Dante Gabriel's paintings.

> Raise me a dais of silk and down;
>   Hang it with vair and purple dyes;
> Carve it in doves and pomegranates,
>   And peacocks with a hundred eyes;
> Work it in gold and silver grapes,
>   In leaves and silver fleurs-de-lys;
> Because the birthday of my life
>   Is come, my love is come to me.

In 'A Shadow of Dorothea', Christina opens a door into the legendary emblematic world of the Pre-Raphaelite painting with its golden-haired, dreaming figures, and richly ornamented backgrounds. It opens with the lily emblem.

> 'Golden-haired, lily white,
> Will you pluck me lilies?'

The figure addressed replies

> 'I pluck young flowers of Paradise,
>   Lilies and roses red:
>   A sceptre for my hand,
> A crown to crown my golden head.
>   Love makes me wise:
>   I sing, I stand,
> I pluck palm-branches in the sheltered land.'

The world of legend again comes alive in the fourth verse, which incorporates the tension of the gothic with its love of mystery and ruined buildings and the beauty of the illuminated manuscript.

> 'There is a heavenward stair –
>   Mount, strain upwards, strain and strain –
>   Each step will crumble to your foot
>   That never shall descend again.
>   There grows a tree from ancient root
>   With healing leaves and twelvefold fruit
>   In musical heaven-air:
>   Feast with me there.'

In 1848 Dante Gabriel, under Holman Hunt's tutelage, began his painting of *The Girlhood of Mary Virgin*. It shows St Anne instructing the Virgin in womanly virtues. She is embroidering an altar cloth with symbolic lilies. To the left of the picture a small angel stands with her hand on a pile of conduct books, their titles illustrating the virtues to be expected of the Virgin – Temperance, Chastity, Fortitude, Hope, Faith and Charity. A lily and a dove occupy central positions in the picture and St Joachim is shown in the background pruning a vine. Gabriel used Christina as his model for the Virgin and his mother for St Anne, making a deliberate analogy. The picture was to be 'a symbol of female excellence', Christina's appearance 'being excellently adapted to my purpose', though he changed her hair colour from brown to gold.

Gabriel's poem printed on the frame of the portrait outlines the Pre-Raphaelite ideal of womanhood, and is a pictorial representation of the influences and pressures that shaped Christina.

Her kin she cherished with devout respect;
A profound simpleness of intellect
Was hers and supreme patience. From the knee
Faithful and hopeful: wise in charity,
Strong in grave peace; in duty circumspect.
So held she through her girlhood: as it were
An angel-watered lily, that near God
Grows and is quiet.

If Christina had learnt to tame her unruly disposition, Gabriel had not, and he was not the easiest person to sit for. The small girl he was using for the angel was rather fidgety and 'so overtired his temper that he revealed his irritation beyond bounds, storming wildly, overthrowing his tools and stamping about, until the poor child sobbed and screamed with fright.'[7]

Other Royal Academy acquaintances were drawn into the Pre-Raphaelite circle which was beginning to assume something of the character of a secret society. There was heated debate on a name before Pre-Raphaelite Brotherhood was fixed on, the initials to be affixed to their signatures on the canvases. Its meaning was to be kept secret. Seven was the number settled on for membership. Gabriel proposed that his brother be elected although William did not paint, only writing occasional verses. It was agreed that he could join provided that he took lessons in drawing. Madox Brown was asked to join but refused. He disliked coteries. The sculptor Thomas Woolner, painter Frederick Stephens and a young painter called James Collinson all became members of the group.

Like most of the Pre-Raphaelites James Collinson not only painted but also wrote poetry 'in the highest church spirit'. He had excited admiration at the Academy for the 'finish' of his canvases, which were mainly in the Victorian genre tradition. Gabriel saw his painting *The Charity Boy's Debut* at the Academy exhibition in 1847 and took possession of him. He was going to be a 'stunner'. The others were less enthusiastic. Millais thought of him as a 'stalwart leader of a forlorn hope'. Hunt dismissed him as 'a meek little chap' and complained that he could rarely 'see the fun of anything', but they were all carried along on the wave of Gabriel's conviction.

Christina already knew Collinson. He had been in the habit of attending Christ Church where Christina and her family worshipped, and had attracted her attention by the apparent sincerity of his devotions. Just before he joined the PRB he became a Catholic convert, like so many High Anglicans. William Bell Scott scathingly referred to his work as an example of the 'feckless dilettantism of the converts who were then dropping out of their places in Oxford and Cambridge into Mariolatry and Jesuitism.'

Collinson was the younger son of a bookseller (deceased) from Mansfield near Nottingham. He had a provincial accent and was small and rather plump. William Rossetti described him as 'subdued and rather timid, and the same was the case with his art'. He came initially to the Rossettis to see Gabriel and William, but it was soon Christina who claimed most of his attention. Some of her biographers have been unable to believe that Collinson was a credible suitor for Christina and the object of so much passionate poetry, but his strict religious code and modest serious disposition were perfectly matched to Christina's own, and his shyness created a bond of sympathy between them. She was also only seventeen and it was her first love affair. It was Christina's nature to love deeply and permanently.

In the early summer of 1848 Collinson approached Gabriel about his feelings for her. Gabriel talked to Christina and she made it clear that, although she cared for Collinson, she could not accept a proposal of marriage while he remained a member of the Roman Catholic Church. On the face of it this decision may seem over scrupulous. Christina was herself the product of a Catholic/Protestant marriage, and her grandparents had also managed such a partnership with apparent success, but it is possible that this first hand knowledge and the experience of her parents' religious differences made her decide against entering a similar relationship.

Collinson's great fault was that he was indecisive and easily swayed by stronger personalities. After Christina's rejection he re-thought his conversion to Rome, decided that it had been a mistake and rejoined the Anglican communion. When he proposed again in the autumn of 1848 Christina gladly accepted him. From then on, her brother William recorded, she 'freely and warmly bestowed her affections on him.'[8]

It was a very happy time. The Pre-Raphaelite Brotherhood painted together and were often in each other's houses. They had very little money, or 'tin' as Gabriel called it, but were young and full of enthusiasm. Collinson and Woolner at twenty-three were the oldest of the group, Millais and William the youngest at nineteen. There was a certain amount of youthful excess – rumours of having labels attached to their jackets on a night out so that they could be returned to their addresses after they had passed out. Collinson was very unwilling to take part in these excursions, and was inclined to fall asleep. Sometimes he was so quiet people couldn't remember afterwards whether he'd been there or not. They were sometimes joined on outings by Walter Deverell and Arthur Hughes.

They discussed art and literature and read poetry. At one meeting they drew up a table of immortality which included artists and poets and awarded stars to the most important. Elizabeth Barrett Browning, the only woman, was awarded one star on a par with Raphael, Shakespeare had three and Robert Browning two. Wordsworth and Milton didn't get any.

William and Gabriel would have liked Christina to be present at some of their meetings, but this was vetoed by the others. It is doubtful if she would have accepted even if the invitation had been extended. She was only able to join in the discussion when members of the brotherhood called at Charlotte Street. Ford Madox Brown continued to be a regular visitor, even though Gabriel was no longer his pupil; Charles Cayley, a young scholar even less communicative then Collinson, came to consult Gabriele on his translations of Dante, and in 1849 W.B. Scott renewed his acquaintance during the few weeks of the year that he spent in London. His wit and easy charm made him something of a favourite with the Rossettis.

Christina was suddenly exposed to a variety of influences and modes of thought. W.B. Scott sent William the poetry of Walt Whitman. Woolner introduced the poet Coventry Patmore and he and his new wife Emily rented a house from Christina's uncle Henry Polydore. Christina liked the Patmores and sometimes walked over with her sister on summer evenings, and they would all go out and ramble in the fields. Emily Patmore was one of the few people privileged to be shown Christina's poetry – probably by Gabriel. She was 'greatly pleased', though Coventry was less complimentary, only admiring one of her bouts-rimés sonnets.

It was Coventry Patmore's poetry that embodied the Victorian vision of Womanhood identified by Virginia Woolf as the primary obstacle for the woman writer. His 'Angel in the House' was inspired by his wife, whom he saw as a model of submission and virtue, juggling motherhood and housekeeping with solicitude for her husband. In fact Emily was herself a gifted writer, whose talent was consumed by the regular arrival of six children and the demands of her husband. John Ruskin, another Pre-Raphaelite acquaintance, was also influential in creating the female myth that has proved so hard to eradicate. His portrait of female perfection in *Sesame and Lilies* and *Of Queen's Gardens* is synonymous with Gabriel's Blessed Damozel leaning on the bar of heaven. Ruskin was hardly a model husband either, and subjected his wife Effie to a loveless, unconsummated marriage. Following its annulment he fell violently in love with a young, barely pubescent girl. Full blown female sexuality seems to have repelled him.

In this early Pre-Raphaelite period it was Christina's face and devout demeanour that embodied the ideals of truth and purity they were trying to express on the canvas. Leslie Parris, deputy keeper of the British Collection at the Tate Gallery, states that 'It was as much the appearance of Christina Rossetti that determined the emaciated and angular style of the Brothers as any return ... to the pre Raphael frescoes in the Campo Santo at Pisa'.[9]

Christina sat for a portrait by James Collinson, and it shows a radically different person to the profile executed by Gabriel a year earlier. She looks strained and serious – her expression little different from that of the Virgin in Gabriel's painting. Several of the group used her as a model. They could rarely afford to pay for professional sitters, and so members of their own families and friends were pressed into service.

As well as sitting for her brother and his friends, Christina was devoting more of her time to poetry. Encouraged by William and Gabriel she submitted some of her poetry to the *Athenaeum*, one of the most influential literary magazines of the time. Two of the poems were rejected by the editor on the grounds that they contained too many Tennysonian mannerisms, but two others were accepted and published on 14 and 21 October. The first was a lament by Anne of Warwick after her husband, the Prince of Wales, had been killed at the Battle of Tewkesbury. Gabriel retitled it 'Death's Chill Between'. The second, written in September 1847 a few days before the other, was called 'The Lost Hope' and Gabriel altered this to 'Heart's Chill Between' to create a link between the poems. They are sentimental accounts of past love – one pair of lovers separated by death, the others by inconstancy, and neither Christina nor her brother William thought them good enough to republish in her lifetime.

In November William accompanied Collinson on a visit to his parents at Pleasley Hill, Mansfield. Christina wrote him a typically lively letter which completely belies the prim and serious girl in Collinson's portrait.

Dear William,
The postman's knock this morning made evident a most humiliating state of my own mind, for though not sufficiently philosophical to regret

the arrival of your letter today, I was quite enough of a baby to mourn over my losing that pleasure tomorrow, when I had calculated upon receiving it. From all this you will draw the conclusion that your hint of a second communication must quite have consoled me, and believe in the sincerity of my thanks for both performance and promise . . . I had fancied Mrs Collinson the very reverse of *prim*; but, as you conjecture, kind-hearted. I am glad you like Miss Collinson, but have a notion that she must be dreadfully clever. Is either of these ladies *alarming*? not to you, of course, but would they be so to me? I wish that they could be convinced that the celebrated portrait is flattering, and that "the thoughtful and pleasing expression" of my face is indeed "as developed in the portrait." You probably not only *profusely banqueted* but surfeited your victims with my *poetry*; but in this you may not have been the sole culprit.[10]

In December Christina wrote one of her most famous lyrics, simply called 'Song' – Christina always struggled with titles. Winter had brought a recurrence of her bronchitis and she was once more forced to be acutely aware of her precarious health. The lines reflect that blend of 'piety and sadness' which W.B. Scott identified as the main character-istic of her poetry. There is an awareness of mortality even in happiness, a portrayal of the seductiveness of death.

> When I am dead, my dearest,
>   Sing no sad songs for me;
> Plant thou no roses at my head,
>   Nor shady cypress tree:
> Be the green grass above me
>   With showers and dewdrops wet;
> And if thou wilt, remember,
>   And if thou wilt, forget.
>
> I shall not see the shadows,
>   I shall not feel the rain;
> I shall not hear the nightingale
>   Sing on as if in pain:
> And dreaming through the twilight
>   That doth not rise nor set,
> Haply I may remember,
>   And haply may forget.

Seven days later Emily Brontë died of tuberculosis at Haworth, after refusing medical attention until a few hours before her death. To those close to her, it seemed to be a wilful act of self-destruction, her longing for death and implacable resolve every bit as strong as Christina's.

CHAPTER FOUR

Throughout 1849 Christina was engaged to James Collinson. Added to the emotional see-saw of a first love affair were the additional worries over her own health and anxiety about her father and family finances. In February she wrote another lyric, also entitled 'Song'.

> Oh roses for the flush of youth,
>   And laurel for the perfect prime;
> But pluck an ivy branch for me
>   Grown old before my time.
>
> Oh violets for the grave of youth,
>   And bay for those dead in their prime;
> Give me the withered leaves I chose
>   Before in the old time.

In May Gabriel exhibited *The Girlhood of Mary Virgin*, not at the Royal Academy with other members of the PRB, but at the 'Free Exhibition' in a picture gallery near Hyde Park. The painting was very well received. A reviewer in the *Athenaeum* talked of 'sacred mysticism inseparable from the works of the early masters'. The personification of the Virgin was much admired and the painting sold to the Marchioness Dowager of Bath for £80.

Christina had begun to write her juvenile novel *Maude*, a story for girls which features four main characters, Maude, her cousins Agnes and Mary Clifton, and their friend Magdalen. Her family regarded the book as autobiographical, and, while there is some danger in adopting this viewpoint unreservedly, there are similarities between Maude and Christina.

Maude Foster was just fifteen. Small though not positively short, she might easily be overlooked but would not easily be forgotten. Her figure was slight and well-made, but appeared almost high-shouldered through a habitual shrugging stoop. Her features were regular and pleasing, as a child she had been very pretty; and might have continued so but for a fixed paleness, and an expression, not exactly of pain, but languid and preoccupied to a painful degree. Yet even now, if at any time she became thoroughly aroused and interested, her sleepy eyes would light up with wonderful brilliancy, her cheeks glow with warm colour, her manner become animated, and drawing herself up to her full height she would look more beautiful than ever she did as a child.

Maude writes furtively, 'original compositions not intended for the public eye, pet extracts, extraordinary little sketches, and occasional tracts of journal.' She keeps her writing book locked, slipping her compositions out of sight whenever someone comes into the room. She knows that people think her clever and 'her little copies of verses' are 'handed about and admired' among family and close friends. Like Christina

> . . . it was the amazement of everyone what could make her poetry so broken-hearted as was mostly the case. Some pronounced that she wrote very foolishly about things she could not possibly understand; some wondered if she really had any secret source of uneasiness; while some simply set her down as affected. Perhaps there was a degree of truth in all these opinions.

The same questions have been asked about Christina's melancholy verses and similar hypotheses put forward to explain them. Perhaps a clue can be found in the work of an earlier poet, Laetitia Landon. Like Maude/Christina she also wrote tragic poetry, though her friends remembered her as a lively, sociable person, without a trace of melancholy. L.E.L. tried to explain it in her preface to *The Venetian Bracelet* in 1829.

> Aware that to elevate I must first soften, and that if I wish to purify I must first touch, I have ever endeavoured to bring forward grief, disappointment, the fallen leaf, the faded flower, the broken heart, and the early grave.

L.E.L.'s statement and those of her friends must not be read too credulously. A difficult childhood, an early scandal with the editor of the

Literary Gazette, several failed love affairs and a broken engagement, coupled with acute financial problems, do not add up to a particularly happy life. Her pursuit of love ended when she made a disastrous marriage at the age of thirty-five to the taciturn governor of Cape Coast Castle on Africa's Gold Coast. She travelled out there with him to discover that she was the only European woman in the settlement. Her relationship with her husband, based on a few months' acquaintance, was a failure and she died from a self-administered dose of prussic acid six months after her marriage. There was a 'degree of truth' in L.E.L.'s poetry, just as there was in Christina's, even though 'affecting poetry' was still in vogue.

Maude includes a sonnet not written until some time in 1850 and added when Christina revised the manuscript, at a time when life seemed bleaker and less full of hope. It is called 'Endurance' and begins

> Yes, I too could face death and never shrink:
> But it is harder to bear hated life;
> To strive with hands and knees weary of strife;
> To drag the heavy chain whose every link
> Galls to the bone;

This became a recurrent theme in Christina's poetry, rooted in early experience and never countered by anything that followed.

> To do is quickly done; to suffer is
> Longer and fuller of heart-sickness:
> Each day's experience testifies of this:

The last line is the bitter cry of one who suffers and asks – why me?

> Thousands taste the full cup; who drains the lees?

There is subtle irony in the novel. The secretive Maud, adept at hiding the truth without ever telling a lie, appears to be untouched by the painful sonnet she has just written. '. . . she yawned, leaned back in her chair, and wondered how she should fill up the time till dinner.'

When Maude visits her cousins Mary and Agnes Clifton her correct breeding and lack of social ease is contrasted with their 'genuine, unobtrusive courtesy'. They play, like the Rossetti family at proverbs, magic music, and bouts-rimés. Christina penned three sonnets using the same rhymes to illustrate the different temperaments of the girls. Agnes has no aptitude for poetry.

> Rather than writing, I would change my pink
> Gauze for a hideous yellow satin gown

Their friend Magdalen writes limpid verse about fairies.

> Or wrapping lilies in their leafy gown,
>   Yet letting the white peep beyond the rim.

Maude's performance is considered by far the best, and thoroughly deserving of the sprig of bay Agnes has fixed in her hair. It is a rather more humorous production than usual.

> If all the world were water fit to drown
>   There are some whom you would not teach to swim;
>   Rather enjoying if you saw them sink;
>   Certain old ladies dressed in girlish pink,
> With roses and geraniums on their gown:

Maude's health is poor and when the second part opens a year later she is pale and thin. Magdalen has entered a convent to the horror of her friends. Maude defends her choice, though admitting that she herself has no desire for it. 'You cannot imagine me either fit or inclined for such a life; still I can perceive that those who are so are very happy.' The debate between life in the world and life in the cloister has begun to appear in Christina's work and seems to reflect both her sister Maria's sense of vocation and Christina's own yearning for a similar certainty at particular periods in her life. The nun haunts her psyche just as it haunted Lucy Snowe in *Villette*.

The Anglicans had begun to set up sisterhoods all over England, offering for the first time a Protestant alternative to the Catholic convent. One of the first orders of the Sisters of Mercy was opened quite close to Christ Church where Maria and Christina worshipped. It offered women opportunities to teach and nurse and give service to others – a practical alternative to the life of the governess, which was all that Victorian society could offer its surplus population of unmarried women.

Remembering the portrait of Christina Rossetti in later life – the shy, reclusive, austere figure she became to those who did not know her, it is easy to forget that as a young girl she could be gay and sociable in the presence of close family and friends, and had a lively sense of humour. Among her favourite books were Thackeray's *Book of Snobs* and the works of Edward Lear. Some of this humour comes through in the description of a party Maude attends where she is pressed to read her poetry.

> Seated between Miss Savage and Sophia Mowbray she was attacked on either hand with questions concerning her verses. In the first place, did she continue to write? Yes. A flood of ecstatic compliments followed this admission: she was so young, so much admired, and, poor thing, looked so delicate. It was quite affecting to think of her lying awake at night meditating those sweet verses – ('I sleep like a top,' Maude put in drily) – which so delighted her friends, and would so charm the public if only Miss Foster could be induced to publish. At last the bystanders were called upon to intercede for a recitation.
>
> Maude coloured with displeasure; a hasty answer was rising to her lips, when the absurdity of her position flashed across her mind so forcibly that, almost unable to check a laugh in the midst of her annoyance, she put her handkerchief to her mouth. Miss Savage, impressed with the notion that her request was about to be complied with, raised her hand, imploring silence; and settled herself in a listening attitude.

Maude refuses, as Christina was persistently to do. Internally, Christina, like Maude was debating the ethics of writing. Was it not a species of vanity involving a love of display? 'No one will say that I cannot avoid putting myself forward and displaying my verses.' It was an argument that beset many High Anglican women. Charlotte M. Yonge in *Womankind*, wrote that women must never '*far la civetta*' – which is an Italian expression meaning to lay oneself out for admiration and attention like 'the little civetta owls which make themselves ridiculous by their airs and graces, on the roofs of houses in Rome'. It is all right to excel if it is done only for the purposes of excellence, but taking pleasure in one's own excellence is the sin of vanity. Charlotte's own father 'subjected her to a grave catechism of her motives for publishing'. She was allowed to do so when she could assure him, with penitent tears, 'that I really hoped I had written with the purpose of being useful to young girls like myself'. 'Wanting to be first, rather than wanting to do one's best' had to be guarded against at all costs.

Christina's struggle with her conscience led her to refrain from Holy Communion because she felt unfit. Maude has a similar crisis.

> "I shall not receive tomorrow," answered Maude; then hurrying on as if to prevent the other from remonstrating. "No: at least I will not profane Holy Things; I will not add this to all the rest. I have gone over and over again, thinking I should come right in time, and I do not come right. I will go no more."

This was the 'wire-drawn scrupulosity' remarked upon by Christina's brother.

The delicate Maude suffers a carriage accident and is confined to bed. The opening of the final chapter is one of the most vivid of the whole book.

> Three weeks had passed away. A burning sun seemed baking the very dust in the streets, and sucking the last remnant of moisture from the straw spread in front of Mrs Foster's house.

Maude sees her illness as a punishment sent by God.

> You remember Mr Paulson told us last Sunday that sickness and suffering are sent for our correction. I suffer very much. Perhaps a time will come when these will have done their work on me also; when I shall be purified indeed and weaned from the world.[1]

It is possible to see the four girls, Maude, Mary, Agnes and Magdalen as representing the four possibilities open to women at the time. Maude seeks literary fulfilment, Mary marries, Agnes remains single and occupies herself with church duties and 'good works', while Magdalen enters an Anglican convent. There is a great deal of significance in the fact that it is Maude – with all her secret ambitions and talents – who is the one to die. The ending is as pessimistic as any of George Eliot's novels. And, as so often happened in real life, Maude's poetry 'dies' with her; either burnt by Agnes, or buried in her coffin, 'with all its words of folly, sin, vanity.' This part of the story was possibly inspired by the account of Keats' funeral, and his request that the letters of Fanny Brawne be buried with him.

Comments by William, coupled with internal evidence, seem to indicate that the first part of Maude may have been written when she was seventeen or eighteen, the last part two or three years later. There is a darkness and very real sadness in the second half of the book and the poems it contains, which suggest that it was composed some time after her engagement to James Collinson had been severed. The poems are dated 1850.

Maude is much too short to be a novel, it is really only a long short story and has all the faults to be expected of such an early attempt at fiction. The dialogue is for the most part convincingly done, if a little stilted, and the descriptions are good, though the characters lack depth. It gives a glimpse of what Christina might have done if she had ever seriously turned to fiction. As Charles Sisson writes in the Carcanet edition of her work 'with any poet the starting point, social as well as literary, is worth finding out about, and as first hand evidence of where Christina set out from *Maude* is worth the short time it takes to read.'[2]

Many of the poems written in early 1849 concern the prospect of young death; but for someone in Christina's state of health this was hardly surprising. She saw 'the countenance of Death very close to her own', being 'compelled, even if not naturally disposed, to regard this world as a "valley of the shadow of death".'[3]

The death of the young was a frequent fact of life in the nineteenth century. Emily Brontë's experience was not unusual. By the age of seven she had lost her mother and her two favourite sisters. The demise of Little Nell was a circumstance many of Dickens' readers could relate to. The tragedy was rationalised by religion. Life was hard and difficult and death a kind of happy ending, the passage to an afterlife of unmitigated delight, expressed by Christina in 'Looking Forward'.

> Then, if you haply muse upon the past,
> Say this; Poor child, she has her wish at last;
>   Barren through life, but in death bearing fruit.

In the summer of 1849 Christina went to stay with Collinson's family at Pleasley Hill. It was a visit she dreaded. She was always shy with strangers, had never been away from home alone before and was anxious to make a good impression. She found the Collinson women friendly but completely alien in their interests and occupations. She wrote to William

The talk of *beaus* is as perpetual as at Mrs Heimann's: however, fewer jokes have been passed on me than might have been anticipated; and of these Mary is entirely innocent. Do you know, I rather like Mary; she is not at all caressing, but seems real. Do you ever see the Kings? news of them, or of the Brotherhood, or of anything else, thankfully received. Apropos of receiving, would you be so kind as to let me have at your convenience "As I lay a-thinking"? In my desperation I knit lace with a perseverance completely foreign to my nature. Yesterday I made a dirt-pudding in the garden, wherein to plant some slips of currant. The unbusinesslike manner in which the process was gone through affords every prospect of complete failure. Ah Will! if you were here we would write bouts-rimés sonnets and be subdued together. Mary has told me a capital story of three bears, with which I may perhaps solace you on my return; you will stand in need of some comfort.[4]

The Brotherhood were all painting their 'vacation' pieces for the Academy. Collinson was working on the *Emigrant's Letter* which was to be one of his most famous studies, and Gabriel had begun to think about a companion piece to *The Girlhood of Mary Virgin – Ecce Ancilla Domini*, a painting of the annunciation, once more using Christina's face for the Virgin. They had begun to read Elizabeth Barrett Browning's *Drama of Exile* and there was much argument about the relative merits of Elizabeth and her husband. Browning was regarded by most of the PRB as totally unintelligible, though Gabriel and Coventry Patmore were convinced of his superiority. They were also discussing the possibility of a publication of their own to be called *Thoughts Towards Nature*. This would contain poetry, fiction and articles expounding their new vision of art. Eventually they decided to call it *The Germ*.

Christina wrote to William on 31 August.

Many thanks for "As I lay, etc". To your rhymes I have written a rather intense sonnet, which cannot miss your approbation. The notion of *life* turning to *must* is not hackneyed. On the back are some rhymes for you to fill up; They belong to one of my old things . . .

I long to see your first *Thought*. That such a magazine as yours will be clever is beyond a doubt, but you must excuse my joining one which numbers among its contributors a "rabid chartist", and one "who thinks of nothing but politics" and 'the negation of religion'. Your plan is far too Blissful for my taste.

Mary desires me to kindly remember, or something of the sort "us" to you. Tomorrow she and I go to Mansfield; she prophesies my being a *favourite* with C[harles] C[ollinson] on account of my unalterable self-possession. Fancy the inflated state in which I shall re-enter London, should this flattering preference result from my visit.[5]

Christina had already met James Collinson's brother Charles in London and he was disliked, not only by her but by her family. The 'unalterable self-possession' mentioned in the letter seems to refer to a comment made to her – probably by Mary Collinson – that she seemed 'to do all from self-respect' not from fellow-feeling with others, or from 'kindly consideration for them'. The Collinsons had completely misinterpreted her reserve. William wrote that in her character there was a 'distance, not remote from *hauteur*' which was at that time quite marked. Christina was deeply hurt, though acknowledging the possibility of truth, and the phrase 'doing all from self-respect' crops up in the poems 'Is and Was' written early in 1850 and in 'Enrica' where she contrasts herself with her Italian friend, Enrica Barile.

Christina seems to have enjoyed her visit on the whole and regarded it as successful. She wrote to William, who was on the Isle of Wight with James Collinson, as soon as she returned.

> I came home on Monday, after exactly a month's stay in Notts. From all acquaintances there I have received unvarying kindness and hospitality; on your return you will probably witness (not watch) the progress of a piece of work of which I hope some day to beg Mrs Charles' acceptance. I have already given Miss Collinson my Nice portfolio, so need not on that account hesitate to make my next present where I like . . .

However she adds that 'my visit was very pleasant for some reasons, but not exclusively so.' It was something of a shock for Christina to learn that Mary Collinson did not want to pursue their newly established intimacy.

> My correspondence with Mary Collinson has come to an end by her desire. Do not imagine we have been quarrelling: not at all: but she seems to think her brother's affairs so unpromising as to render our continuing to write to each other not pleasant. Does not this sound extraordinary? We are all much surprised.[6]

Why the Collinsons found the affair unpromising can only be conjectured. Neither James nor Christina had any money. He lived on an allowance from his family and was a long way from the prospect of earning a living by painting, but this need not have been a bar. Long engagements were almost the norm. Christina's imperfect health may have been a factor, also too her 'difference'. It is quite possible that they disapproved of her. But the Collinsons may have been privy to James's vacillations with regard to religion and it is possible that he had said something to them when he visited Mansfield in May about reconsidering his position in the Anglican communion. He obviously still cared for Christina. On 17 September, the day after she returned from Pleasley Hill, he left Cowes to come back to London and promptly presented himself at 50 Charlotte Street.

'From House to Home', a long poem completed in 1858, charts the journey of the soul from dependency upon earthly love, through bitterness and torment to realisation of divine love. It describes a state of relationship where one person is happy without perceiving the doubt and hesitation of the other.

We sang our songs together by the way,
   Calls and recalls and echoes of delight;
So communed we together all the day,
   and so in dreams by night.

I have no words to tell what way we walked.
   What unforgotten path now closed and sealed;
I have no words to tell all things we talked,
   All things that he revealed:

This only can I tell: that hour by hour
   I waxed more feastful, lifted up and glad;
I felt no thorn-prick when I plucked a flower,
   Felt not my friend was sad.

Tomorrow, once I said to him with smiles.
   Tonight, he answered gravely; and was dumb,
But pointed out the stones that numbered miles
   And miles to come.

Not so, I said: tomorrow shall be sweet:
   Tonight is not so sweet as coming days.
Then first I saw that he had turned his feet,
   Had turned from me his face.

Something of the sort seems to have happened to Christina, for Collinson's change of heart found her totally unprepared, despite all the warning signs from the Collinson family.

Christina became closely involved in the production of *The Germ*. The 'rabid chartist', whose contribution she had objected to was excluded and she was persuaded to allow Gabriel to select some of her poems for inclusion. She discussed the magazine's progress by letter with William who was still on holiday on the Isle of Wight.

Gabriel, being pressed for time, has commissioned me to write as follows.

   You need not hasten your return home on account of the magazine, as the prospects can wait. You already know all the contributions except Mr Stephens'; which is at present on divers scraps, in a highly chaotic state. Mr Hunt's etching is in two compartments; the first represents Mr Woolner's man and woman gathering flowers by the water-side; the second, the man throwing himself on a woman's grave. These are all his messages, to the best of my remembrance . . .

   P.P.S. Several are thinking of calling it the P.R.B. Journal. Think maturely and write result at once to Stephens. You need not hasten back, as he will manage till your return. All communications are to be addressed to him.[7]

Dante Gabriel was spending part of his time in the British Library reading old romances in search of 'stunning words' for poetry and planning a trip to Paris with Holman Hunt. By October, William was back in London and there are no more letters.

In December they decided to call the magazine *The Germ* and on 31 December William collected the first copies from the publisher. It included contributions from Woolner, Ford Madox Brown and Coventry Patmore as well as the Rossettis. Gabriel printed 'My Sister's Sleep', and a prose piece called 'Hand and Soul'. Christina published 'Dreamland' and 'An End', neither of them particularly distinguished. She did not include her beautiful sonnet 'Remember', written in July 1849 because she did not want to publish anything that might be construed as a 'love personal'. All the contributors were anonymous in this first edition. Subsequently names and pseudonyms were affixed. Christina's work appeared under the name Ellen Alleyne, invented by Gabriel.

They optimistically printed 700 copies, of which only about 200 were sold. The print run was reduced to 500 for the second which sold even more badly than the first. Christina's 'Pause of Thought', 'Testimony' and 'Song' – 'Oh Roses for the Flush of Youth' appeared alongside W.B. Scott's 'Morning Sleep', Coventry Patmore's 'Stars and Moon' and Gabriel's 'Blessed Damozel'.

The title was changed to *Art and Poetry*, but after the fourth issue in April 1850 the magazine lapsed, leaving a debt to the publisher, George Tupper, which took a long time to discharge. It was however a critical success and copies changed hands later on for inflated sums of money.

Collinson had for some months been prey to religious doubt. William had described him as a 'man of timorous conscience' and he was certainly indecisive, finding it difficult to choose even which picture he wanted to work on. Early in 1850 he reverted to the Church of Rome and, according to William, 'struck a staggering blow at Christina Rossetti's peace of mind . . . a blow from which she did not fully recover for years.'[8]

'From House to Home' records the ending of earthly love.

> That night destroyed me like an avalanche;
> One night turned all my summer back to snow:
> Next morning not a bird upon my branch,
> Not a lamb woke below,

She felt that she had no option but to terminate the engagement. Some of her biographers have thought that she did so with relief, attributing the subsequent poetry delineating the agony of choice to an affair with William Bell Scott. But there is nothing to support an alternative view to that of her close family and no breath of scandal has survived to even hint at it, among a group of people who wrote about each other pretty freely.

Christina's internal struggle is chronicled in her poetry in terms as bare and brief as Emily Dickinson, and more implacable than anything written by Emily Brontë. An addition to 'A Pause of Thought', written in 1854 describes how

> I thought to deal the death-stroke at a blow
> To give all, once for all, but never more:-

And the fifth stanza recalls Emily Dickinson's 'My Life closed Twice Before its Close'.

> I said so in my heart: and so I thought
> My life would lapse, a tedious monotone:
> I thought to shut myself and dwell alone
>   Unseeking and unsought.

For Emily Dickinson becoming a Queen, with its implications of triumph and pre-eminence, had special significance connected with womanhood and poetry. For her, Elizabeth Barrett Browning and George Sand were 'women now, Queens now'. And Elizabeth Barrett Browning's Aurora Leigh was also 'a woman and a queen'. Christina cannot see such a great event happening to her. Instead only failure seems a reality, in love and in poetry.

> Alas, I cannot build myself a nest,
>   I cannot crown my head
>
> With royal purple blossoms for the feast,
> Nor flush with laughter, nor exult in song:-
> These joys may drift, as time now drifts along;
>   And cease, as once they ceased.
>
> I may pursue, and yet may not attain,
> Athirst and panting all the days I live:
> Or seem to hold, yet nerve myself to give
>   What once I gave, again.

Christina was extremely secretive where her affections were involved. William wrote that 'it would have been both indelicate and futile to press her with inquiries'.[9] She buried her feelings deep inside her, where they corroded her spirit.

In 'Three Moments', written in March 1850 the young girl in the poem laments that she is unable to weep.

> She cried: O mother, where are they,
> The tears that used to flow
> So easily? One single drop
> Might save my reason now, or stop
> My heart from breaking . . .

In 'Seeking Rest', mother and sister press the young girl to reveal first the secret source of her joy, and then her sorrow so that they can share it and give her comfort. She answers:

> How should I share my pain, who kept
>   My pleasure all my own?
> My Spring will never come again;
>   My pretty flowers have blown
> For the last time; I can but sit
>   And think and weep alone.

Later, as she looked back at the event, an implacable stoicism crept into her poetry. The decision to terminate her relationship with Collinson had been hers alone, the cost one that only she could estimate. In putting her duty to God before her own personal happiness she faced the possibility that she might never have the chance to marry and have children. The resolution in the stark lines of 'Memory' resembles Emily Brontë's in her poems 'Remembrance' and 'No Coward Soul is Mine'.

> I nursed it in my bosom while it lived,
>   I hid it in my heart when it was dead;
> In joy I sat alone, even so I grieved
>   Alone, and nothing said.
>
> I shut the door to face the naked truth,
>   I stood alone – I faced the truth alone,
> Stripped bare of self-regard or forms or ruth
>   Till first and last were shown.

I took the perfect balances and weighed;
   No shaking of my hand disturbed the poise;
Weighed, found it wanting: not a word I said,
   But silent made my choice.

None know the choice I made; I make it still.
   None know the choice I made and broke my heart,
Breaking mine idol: I have braced my will
   Once, chosen for once my part.

I broke it at a blow, I laid it cold,
   Crushed in my deep heart where it used to live.
My heart dies inch by inch; the time grows old,
   Grows old in which I grieve.

PART TWO

Renunciation

He chose what I had feared to choose
  (Ah, which was wiser, I or he?)
He chose a love-warm priceless heart
  And I a cold bare dignity.

      *   *   *

He chose a garden of delights
  Where still refreshing waters flow;
I chose a barren wilderness
  Whose buds died years ago

CHRISTINA ROSSETTI
Deleted stanzas from
'Two Choices'
October 1854

CHAPTER FIVE

In May 1850 Collinson resigned from the PRB in a prim letter to Gabriel explaining that as a Catholic his conscience would not allow him to continue to promote the artistic opinions and ideals of those who were not. He continued to paint – working on a long discussed portrayal of St Elizabeth of Hungary, the queen who gave up her crown to become a nun. The following year he entered a Jesuit training college, but left without being ordained.

Despite Christina's courage in renouncing Collinson she still loved him and longed for news of him. At times her resolution wavered. When she went with some members of her family to Brighton for the summer, a practice begun for the sake of Gabriele's health and continued for Christina's own, she wrote secretly to William. It is a sad dejected note, contrasted with the lively letters of the previous year.

My dear William,
Seized with my usual longing for news, I as usual resort to you; somewhat ashamed indeed of the empty letter system, yet not enough to make me give it up. . .

Have you seen the St. Elizabeth lately? and do you yet know what is to be done with the figure of the old woman whose position was not liked? Whilst I am here, if you can manage without too much trouble, I wish you would find out whether Mr Collinson is as delicate as he used to be: you and Gabriel are my resources, and you are by far the more agreeable.

I direct this to the Excise that Mamma may not know of it. Do not be shocked at the concealment; this letter would not give her much pleasure. Do have patience both with the trouble I occasion you and with myself. I am ashamed of this note, yet want courage to throw it away; so must despatch it in its dreary emptiness . . .[1]

A few months later when Christina saw James Collinson in the street she fainted. Nor could she at this point, find any comfort in writing. Only three rather pedestrian poems can be identified as belonging to the months after April 1850. 'Song' – 'We buried her among the flowers' on 14 May, a narrative poem of rejected love called 'Annie' in September, and two stanzas on St Elizabeth of Hungary begun in 1850 but not finished until 1852. Christina referred to writing 'two or three scraps, none of which may very likely be finished.' She wrote to William that 'altogether our days and nights and days go by, bearing a considerable resemblance between themselves'.[2]

William had gone north on holiday first to Edinburgh, and then to Newcastle to stay with W.B. Scott. A letter sent by Christina from Brighton arrived in Charlotte Street after his departure and appears to have been opened by Mrs Rossetti. Christina wrote to her brother that 'As a whole it was not perhaps a peculiarly interesting document; but it contained an unhappy little fragment which so totally disgusted Mamma that I very speedily made away with it.'[3]

Christina had begun to build her love affair with Collinson and her renunciation of him into a major tragedy. His importance and the depth of her love for him expanded to fill the emotional vacuum that he left behind. If she had had any kind of absorbing occupation, or a wider social life with the possibility of other relationships, Collinson would quickly have been relegated to his proper place in Christina's mind, as her first love affair, a teenage romance that had failed to mature. As it was, she became emotionally maimed by the experience.

With the demise of *The Germ* there was little for Christina to look forward to and she appears to have been deeply depressed. Her father's health had continued to decline, and a succession of strokes weakened his constitution. He was continually at odds with Gabriel, accusing him of wasting his talent by lack of application and what William describes as 'desultory' habits.

Gabriel seemed to be unable to make up his mind whether to be a poet or a painter. His father felt that Gabriel had failed him and there were distressing scenes. Gabriel was also in trouble elsewhere. He had rented a studio above a dancing academy – referred to as the 'hop shop' – and when the proprietor defaulted on the rent the landlord seized all Gabriel's property. As a sub-tenant there was little he could do.

Gabriel had recently met Elizabeth Siddal who was eventually to become his wife. The Pre-Raphaelites were fascinated by a particular shade of red gold hair and were always looking for models. Walter Deverell accompanied his mother on a visit to a milliner's shop, and glancing through the door into the workroom saw Elizabeth, lifting down a hatbox. She was tall, long necked, with agate coloured eyes and the requisite shade of red hair. After discreet enquiries by Deverell's mother she consented to model for him. A professional model earned considerably more than a milliner's apprentice and she was soon modelling full time, posing in a bath of water for Millais' painting *Ophelia*. Gabriel saw her in Deverell's studio and fell in love with her. The affection was eventually returned, although initially there seems to have been some kind of bond with Deverell.

Elizabeth was still only sixteen, the daughter of a cutler. She had considerable artistic talent, which because of her lack of education and social position had never been developed. William described her character as

> somewhat singular – not quite easy to understand, and not at all on the surface . . . All her talk was of a "chaffy kind" – its tone sarcastic, its substance lightsome . . . she seemed to say "My mind and my feelings are my own, and no outsider is expected to pry into them".[4]

Gabriel undertook to teach her to paint and under his tuition she painted gloomy portraits and wrote poetry which was bleak and sad. He painted her as Beatrice and she became the paradigm of what we now think of as the Pre-Raphaelite woman. Elizabeth, unsure of her gifts and of Gabriel's fidelity, suffered from depression and exhibited the symptoms of consumption, though her condition may have had psychosomatic origins.

The Brotherhood had in 1850 suffered the first test of its principles. Gabriel had divulged to his friend Alexander Munro the secret of the initials PRB; Munro told other people, an article was printed in *The Illustrated London News* and the consequences were disastrous. Hunt and Millais were ridiculed when they submitted their paintings to the Academy and Gabriel, who had once more chosen to exhibit at the Free Exhibition, found himself unpopular with his colleagues and the public. A coolness developed between him and the others. They blamed him for not exhibiting with them at the Academy and presenting a solid front, and for revealing their secret to Munro. Gabriel, heavily criticised by the public for his *Annunciation*, resolved not to exhibit in public again.

The *Athenaeum* published a direct attack on Gabriel and the PRB. The *Annunciation* was described as 'an unintelligent imitation'. The one redeeming feature was that 'A certain expression in the eyes of the ill-drawn face of the Virgin affords a gleam of something high in intention', but the workmanship is 'timid', the picture flawed by affectation and 'infantine absurdities'.[5]

For the artists this meant ruin, for they were suddenly unable to sell their paintings. William and Aunt Charlotte jointly funded Gabriel who was reduced to borrowing from the hard pressed Frances so that he could continue, and this put even more of a strain on family relationships. Aunt Charlotte, for one, felt that he wasn't sufficiently grateful for the sacrifices made for him. Gabriel decided to abandon poetry and devote himself entirely to painting in order to perfect his technique, which he knew was flawed. But at one point he almost gave up altogether and even considered a post as a telegrapher on the North Western Railway. Things did not improve until Ruskin decided to take up the PRB cause some years later.

William, through the influence of Madox Brown, became at twenty-one the art critic of the *Spectator*. This brought him an extra £50 a year on top of his Inland Revenue salary. The strain of supporting the family was beginning to tell on him, and at one point he lost his hair and had to wear a wig. Friends and family teased him that the hair loss was due to dissipation!

The editor of the *Spectator*, R.S. Rintoul, had a daughter Henrietta who became a close friend of Christina's. Although Henrietta was rather older than William, he fell deeply in love with her, and Christina became something of a go-between in her brother's affairs. Maria was also in the throes of a love affair. She had met Charles Collins, brother of the novelist Wilkie Collins. Charles was a painter who had been introduced to the PRB by Madox Brown. He was also a High Anglican and his courtship of Maria proved to be the first test of her vocation. But although she loved him she chose not to marry him, putting God first. Tradition has it that after his rejection Collins altered the figure of a lady that he was painting to that of a nun in the painting that became *Convent Thoughts*.

It was no comfort to Christina in her depressed state to watch her sister and her brothers finding their own personal happiness in love. Several of her poems describe a state of emotional and spiritual aridity and the sense of isolation among people who are happy. 'Downcast', written in 1856 ends

> I, only I,
> Am changed and sad and cold, while in my soul
> The very fountain of delight is dry.

In the autumn of 1850 Frances Rossetti formulated a new plan to improve family finances and at the beginning of 1851 the family moved to a new house at 38 Arlington Street. It was not as pleasant as 50 Charlotte Street, but it did have a garden which was essential for the school Frances set up with Christina's help. Unfortunately the accommodation and type of education they were able to offer attracted only the daughters of local tradesmen – the hairdresser and the butcher among others – and not the wealthier children of professional parents who might have turned the school into a paying proposition.

Christina turned increasingly to Christianity to find consolation. The second half of 1851 marks the beginning of a stream of religious poetry which gradually increases throughout her life. In 1852 the theme is predominantly one of suffering now in the hope of bliss to come. 'The Heart Knoweth its own Bitterness', written in December illustrates the kind of faith she clung to.

> Weep, sick and lonely,
> Bow thy heart to tears,
> For none shall guess the secret
> Of thy griefs and fears.
> Weep, till the day dawn,
> > Refreshing dew:
> > Weep till the spring:
> > For genial showers
> > Bring up the flowers,
> And thou shalt sing
> In summertime of blossoming.
>
> Then love rejoicing
> Shall forget to weep:
> Shall hope or fear no more,
> > Or watch, or sleep,
> But only love and cease not,
> > Deep beyond deep.
> Now we sow love in tears,
> > But then shall reap.
> Have patience as the Lord's own flock of sheep:
> > Have patience with his love
> Who died below, who lives for thee above.

Bleak lines such as 'Yet how could I keep silence when I burn/And who can give me comfort?' testify to inner torment. She seems at times to have despaired of salvation for herself and her horror of worldliness intensified. A poem called 'The World' anticipates some of the themes and images that appeared in 'Goblin Market' and is an example of how powerfully she was beginning to write, in full command of her technique, able to express the divisions that were tearing her apart with vivid gothic imagery rooted in the Book of Revelations.

> By day she woos me, soft, exceeding fair:
>   But all night as the moon so changeth she;
>   Loathsome and foul with hideous leprosy
> And subtle serpents gliding in her hair.
> By day she woos me to the outer air,
>   Ripe fruits, sweet flowers, and full satiety:
>   But thro' the night, a beast she grins at me,
> A very monster void of love and prayer.
> By day she stands a lie: by night she stands
>   In all the naked horror of the truth
> With pushing horns and clawed and clutching hands.
> Is this a friend indeed; that I should sell
>   My soul to her, give her my life and youth,
> Till my feet, cloven too, take hold on hell?

Christina had not only found her technique, she had found her subject and that subject was suffering – her best poetry ranking with the so-called 'terrible sonnets' of John Donne and Gerard Manley Hopkins. Her great gift was to take us inside ourselves, to that inner space, to describe that moment of truth when we have to face what we are.

In the summer of 1851 Christina was sent to stay with her Aunt Charlotte at Longleat, the Somerset home of the Marchioness Dowager of Bath. It was hoped that the change of air and country scene would do her good. Christina was treated very kindly, and Lady Bath let her ride back from church in her own carriage while she walked in the rain. Christina reported that she was taking arrowroot for her health and mixing her wine with 'hop tea' and that this was 'unpleasant and salutary'.

William was unsuccessfully trying to find a publisher for *Maude* which Christina had managed to finish, and he was preparing for a second visit to W.B. Scott in Newcastle. On his first visit he had discovered to the surprise of the Rossettis that Scott was married. Mrs Scott was a cheerful chatterbox, quick-witted without being clever and something of a religious butterfly, trying several creeds before she settled on Anglicanism. The Scotts' marriage had not been a success and they were living separately under the same roof, though apparently the arrangement was amicable. Laetitia Scott also wrote poetry and William sent some of her verses to Christina in Somerset. She was cautiously complimentary, and wrote that they indicated 'talent and feeling: if such poetry may be trusted for telling a true tale.'

Christina's biographer L.M. Packer postulates the discovery of Mrs Scott's existence as the crisis in Christina's life which caused the breakdown in her health and produced her most impassioned poetry. However, the documentary evidence shows that this discovery took place after Christina's health had deteriorated. The idea that she might have been in love with W.B. Scott is also negated by Christina's own letters, which not only reveal Collinson as her prime concern but also seem to indicate that she did not know Scott particularly well at this time. In July 1851 she wrote to William

> When next you see him, you may remember me not only to Mrs but also to Mr Scott. This is avoiding the hurry of the last moment. Is Mr Scott a good judge in art? Of course, if not, his opinion may still occasionally be right.[6]

She may, at this point, have met Scott no more than half-a-dozen times. He was in London for only a few weeks of each year and made only courtesy calls to Charlotte Street. His main meetings with William and Gabriel took place at Gabriel's studio or at friends' houses. Scott comes over as rather vain and self-congratulatory. He refers disparagingly to the 'Oxford Tractarianism just then distracting weak intellects' including presumably his wife's – a sentiment that would not have endeared him to Christina, however he sought to cloak it with charm. Christina was fond of Scott, as was her mother, but it was his wife who was Christina's particular friend and, after she returned to London, often her chaperone. Laetitia's letters are full of Christina; their outings and discussions.

In August 1852 Christina went to Darleston Hall in Staffordshire for a few weeks to coach the daughters of a Mr Jervis in Italian. Swynfen Jervis was an MP and Shakespearian commentator, and an old acquaintance of Gabriele's. Christina took up drawing again while she was there and Gabriel wrote to her from London.

> Maria has just shown me a letter of yours by which I find that you have been perpetrating portraits of some kind. If you answer this note, will you enclose a specimen, as I should like to see some of your handiwork. You must take care however not to rival the Sid, but keep within respectful

limits. Since you went away, I have had sent me, among my things from Highgate, a lock of hair shorn from the beloved head of that dear, and radiant as the tresses of Aurora, a sight of which perhaps may dazzle you on your return. . . I am rejoicing to hear of your improved health, and hope it may prove lasting. I was lately in company with Mrs and Miss Howitt, with whom you are a considerable topic. I believe Mamma forwarded you an intelligent magazine by Mrs H. to which you are at liberty to contribute. That lady was much delighted with your printed performances, and wishes greatly to know you.[7]

Gabriel was now engaged to Lizzie Siddal and Christina seems to have had mixed feelings towards her. The fact that Gabriel was intent on tutoring Lizzie's genius, and had turned his attention to her at Christina's expense, may have had something to do with it. Christina did not have a jealous disposition, but Gabriel's playful phrase 'take care not to rival the Sid' is very provocative. There was also the knowledge that Lizzie had replaced Christina as the face of Pre-Raphaelitism – a move from ascetism towards the more erotic images of the later paintings. Whatever it was, Madox Brown's diaries recorded a disagreement between Gabriel and Christina over Lizzie.

Christina was extraordinarily clear eyed about Gabriel's relationship with Lizzie. She saw the way he projected her onto canvas, recreating her, seeing her as an idealised being, and she saw that ideal replace the real Lizzie in his mind. The first lines of Christina's poem 'In an Artist's Studio' are ambiguous in that they refer to the proliferation of paintings and drawings featuring Lizzie Siddal that Gabriel was turning out at the time, but her poem also refers to the fact that whoever Gabriel now used as a model would take on the same idealised form – the long fingers and neck, the crimped red-gold hair, large dreaming eyes and angular countenance. Even Holman Hunt remarked on Gabriel's tendency to 'convert the features of his sitter to his favourite ideal type.' Gabriel, inspired by Lizzie, had created a new Pre-Raphaelite Woman and whoever he painted now was transfigured into that image on the canvas.

> One face looks out from all his canvases,
>   One selfsame figure sits or walks or leans:
>   We found her hidden just behind those screens,
> That mirror gave back all her loveliness.
> A queen in opal or in ruby dress,
>   A nameless girl in freshest summer-greens,
>   A saint, an angel – every canvas means

The same one meaning, neither more nor less.
He feeds upon her face by day and night,
   And she with true kind eyes looks back on him,
Fair as the moon and joyful as the light:
   Not wan with waiting, not with sorrow dim;
Not as she is, but was when hope shone bright;
   Not as she is, but as she fills his dream.

Images of women dominated Pre-Raphaelite art, as Jan Marsh points
out in her excellent book *Pre-Raphaelite Women*. The Pre-Raphaelite
painters had very definite ideas about how women ought to look and
behave and were in the habit of taking up young girls and shaping them
to suit. As Gabriel groomed Lizzie Siddal, Holman Hunt educated the
illiterate Annie Miller. Ford Madox Brown fell in love with his young
model Emma Hill in 1848 and, though only fifteen, she lived with him
as his mistress, giving birth to a daughter, Cathy, in 1850. They married
secretly in 1853 and Brown sent her to a finishing school to learn good
manners and social expertise. Emma pretended that her father was dead
and claimed that he had been a farmer, though both her parents were
alive and living in the East End of London.

The school at Arlington Street failed, and a new plan was put forward
with the assistance of Lady Bath and Aunt Charlotte. Christina and her
mother were to move to Frome in Somerset – a small market town not
very far from Longleat. The Anglo-Catholic priest Dr W.J. Bennett had
just been presented with a living there by Lady Bath after he had been
ousted from St Barnabas, Pimlico, because of his High Church
inclinations. It was felt that under such patronage a school would have
a better chance of success.

They moved into Brunswick Terrace, Fromefield, in March 1853 and
as soon as the house was in order they sent for Gabriele. He was not
really well enough for such an upheaval, and once settled fretted for
London and the family and friends who had visited him every evening.
Deprived of stimulation, he began to decline. William and Maria stayed
in Arlington Street until the lease ran out and Gabriel left home entirely
to rent what Ruskin unkindly called 'a garret in Blackfriars'. The PRB
was all but defunct. Woolner emigrated to Australia with his wife, Hunt
decided to go to Egypt in search of new ideas, and Millais made the
decision to apply to the Academy for an associateship. The other
members of the Brotherhood saw Millais' action as a betrayal. Christina
wrote a satirical sonnet which Hunt thought had actually helped cause
their disintegration.

> The P.R.B. is in its decadence:
>   For Woolner in Australia cooks his chops,
> And Hunt is yearning for the land of Cheops;
>   D.G. Rossetti shuns the vulgar optic;
> While William M. Rossetti merely lops
>   His B's in English disesteemed as Coptic;
> Calm Stephens in the twilight smokes his pipe,
>   But long the dawning of his public day;
>   And he at last the champion great Millais,
> Attaining academic opulence,
>   Winds up his signature with A.R.A.
> So rivers merge in the perpetual sea;
> So luscious fruit must fall when over-ripe;
> And so the consummated P.R.B.

Only a month after their arrival in Frome Christina's grandmother Anna Polidori became seriously ill and Frances had to travel back to London. A few days later Anna died aged eighty-four. Christina went home for the funeral, writing to her mother that she would like to see her grandmother's body before the coffin was closed. 'Pray do not be afraid of the effects of such a sight on me. I really wish it, unless the lapse of so many days renders it inadvisable.'[8]

Back in Frome again Christina and her mother struggled to make the school pay. Unfortunately the Rev. Dr Bennett failed to promote the school in any way and they were only able to attract children from local tradespeople and farmers. Although Frances was a natural teacher, Christina found the occupation tiresome. Already low in spirits she became even more unhappy, and missed other members of her family. She put on a good front for her mother, and Gabriel chaffed her about her 'stereotyped smile'. Christina filled her spare time with drawing and water colouring, painting a portrait of her mother than won approval from the rest of the family. But without tuition she found it hard to improve her skills and eventually she abandoned it. Her poetic inspiration was beginning to return and there was a steady flow of verses throughout the year.

Most rehearse the themes of the previous two years – what Gabriel called 'the old shop' – disconsolate verses longing for death to relieve suffering, but some of them are exceptional. One, 'A Pause', written in June, echoes the mystic power of Emily Brontë's 'He comes with Western Winds', and shows how Christina's style had matured.

They made the chamber sweet with flowers and leaves,
  And the bed sweet with flowers on which I lay;
  While my soul, love-bound, loitered on its way.
I did not hear the birds about the eaves,
Nor hear the reapers talk among the sheaves:
  Only my soul kept watch from day to day,
  My thirsty soul kept watch for one away:-
Perhaps he loves, I thought, remembers, grieves.
At length there came the step upon the stair,
  Upon the lock the old familiar hand:
Then first my spirit seemed to scent the air
  Of Paradise; then first the tardy sand
Of time ran golden; and I felt my hair
  Put on a glory, and my soul expand.

Two Italian poems were printed in a publication called *The Bouquet Culled from Marylebone Gardens*, and an almanac called *Aikin's Year* accepted 'Behold I stand at the Door and Knock'. Christina was also working on prose tales, although William had not been able to sell *Maude*, and tried unsuccessfully to market a gothic tale called *Nick*. Gabriel was still trying to dominate Christina and influence her output.

> I have written lately to Papa and Mamma . . . but it is some time since I have enlightened you. Maria showed me the other day two poems of yours which are among the best you have written for some time: only the title of one Something Like Truth – seems "very like a whale". What does it mean? The latter verses of this are most excellent; but some, which I remember vaguely, about "dreaming of a lifelong ill" (etc etc *ad libitum*) smack rather of the old shop. I wish you would try any rendering either of narrative or sentiment from real abundant Nature, which presents much more variety, even in any one of its phases, than all such "dreamings".[9]

The beauties of nature were seen as very much the province of the female poet. The passionate, internal 'dreamings' of Brontë, Dickinson and Rossetti, the polemics of Barrett Browning, were something quite new.

Dante Gabriel was not alone in wishing that Christina's poetry had been more strongly rooted in nature, and she was often compared unfavourably to Jean Ingelow in this respect. Gabriel's friend Theodore Watts-Dunton thought that the problem was that Christina had been brought up in town. He wrote in the *Athenaeum* that:

It is here that Miss Ingelow has such an advantage over Christina Rossetti. Her love of flowers, and birds and trees, and all that makes the earth so beautiful, is not one whit stronger than Christina's own, but it is a love born of an exhaustive, detailed knowledge of Nature's life.[10]

The idea that Christina might have preferred to write of internal rather than external landscapes was not considered.

Anna Mary Howitt, whose mother had solicited Christina's poems for *Aikin's Year* and various other periodicals she was connected with, continued to be enthusiastic – something Christina needed very much at the time. It was at the Howitts' that Gabriel first met the feminist Barbara Leigh Smith (a cousin of Florence Nightingale's) and introduced her to Christina. He wrote

Allingham [William Allingham the poet] had just come to town and with him and William I went last night to the Howitts. Anna Mary's excitement on your subject has not subsided, and she still hoped, when you come to town not to miss you again. She has painted a sunlight picture of Margaret [Faust] in a congenial wailing state, which is much better than I fancied she could paint. I am going down some time by daylight to give her some hints about the colour. I wish there were any chance of my doing the same for you, but I am afraid you find art interferes with the legitimate exercise of anguish. Ah, if only you were like Miss Barbara Smith! a young lady I met at the Howitts', blessed with large rations of tin, fat, enthusiasm, and golden hair, who thinks nothing of climbing up a mountain in breeches, or wading through a stream in none, in the sacred name of pigment. Last night she invited us all to lunch with her on Sunday, and perhaps I shall go, as she is quite a jolly fellow . . .[11]

Just before Christmas Gaetano Polidori died and the Polidori family separated. Eliza decided that she wanted untrammelled independence and went to live on her own. William and Maria had taken temporary lodgings over a chemist's shop near Regents Park and Philip and Margaret took lodgings nearby. The Polidoris had all inherited a small sum of money after their parents' death, enough for modest subsistence.

William was promoted at the Excise Office with an increased salary of £250. With his *Spectator* fees, Maria's income from private lessons, and the money Frances had inherited William calculated that they could all live comfortably again under one roof. He was eager to reunite the family, and wanted to spare his mother the drudgery of school teaching. He rented a house at 166 Albany Street and insisted that she move in by Lady Day 1854.

Although Christina and her mother missed the countryside they were very glad to return to London. The Albany Street house was bigger than any they had previously occupied and although the outlook was a little dismal, it faced the rear of a terrace of houses fronting the park, it was so close to Regents Park that this compensated for any of its drawbacks. Eliza and Margaret were regular callers, and, after Philip (who had become very strange in the last few years) died, Margaret was offered two rooms at the top of the house and came to live with them, though she was always careful to remain aloof and not intrude on the others. She was apparently subject to hysterical fits, when she rolled on the floor and screamed with laughter.

The removal was too much for Gabriele, and he was very ill after their return. On Easter Sunday the family doctor was summoned and a week later he called in the more senior Dr Hare.

On 24 April Gabriele seemed to be rather better, and insisted that Frances get him up and dressed, but after breakfast he collapsed and Frances noticed an alarming change in his countenance. After that he did not get out of bed again. The children took turns to be with him and Frances read to him from the Italian Liturgy. At times he imagined his mother was in the room with him. He died at 5.30 p.m. on the 26th, very quietly, being conscious almost to the last. His cousin Teodoro Pietrocola-Rossetti, Margaret, Eliza and Charlotte Polidori were all present as well as his children. Gabriel had been dining with John Ruskin when he was called back to the house.

Charles Cayley, whose translation of Dante had been supervised by Gabriele, called twice while he lay dying, and endeared himself to Christina and the family by waiting respectfully in a downstairs room until the end.

Gabriele was buried at Highgate cemetery next to Ford Madox Brown's first wife. Everything (the little that there was) was left to Frances. One of the first things she did when she had recovered from her initial grief was to burn all surviving copies of a book he had written called *Mistero dell'Amor Platonico*, which she considered heretical and dangerous.

CHAPTER SIX

Gabriel was hoping to use his connection with the poet William Allingham to get a small volume of Christina's poems published, but it is difficult to tell whether he was trying to promote Christina or Lizzie. He wrote to William in March 1854

> Tell Christina that, if she will come here on Thursday Lizzy will be here . . . I shall be glad if she will come, as I have told Lizzy she mentioned her wish to do so.
>
> Allingham has been looking over her poems, and is delighted with many of them. I am going to lend them him (trusting in her permission to do so) that he may give his opinion as to which will be best for a volume. Lizzy will illustrate, and I have no doubt we shall get a publisher.[1]

A month later, Lizzie became ill again and went to Hastings for her health, accompanied for some of the time by Gabriel, and the idea never came to anything. Lizzie's illness was never really diagnosed and a variety of physicians were consulted, even a homeopath, without success. She had a weak chest and suffered from depression as well as digestive problems. Her situation was unenviable. Gabriel was in love with her, but could not, or would not, marry her. And there was also artistic frustration, as she tried to realise her creative capacities. One of her doctors suggested that the chief cause of her illness was 'mental power long pent up and lately overtaxed.'

Barbara Leigh-Smith tried to persuade Gabriel to admit her to Florence Nightingale's sanatorium in Harley Street, but in September 1855 she went abroad to Nice and Paris accompanied by a relative of Frances Rossetti.

Christina was at work helping William with a translation of the Memoirs and Correspondence of Mallet du Pan. This included an account of the French Revolution from an aristocrat's point of view, and had been undertaken by William in partnership with Dr Benjamin Paul. Mrs. Rossetti and Maria also did some of the translating, but Christina's share of the enterprise seems, on William's own admission, to have been considerable. Her name, however, does not appear on the title page though her biographer MacKenzie Bell lists the book under Christina's works in his bibliography. She is, however, listed among contributors to Dr Waller's *Imperial Dictionary of Universal Biography*, for which she supplied the entries on Italian writers.

Christina was by now very sure of her gifts. According to her brother she considered herself 'Truly a poetess, most decidedly, yes; and, within the range of her subject and thoughts and the limits of her executive endeavour, a good one'. She tried very hard to guard against the sin of vanity, while at the same time preserving standards and critical judgement. William observed that the sense of her own worth

> did not make her in the least conceited or arrogant as regards herself, nor captious as to the work of others: but it did render her very resolute in setting a line of demarcation between a person who is a poet and another who is a versifier.[2]

Constantly in Christina's mind was the text 'Judge not, that ye be not judged'. She would often remain silent rather than utter a critical remark. When people sent her their poetry she dashed off a thank you note straight away to relieve herself of the necessity of writing a possibly critical letter after she had read their work.

The other creed by which she lived and which shaped her talent more than any other was the Biblical injunction not to do 'anything whereby thy brother stumbleth or is offended, or is made weak'. William wrote candidly that he had often thought

> that this tramelled her to some extent in writing, for she was wont to construe the biblical precepts in a very literal manner; and that she would in some instances have expressed herself with more latitude of thought and word, and to a more valuable effect, but for the fear of saying something which would somehow turn to the detriment of some timorous or dim-minded reader.

Christina felt that 'to write anything for publication is to incur a great spiritual responsibility'.[3]

Some of the tension in her poetry is produced by these pressures and conflicts – the struggle between self-effacement and literary achievement. It was this over-scrupulosity which persuaded her to withdraw her poem 'A Triad' after it had been published in *Goblin Market*. Someone drew her attention to the unflattering picture she had drawn of an otherwise virtuous married woman, comparing her unfavourably with the mistress – the former growing 'gross in soulless love, a sluggish wife' while the other glows 'Flushed to the yellow hair and finger tips.'

Christina spent some of her time during the week doing parish visiting for the church in poor areas of London. There is a consciousness in her poetry of *waste*. In a terse poem, similar to some of Emily Dickinson's in both sentiment and style, she describes the feeling of uselessness and inertia felt by many women at the time.

> It's a weary life, it is, she said:-
> Doubly blank in a woman's lot:
> I wish and I wish I were a man:
> Or better than any being, were not:

During this period Florence Nightingale was putting together a party of nurses to take out to the Crimea. She too had had to fight her way through psychosomatic illness, and the loving tyranny of her family. She too had refused to marry the man she loved because of her principles. In a statement which illuminates Christina's own decision a few years earlier Florence Nightingale writes that though he would satisfy her 'intellectual nature' and her 'passionate nature', yet she also has 'a moral, an active nature which requires satisfaction, and that would not find it in his life'.

Christina's unconventional Aunt Eliza was one of the first to volunteer for Scutari and be accepted. Her cheerful philosophy and resolution was just what was required, though she was disappointed to discover when she arrived that she had been appointed as a store-keeper, handing out linen and supplies instead of nursing the sick. She was, however, very proud of the part she had played and wrote a memoir of her time at Scutari. Christina had wanted to go too, and put her name forward to accompany her aunt, but she was refused because, at twenty-four, she was too young.

Christina was searching for fulfilment. In what Gabriel describes as her 'dreamings' – beautiful, mystical poetry that can be compared with Emily Brontë's, Christina portrays a woman in a trance-like state, waiting to be awakened. Titles like 'Dead Before Death', and 'Dream

Love', describe a kind of death-in-life, an emotional limbo. Two poems 'Long Looked For' and 'Echo' closely follow Emily Brontë's 'The Prisoner'. The opening lines of the first

> When the eye hardly sees,
> When the pulse hardly stirs,
> And the heart would scarcely quicken
> Though the voice were hers:

seem almost to be a borrowing from Emily's vision. 'Echo' has the same visionary quality in the invocation to the lover, the same supernatural overtones, the same ambiguity (is the lover spiritual or sexual?). The reader is reminded of Heathcliff in *Wuthering Heights* waiting for Cathy, as well as the poems in which Emily either as a Gondal character, or as herself, longs for the night, for the return of

> My blissful dream that never comes with day.
> A vision dear, though false, for well my mind
> Knows what a bitter waking waits behind.[4]

Christina's poem is poignant, the invocation passionate.

> Come to me in the silence of the night;
> Come in the speaking silence of a dream;
> Come with soft rounded cheeks and eyes as bright
> As sunlight on a stream;
> Come back in tears,
> O memory, hope, love of finished years.
>
> O dream how sweet, too sweet, too bitter sweet,
> Whose wakening should have been in Paradise,
> Where souls brimfull of love abide and meet;
> Where thirsting longing eyes
> Watch the slow door
> That opening, letting in, lets out no more.
>
> Yet come to me in dreams, that I may live
> My very life again though cold in death:
> Come back to me in dreams, that I may give
> Pulse for pulse, breath for breath:
> Speak low, lean low,
> As long ago, my love, how long ago.

Some of her dreams were more sinister and pictorially very vivid. Gabriel said that Christina wrote with an artist's eye. One of her strangest poems, called simply 'My Dream', perfectly illustrates what William called 'the exceptional turn of mind of Christina Rossetti – the odd freakishness which flecked the extreme and almost excessive seriousness of her thought'.[5] Christina denied that the poem referred to a real dream in the sense of being dreamt in sleep.

The poem is patterned like a fable, and is based on the prophetic dreams of Pharaoh interpreted by Joseph in Genesis. There seems also to be some reference to contemporary cartoons of the Tzar of Russia – sometimes portrayed as a crocodile. The dreamer stands beside the Euphrates and watches a band of young, newly-hatched crocodiles emerge from the waves.

> Each crocodile was girt with massive gold
> And polished stones that with their wearers grew:

One crocodile more magnificent than the rest grows faster than the others

> And special terror weighed upon his frown;
> His punier brethren quaked before his tail,

Eventually he turns on them, and, like the lean cows who emerged from the river in Pharaoh's dream, devours the others.

> He battened on them, crunched and sucked them in,
> He knew no law, he feared no binding law,
> But ground them with inexorable jaw.
> The luscious fat distilled upon his chin,
> Exuded from his nostrils and his eyes,
> While still like hungry death he fed his maw;

When the crocodile goes to sleep he suddenly dwindles to the normal size and his coat fades. A mysterious, winged vessel approaches – 'white it was as an avenging ghost' – and before this judgemental force

> The prudent crocodile rose on his feet,
> And shed appropriate tears and wrung his hands.

What can it mean? Christina asks at the end of the poem and declines to give an explanation. 'I answer not/For meaning, but myself must echo, What?' But she herself must have known that it was a moral fable with its roots deep in the old Testament. There is a strong element of didacticism running through all Christina's work, implicit if not explicit. Her gift was to clothe it in poetry. 'My Dream' is also a good example of Christina's sense of humour. Not all her poems are sad. The prudent crocodile was a great favourite with her family and the subject of many jokes. Gabriel nicknamed his friend William Morris 'The Prudent' and to Morris's annoyance it stuck.

Ruskin had now taken up the PRB cause, writing articles in their defence which helped to encourage the sale of their work. He was a frequent visitor to Gabriel's studio, and Maria and Christina were asked to dine with Ruskin's family. 1854 was a difficult year for Ruskin and the PRB. Hunt was making solitary expeditions to the Middle East, and Walter Deverell died from Bright's disease, after a long illness. Ruskin's wife Effie had fallen in love with John Millais and, on the advice of friends, had applied to have their unconsummated marriage annulled. She and Millais later married, and this caused an awkwardness between the Millais and Rossetti families because of their continuing relationship with Ruskin. Dante Gabriel and John Millais, though still cordial, saw less and less of one another.

Ruskin was very impressed by Lizzie Siddal's talent. Her youth and fragility appealed to him, and he offered to settle £150 a year on her, to enable her to live comfortably, on condition that she gave him all her drawings. Gabriel was very enthusiastic – there is no record of Lizzie's feelings – and the arrangement was entered into. Why he did not marry her at this point is hard to understand, since he was earning at least as much as William and with Lizzie's money they would have had more than enough. Gabriel, however, the most generous of men towards his friends and family, was one of those for whom 'money never stuck to his fingers' and he was always in need of it. Ruskin wrote to him that

> my feeling . . . is that it would be best for you to marry . . . putting an end to the peculiar sadness and 'want of you hardly know what' that there is in both of you.[6]

A crisis undoubtedly did occur, for Dante Gabriel tore out entries in William's diary for the years 1854/5 which William believed had referred to Lizzie. The rest of his family also seem to have thought that he was not acting as he should towards her. There are references in Gabriel's letters to William Allingham of a flirtation with a *'Belle pas Sauvages'* throughout 1854 and 1855. According to him she was a 'stunner'.

Christina also witnessed a growing attachment between Maria and John Ruskin. How much of this was on Maria's side only is difficult to know. Ruskin tended to be attracted to adolescent girls rather than mature and intellectually powerful women. However, Gabriel's letters record that it was Ruskin who particularly asked to meet Maria, and that Gabriel and Lizzie took her to dine with them at Ruskin's house on more than one occasion. Christina wrote in *Time Flies*, a religious prose work, that 'One of the most genuine Christians I ever knew, once took lightly the dying out of a brief acquaintance which had engaged her warm heart, on the ground that such tastes and glimpses of congenial intercourse on earth wait for their development in heaven.' The margin of the text is annotated 'Maria with Ruskin'.[7]

In the summer of 1855 the Brownings came to London and both William and Dante Gabriel visited them at their lodgings in Dorset Street. They had been admirers of Elizabeth's gifts since the publication of her first collection – William dated their first enthusiasm as early as 1844 when he would have been only fifteen. Gabriel's admiration for Robert Browning came later, and characteristically he had written to the poet in Italy and been invited to meet him in London. The Brownings admired his paintings, and borrowed one – called *Dante's Dream* – for their lodgings.

In September the Brownings invited William and Gabriel to meet Tennyson and hear him read his work. Sadly Christina did not go with them. It was her habit to spend the summer at Hastings or Brighton, and in the autumn of 1855 she took a post as a governess with a family who lived on Hampstead Heath. William regretted that she did not meet Elizabeth Barrett Browning. Elizabeth was working on *Aurora Leigh*, and William was apparently shown the manuscript. He believed that Gabriel had shown some of Christina's poetry to Elizabeth, but no comments survive. In 1850 Elizabeth had been jokingly proposed as Poet Laureate in an *Athenaeum* article. By her appointment, the author suggested, two poets would be remunerated instead of one.

The following year Robert Browning wrote from Italy to ask William to organise the engravings for the frontispiece of *Aurora Leigh*. He was very glad to be involved, even in such a minor capacity, though the Brownings were not particularly happy with the result of his efforts. William thought that *Aurora Leigh* was 'stuffed and loaded with poetic beauty and passionate sympathy and insight,'[8] but was rather daunted by the length of it. Christina's comments were not recorded.

Christina was temperamentally unsuited to being a governess, and was as unhappy as Emily Brontë in the short time she spent at Law Hill.

Like Emily, Christina's health broke down. With the onset of winter her chest became troublesome and she was confined to bed. On 13 November she wrote to William.

I hope you are glad to know that I am very comfortable in my exile; but at any rate I know I am rejoicing to feel that my health does really unfit me for miscellaneous governessing en permanence. For instance yesterday I indulged in breakfast in bed, having been very unwell the day previous; now I am very tolerable again, but do not feel particularly to be depended upon.[9]

She makes a teasing reference to William's affection for Henrietta Rintoul in the letter and is obviously delighted at the prospect of being at home again. All that winter she was ill, and tried to accept it was the will of God. 'I Have a Message unto Thee', dated 26 March 1855, is subtitled 'Written in Sickness'.

> Sweet jasmine branches trail
> A dusky starry veil;
> Each goodly is to see,
> Comely in its degree:
> I, only I, alas that this should be
> Am ruinously pale.

She laments that 'I only in my spring/Can neither bud nor sing,' and faces the fact that she 'may be immortally made fair' by death. The family sent her to Hastings to recuperate, and on her return she stayed with the Madox Browns.

In January 1856 William proposed to Henrietta Rintoul and, although she was older than him, she accepted. However, her parents objected very strongly to the engagement and she obediently broke it off. Later Henrietta – against the wishes of her family – re-accepted William's proposal and entered an indefinite engagement. If William had not been supporting his family he could have married Henrietta, and the fact that he seems to have felt no bitterness on this point says a great deal for his character, and also for the sense of duty which all the Rossettis seemed to have. As a family they were exceptionally close and this may partly account for the fact that they married either very late or not at all.

In 1856 Christina was twenty-six. As she looked back on her life she saw herself increasingly cut off from the ordinary pleasures of human happiness. In a series of poems, but particularly in 'Shut Out', she describes looking through the gates into Paradise, from which, like Eve, she has been cast out. There is a dual meaning in the poems – a fear that she may also, because of sins committed in the past, be denied the spiritual paradise of her faith. 'Shut Out', titled 'What Happened to Me' in manuscript, is Blakean in its simplicity and symbolism.

> The door was shut. I looked between
>   Its iron bars; and saw it lie,
>   My garden, mine, beneath the sky,
> Pied with all flowers bedewed and green.

The garden is lost to her, and the 'shadowless spirit' who guards the gate will give her not even one twig as a remembrance. Instead

> The spirit was silent; but he took
>   Mortar and stone to build a wall;
>   He left no loophole great or small
> Through which my straining eyes might look.

Sitting alone, she is blinded with tears and impervious to the consolations of Nature outside Paradise.

> A violet bed is budding near,
>   Wherein a lark has made her nest;
>   And good they are, but not the best;
> And dear they are, but not so dear.

CHAPTER SEVEN

In the years between 1856 and 1862, Christina wrote much of her best poetry. She was in full control of her technique and its perfection ordered the raw and sometimes turbulent emotions she expressed, providing a dramatic tension between the powerful emotion and the tight form that contained it.

Christina herself believed that her early work was technically superior to the religious prose and poetry she wrote later on. She told Edmund Gosse that she was 'a great believer in the genuine poetic impulse belonging (very often) to the spring and not to the autumn of life'.[1] The 'genuine lyric cry' which was her own natural voice came less frequently as she grew older, but was in full flood during the decade 1855 to 1865.

Christina was often at the home of Ford Madox Brown and his wife Emma, and through Madox Brown she met many other people. As well as making frequent visits to Dr and Mrs Heimann, she was also a regular visitor at the Patmores. It was there that she met Adelaide Proctor, celebrated for her famous lyric 'The Lost Chord'. Shyness prevented her from becoming a close friend, and she later described their relationship as a 'surface acquaintance only'. W.B. Scott had introduced his wife Laetitia, whose gift for conversation fully compensated for Christina's lack of small talk. Mrs Scott had recently become an Anglican and they had much in common. Another female friend was Henrietta Rintoul, now engaged to William and whom Christina already regarded as a sister. The lively, gifted Henrietta became the centre of a literary circle, to which Christina could occasionally be persuaded to go.

Her relationship to Henrietta was in marked contrast to that with Lizzie Siddal, but her inability to make friends with 'The Sid' may have had more to do with Lizzie's enigmatic, melancholy disposition than with any kind of friction. Lizzie's only close female friend was Emma

Brown, whose position had been very similar to her own. Though both Lizzie and Christina painted and wrote poetry, two more dissimilar women can hardly be imagined. Dante Gabriel was also very possessive where Lizzie was concerned and William complained that the family saw the couple rarely and felt discouraged from making visits.

Aurora Leigh was published in the autumn of 1856 after Elizabeth Barrett Browning and her husband had gone back to Italy. It caused a great deal of excitement in London and was the subject of much argument throughout the winter. Ruskin thought it was perfect, but reviews were mixed. Some critics made the connection between Aurora Leigh and Jane Eyre, which Elizabeth may not have intended but which is definitely there, in the independent heroine who won't marry where she ought, an orphan brought up by an unsympathetic aunt who eventually marries the hero only after he has been disfigured. There were also flattering comparisons with George Sand, whom Elizabeth admired, and whose real name, Aurora, she had used for her heroine.

The poem also owes something to Laetitia Landon's *Improvatrice* – superficially at least, using the idea of a passionate figure, with Italian blood, who is also a poet. It is as ambitious in its own way as Wordsworth's *Prelude*, sharing the same theme, the story of a young poet, here a woman, growing to maturity, and it suffers from similar problems. There is insufficient variation of pace and tone, and there is always the difficulty of sustaining quality through such a long, narrative poem. But, like the *Prelude*, it is a major work of literature.

Although Christina, like Emily Dickinson, admired Elizabeth Barrett Browning more than any other living poet, she denied consciously trying to emulate her. She did, however, attempt to write 'political' poetry from time to time – poems such as 'A Royal Princess', 'The Lowest Room' and 'The Iniquity of the Fathers Upon the Children'. Christina, like Elizabeth, was drawn by the plight of the 'fallen woman', and it became almost an obsession. It was a typically Victorian occupation, approached with a mixture of prudery and prurience, and one of the subjects which fascinated the Pre-Raphaelites. Holman Hunt painted *The Awakening Conscience* in 1853 and it shows a mistress suddenly gripped by pangs of conscience as her lover strums idly on the piano. It is contemporary with W.B. Scott's poem 'Rosabell' on the same theme. Dante Gabriel's 'Jenny', 'Lazy, laughing, languid Jenny,/Fond of a kiss and fond of a guinea' with her loosened hair, her silks 'ungirdled and unlac'd,/And warm sweets open to the waist', was a portrait of Fanny Cornforth whom he met, according to one report, cracking nuts in her teeth as she solicited in the Strand. She became his mistress and modelled for some of his more erotic paintings. *Found*, in which she appears as a country girl discovered in her 'shame' by a young man in a farmer's smock, was never finished.

Christina was rare among Victorian women in that she not only dared to write about prostitution, something her brother, true to the Victorian double standard, disapproved of her doing, but she was actively engaged in practical social work as well. Though it may seem incongruous to us that young single women whose knowledge of the facts of life was extremely rudimentary, and whose knowledge of the temptations of sex even more so, should be considered ideal to help and counsel those who had transgressed the moral code, it was considered highly appropriate by the Victorians. Dora Greenwell, in her essay 'Our Single Women' echoed the sentiments of the day when she wrote that fallen women should be reclaimed by those 'to whom the coin, long lost and trodden underfoot, is still precious, for the sake of Him, whose image and superscription it bears.'[2]

Christina was not always tempted to draw a moral in her poems, at least not in the early ones. In 'Look on This Picture and on This' written in 1856 she depicts the alluring Zara.

> You have seen her hazel eyes, her warm dark skin,
> Dark hair – but oh those hazel eyes a devil is dancing in;-
> You, my saint, lead up to heaven, she lures down to sin.
>
> She's so redundant, stately:- in truth now have you seen
> Ever anywhere such beauty, such a stature such a mien?
> She may be queen of devils, but she's every inch a queen.
>
> If you sing to me, I hear her subtler sweeter still
> Whispering in each tender cadence strangely sweet to fill
> All that lacks in music, all my soul and sense and will.

The lover, denied physical union in this world, wishes for union after death, and he confronts the one he is legally bound to (Eva) with the knowledge of his love.

> I would that one of us were dead, were gone no more to meet,
> Or she and I were dead together, stretched here at your feet
> That she and I were strained together in one winding-sheet.

> Did I love you? Never from the first cold day to this:
> You are not sufficient for my aim of life, my bliss:
> You are not sufficient, but I found the one that is.

William in his notes wrote that 'Were it not for the name "Eva", I should be embarrassed to guess what could have directed my sister's pen to so singular a subject and treatment;' however, the name satisfied William that the poem was a reference to Maturin's novel *Women* and as such could be excused.[3]

If Elizabeth Barrett Browning's concern was with Marion Erle, the character in *Aurora Leigh* who has transgressed society's moral code, Christina's was with the innocent child of the illicit union. But although they shared similar concerns, in Christina's mature work the ideas and the metrical and verbal patternings are all her own. There are however close links between their poetry – not so much borrowings, as a system of cross referencing.

This is evident in the poem 'L.E.L.', written in February 1859. In manuscript Christina titled the poem 'Spring', with a note 'L.E.L. by Elizabeth Barrett Browning'. The epigraph is a single line 'Whose heart was breaking for a little love'. The poem is one of Christina's finest, articulating not only her own loneliness and fears of unfulfilment, but also making connections with three other women poets, Elizabeth Barrett Browning, Laetitia Elizabeth Landon, and Felicia Hemans.

Christina's brother William in his notes on the poem thought that the poem of Elizabeth Barrett Browning's referred to was 'L.E.L.'s Last Question', in which Elizabeth describes her as 'one thirsty for a little love' – the line William connects with Christina's epigraph. But Christina could equally well have been thinking of Elizabeth Barrett Browning's poem 'Felicia Hemans' which is subtitled 'To L.E.L. referring to her monody on the poetess'. This refers to L.E.L.'s famous poem on the death of Felicia Hemans, who was also 'not half enough beloved' and experienced the same isolation as Christina and L.E.L.

Christina seems to have identified so strongly with Laetitia Landon's poem to Felicia Hemans that references to it, close enough to be quotations, can be found in her work, (particularly in 'Passing Away'). Part of the poem is worth quoting in order to understand the background to Christina's 'L.E.L.', and the thoughts that might have been in her mind at the time, thoughts which must have included L.E.L.'s solitary, painful suicide.

Ah dearly purchased is the gift,
The gift of song like thine:
A fated doom is her's who stands
The priestess of the shrine.
The crowd – they only see the crown,
They only hear the hymn;
They mark not that the cheek is pale,
And that the eye is dim.

Wound to a pitch too exquisite,
The soul's fine chords are wrung;
With misery and melody
They are too highly strung.
The heart is made too sensitive
Life's daily pain to bear;
It beats in music, but it beats
Beneath a deep despair.

It never meets the love it paints,
The love for which it pines;
Too much of Heaven is in the faith
That such a heart enshrines.
The meteor wreath the poet wears
Must make a lonely lot;
It dazzles, only to divide
From those who wear it not.

Didst thou not tremble at thy fame,
And loathe its bitter prize,
While what to others triumph seemed,
To thee was sacrifice?
Oh, Flower brought from Paradise,
To this cold world of ours,
Shadows of beauty such as thine
Recall thy native bowers.[4]

Christina's epigraph is not a direct quotation from either Elizabeth
Barrett Browning or L.E.L. – it is a statement which makes an
emotional connection between Christina's work and L.E.L.'s own
poetry, where she describes her heart as breaking from the failure of love
on numerous occasions. In 'Song' from *The Golden Violet* she writes:

And my own heart is as the lute
I now am waking:
Wound to too fine and high a pitch,
They both are breaking.

And again in another 'Song'

> I'll turn me to the gifted page,
> Where the bard his soul is flinging;
> Too well it echoes mine own heart
> Breaking e'en while singing.

The themes of Laetitia Landon's poetry are very similar to Christina's. In *The Golden Violet* she acknowledges that the keys which 'Yield to my hand their sympathies' are 'Woman's Love and Sorrow's own'. L.E.L.'s range is narrower than Christina's and her poetry is a conflation of the ideals of Romanticism and the cult of Sensibility – it looks back to the eighteenth century rather than forward and offers nothing new. 'A Night in May' from *The Venetian Bracelet* is typical and gives a useful parallel for comparison with Christina's poem to L.E.L. In it, as in Christina's, the poet gazes on a scene of gaiety where 'the young and lovely' are gathered.

> I left the gay circle:- if I found it dreary
> Were all others there, then, the thoughtless and glad?
> Methinks that fair cheek in its paleness look'd weary,
> Methinks that dark eye in its drooping was sad.
>
> I went to my chamber, – I sought to be lonely –
> I leant by the casement to catch the sweet air;
> The thick tears fell blinding; and am I then only
> Sad, weary, although without actual care?

In Christina's poem 'L.E.L.' the theme is more than just a lament for the failure of human love, or the loneliness that is felt most in a crowd, it is George Herbert's cry for the lack of spiritual fruitfulness felt most at springtime when the earth blossoms with promises of coming harvest and spiritual barrenness is thrown up into sharp relief.

> Downstairs I laugh, I sport and jest with all;
> But in my solitary room above
> I turn my face in silence to the wall;
> My heart is breaking for a little love.
> Though winter frosts are done,
> And birds pair every one,
> And leaves peep out, for springtide is begun.

I feel no spring, while spring is well-nigh blown,
   I find no nest, while nests are in the grove:
Woe's me for mine own heart that dwells alone,
   My heart that breaketh for a little love.
     While golden in the sun
     Rivulets rise and run,
While lilies bud, for springtime is begun.

All love, are loved, save only I; their hearts
   Beat warm with love and joy, beat full thereof:
They cannot guess, who play the pleasant parts,
   My heart is breaking for a little love.
     While bee-hives wake and whirr,
     And rabbit thins his fur,
In living spring that sets the world astir.

Christina, seeing her brothers finding happiness in love, her sister Maria finding fulfilment in the church, was conscious of a great gap in her life. Her poetry, enjoyed and highly praised by friends, had not yet found a wider audience, and her charity work, visiting 'fallen women' at a religious establishment in Highgate, brought less satisfaction than she had hoped. Collinson had left the Jesuit college to resume painting, and was married with a baby daughter. Christina felt it unlikely that she would ever be given the chance to marry again. The surplus of women over men, the ineligibility of most of the men she met, her own poverty and the high standards by which she judged all made it improbable. There is a lack of purpose evident in her work, a sense of living in a vacuum. For Christina the only hope was in the world to come, for herself, for Felicia Hemans and Laetitia Landon.

Yet saith a saint, 'Take patience for thy scythe';
   Yet saith an angel: 'Wait, and thou shalt prove
True best is last, true life is born of death,
   O thou, heart-broken for a little love.
     Then love shall fill thy girth,
     And love make fat thy dearth,
When new spring builds new heaven and clean new earth.'

William suggested that the title 'L.E.L.' was simply a 'cloud' to hide the autobiographical nature of the poem, but while the poem is extremely personal, the connections are there to be made.

Dante Gabriel read the poem in manuscript and suggested the rhymes for lines one and three, which had previously been unrhymed.

Christina accepted his suggestions, agreeing that they 'greatly improved' the piece.

Another poem written in 1859, 'Spring', repeats the theme of barrenness, and 'An Apple Gathering' describes a maiden who plucks apple blossom in spring to decorate her hair, and then goes back in autumn to find no apples on her tree. 'Autumn' reiterates her loneliness in a poem studded with the alliteration, inversion, repetition and internal rhyme that Gerard Manley Hopkins was later to use with such effect.

> I dwell alone – I dwell alone, alone,
>   Whilst full my river flows down to the sea,
> Gilded with flashing boats
>   That bring no friend to me:
> O love-songs, gurgling from a hundred throats,
>   O love-pangs, let me be.
>
> Fair fall the freighted boats which gold and stone
>   And spices bear to sea:
> Slim gleaming maidens swell their mellow notes,
>   Love-promising, entreating –
>   Ah sweet but fleeting –
>   Beneath the shivering, snow-white sails.
>   Hush! the wind flags and fails –
> Hush! they will lie becalmed in sight of strand –
>   Sight of my strand, where I do dwell alone;
> Their songs wake singing echoes in my land –
>   They cannot hear me moan.

These are some of her bleakest poems. 'Autumn' ends

> My trees are not in flower,
> I have no bower,
> And gusty creaks my tower,
> And lonesome, very lonesome, is my strand.

Christina appears to have been deeply depressed. Both she and her brother Gabriel suffered from intense mood swings and frail nerves. Gabriel envied Maria and William their more even temperaments. Maria was particularly calm and practical – the sanest of them all, Gabriel wrote in a letter, whereas he and Christina were 'nowhere' in comparison. Maria ordered everything by strict logic. Her approach to everything, even her religion was that of the scholar. She reasoned things out. Christina on the other hand had an instinctive approach. Christina's religion was a matter of belief, an affair of the emotions, and therefore less easy to sustain in the face of doubt and personal despondency. Maria's faith had the certainty of a proven argument; for Christina it was a matter for the heart and imagination.

Her brother William, a lifelong agnostic, tried to argue the subject with her. He recorded that

> To learn that something in the Christian faith was credible *because it was reasonable* or because it rested upon some historic evidence of fact, went against her. Her attitude of mind was: "I believe because I am told to believe, and I know that the authority which tells me to believe is the only real authority extant, God". To press her, "How do you know that it is God?" would have been no use; the ultimate response could only have come to this – "My faith is faith; it is not evolved out of argumentation, nor does it seek the aid of that".[5]

The most beautiful expression of Christina's faith is her poem 'A Birthday', probably the most frequently quoted and anthologised of all her works. It describes the birthday of the soul, what we would call today, being 'born again', and is a love lyric to Christ the Saviour, with imagery from the Song of Solomon and the Psalms. As in the Song of Songs the lover is never specifically identified, lending the poem an ambiguity which has given it such universal appeal.

> My heart is like a singing bird
>   Whose nest is in a watered shoot:
> My heart is like an apple-tree
>   Whose boughs are bent with thickset fruit;
> My heart is like a rainbow shell
>   That paddles in a halcyon sea;
> My heart is gladder than all these
>   Because my love is come to me.

It was also very easily parodied. One of these, which appeared in an illustrated comic paper, was called 'An Unexpected Pleasure' and appealed to Christina's sense of humour so much that she cut it out and pasted it inside the cover of her collected *Poems*. It begins

My heart is like one asked to dine
Whose evening dress is up the spout;
My heart is like a man would be
Whose raging tooth is half pulled out.
My heart is like a howling swell
Who boggles on his upper C;
My heart is madder than all these –
My wife's mamma has come to tea.[6]

Christina was always ready to laugh at herself. A family joke about her
melancholy demeanour – her 'bogeyism' – was incorporated into her
poetic drama 'A Pageant' as part of October's dialogue.

Here comes my youngest sister, looking dim
And grim,
With dismal ways.

She wrote to Gabriel that 'I have had a quiet grin over October's
remark which ushers in November, as connecting it with my own
brothers and myself! Pray, appreciate the portrait.'[7]

*   *   *

The year 1858 marked a particularly low point for Christina. In contrast
to her own lack of success, her brother Gabriel had begun to make a
name for himself as a painter. He was in Oxford with a group of friends
painting the Oxford murals. He was now at the head of a new Pre-
Raphaelite Brotherhood, which included Edward Burne-Jones and
William Morris, both younger men attracted by his charisma. Max
Beerbohm described Dante Gabriel's fascination. 'In the great days of a
deep, smug, thick, rich, drab, industrial complacency, Rossetti shone for
the men and women who knew him, with the ambiguous light of a red
torch, somewhere in a dense fog.'[8]

His personal life was still troubled. Despite earning large sums of
money he was constantly in debt, being dunned for the rent and reduced
to writing begging letters to Aunt Charlotte. Lizzie Siddal had broken
off her engagement, after despairing of any hope of marriage, and he
had quarrelled with Holman Hunt over a woman – the two circumstances possibly connected. The family thought Gabriel's behaviour highly
culpable.

In Oxford Swinburne's blaze of red hair and 'stunning' poetry
attracted Gabriel's attention. He also met Jane Burden, whose face was
to dominate his later canvases. She was described by William as 'at once

tragic, mystic, passionate, calm, beautiful, and gracious – a face for a sculptor, and a face for a painter.'[9] Jane married William Morris, and was herself a fine artist, designing and working many of the exquisite tapestries turned out by the Morris workshop.

Christina was invited to stay with William Bell Scott's wife in Newcastle. Both her brothers and Maria had already been there for extended visits, and Christina's reluctance to accept an invitation has sometimes been ascribed to an unrequited love for W.B. Scott. The fallacy of this hypothesis has already been exposed in Georgina Battiscombe's meticulous biography and, like her, I have not found one shred of evidence to support such a theory. Christina did not care to be away from home, was shy of strangers and dreaded having to deal with other people's servants. She agonised over small things such as how much money to leave in 'vails', getting conflicting advice from her mother and Gabriel. This was quite enough to account for her reluctance to accept an invitation until she felt that she knew Laetitia well enough to be comfortable. If there had been any truth in the theory of her love for Scott she would not have gone at all. In *Letter and Spirit* she wrote that where sensual temptation was concerned she regarded the commandments as imposing an absolute 'rule of avoidance, rather than of self-conquest, or even of self-restraint'.

At Newcastle she came into contact with the poet Dora Greenwell, a friend of Laetitia Scott's, and they began to correspond. Dora, nine years older than Christina, was the daughter of a gentleman who had been forced to sell his inheritance to pay off debts. The family subsequently had no settled home and lived in comparative poverty. After her father's death, Dora lived with her mother, a woman described by Jean Ingelow as having 'an almost Roman air of decision and energy', and who dominated her daughter totally. Dora, like Christina was deeply religious, and this characterises all her poetry. Her first volume was published in 1848, followed by a collection of *Stories That Might be True* in 1850. Christina liked Dora, responding to her with just the right amount of deference due to an older woman with an established reputation. She wrote the poem 'Autumn Violets' for her, sending it 'with love, and in the hope of our meeting ere long,' and Dora addressed a poem to Christina which begins

> Thou hast filled me a golden cup
> With a drink divine that glows,
> With the bloom that is flowing up
> From the heart of the folded rose.

Dora was slim, dark and rather tall with a melodious speaking voice and a quiet elegance that suited her serious disposition. She wrote lively, amusing letters to her friends covering a wide range of social and literary topics, always permeated by her fervent Christianity. She felt that 'she needed the addition of a large literary circle', and 'desired to influence and be influenced by other intellectual people'. A friend observed that she 'had the power of attracting to herself young and ardent spirits' like Christina. The tragedy of her life was that she loved a man who was already married, and she remained devoted to him until she died. Dora's health was poor, but this was something she regarded at times as an advantage, writing to a friend that 'a *professed* invalid has many social immunities, which I mean to take full advantage of for the time being.' It gave her the leisure to write, and freedom from domestic chores.[10] Christina met Dora when she came to London and they corresponded regularly.

Christina also spent twenty-four hours at Wallington Hall with Mrs Scott, visiting Pauline Trevelyan and her husband. Pauline was fourteen years older than Christina, a talented artist and writer, who was also a Tractarian. She was only five feet tall, pretty and rather fragile. W.B. Scott described her as 'light as a feather and as quick as a kitten'.[11] She was also extremely acute, and her penetrating grey eyes occasionally made people uneasy. She was married to a much older, scholarly man – a teetotaller and non-smoker – and the relationship appears to have been platonic, if not initially, then certainly by the time she met Christina. Pauline was cultured and discreet and had acted as confidante to Ruskin, Effie and Millais a few years earlier. W.B. Scott had been very much in love with her, and Swinburne regarded her as a mother figure and patroness.

Christina liked Pauline, though she was a little envious of her social ease. Pauline was a natural hostess, with the gift of making people feel relaxed and at home. Christina found social events an ordeal, and while she stayed with the Scotts her sense of isolation deepened. After a picnic on 29 June 1858 she wrote 'At Home'.

> When I was dead, my spirit turned
>   To seek the much-frequented house.
> I passed the door, and saw my friends
>   Feasting beneath green orange-boughs;
> From hand to hand they pushed the wine,
>   They sucked the pulp of plum and peach;
> They sang, they jested, and they laughed,
>   For each was loved of each.

* * *

'Tomorrow,' said they, strong with hope,
   And dwelt upon the pleasant way:
'Tomorrow,' cried they one and all,
   While no one spoke of yesterday.
Their life stood full at blessed noon;
   I, only I, had passed away:
   'Tomorrow and today,' they cried;
   I was of yesterday.

I shivered comfortless, but cast
   No chill across the tablecloth;
I all-forgotten shivered, sad
   To stay and yet to part how loth:
I passed from the familiar room,
   I who from love had passed away,
Like the remembrance of a guest
   That tarrieth but a day.

On the same day, and in the grip of the same depression, she wrote the
stoic and beautiful 'Up-Hill', and 'Today and Tomorrow', the most
bleak and savage of her poems. Like 'At Home' it makes the contrast
between one who is alone and miserable while the world burgeons and
blossoms.

In 'Today and Tomorrow' she observes the spring and longs for the
wind of life to stir her branches. It comes as near as Christina could get
to the admission of unsatisfied sexual desire.

All the world is making love:
   Bird to bird in bushes,
Beast to beast in glades, and frog
   To frog among the rushes:
Wake, O south wind sweet with spice,
   Wake the rose to blushes.

It is not hard to imagine, reading the poem that Christina might have
wished for death. It ends

I wish I were dead, my foe,
My friend, I wish I were dead,
With a stone at my tired feet
And a stone at my tired head.

> In the pleasant April days
> Half the world will stir and sing,
> But half the world will slug and rot
> For all the sap of Spring.

A month later, during this period of emotional and spiritual conflict, Christina wrote 'The Convent Threshold'. Alice Meynell, writing an essay on Christina after her death, thought that there was more passion in this poem 'than in any other poem written by a woman. It seems as though the lines were shaken by the force of feeling that never breaks into the relief of violence.'[12] The theme of the poem is one of forbidden love.

> There's blood between us, love, my love,
> There's father's blood, there's brother's blood;
> And blood's a bar I cannot pass:

It is not certain whether this is a reference to an incestuous love affair, or a blood feud similar to the story of Heloise and Abelard. Like Heloise the 'I' of the poem has chosen escape into the cloister.

> I choose the stairs that mount above,
> Stair after golden skyward stair,
> To city and to sea of glass.

Racked by guilt – the scarlet mud which stains her lily feet – she seeks redemption in penitence, urging her lover to take the same course so that they may be reunited in Paradise. She is haunted by conflicting dreams.

> I tell you what I dreamed last night:
> A spirit with transfigured face
> Fire-footed clomb an infinite space.
> I heard his hundred pinions clang,
> Heaven bells rejoicing rang and rang,
> Heaven-air was thrilled with subtle scents,
> Worlds spun upon their rushing cars:
> He mounted shrieking 'Give me light.'
> Still light was poured on him, more light;
> Angels, Archangels he outstripped,
> Exultant in exceeding might,
> And trod the skirts of Cherubim.
> Still, 'Give me light,' he shrieked; and dipped
> His thirsty face and drank a sea,
> Athirst with thirst it could not slake.

The spirit craves knowledge, but the sum of all the knowledge he gains is that 'love is all in all'. She dreams that her lover comes to her after death.

> I tell you what I dreamed last night:
> It was not dark, it was not light,
> Cold dews had drenched my plenteous hair
> Through clay; you came to seek me there.
> And 'Do you dream of me?' you said.
> My heart was dust that used to leap
> To you; I answered half asleep:
> 'My pillow is damp, my sheets are red,
> There's a leaden tester to my bed:
> Find you a warmer playfellow,
> A warmer pillow for your head,
> A kinder love to love than mine.'
> You wrung your hands; while I, like lead
> Crushed downwards through the sodden earth:
> You smote your hands but not in mirth,
> And reeled but were not drunk with wine.

The sheer physicality of the poem and its relentless, erotic energy, bears comparison to Pope's *Eloisa and Abelard*. There are many thresholds in the poem – between the convent and the world, between heaven and hell, earthly love and heavenly love, life and death, sin and redemption – and they reflect the conflicts of Christina's own life.

The poem made a deep impression on Gerard Manley Hopkins, whom Christina met for the first time in 1864 through a mutual acquaintance. Hopkins wrote a reply to Christina's poem from the lover's point of view, called 'A Voice from the World'. It lacks the nightmare quality of Christina's. In it, the lover wanders, hearing his beloved's voice and longing to see her again.

> Your comfort is as sharp as swords;
> And I cry out for wounded love.
> And you are gone so heavenly far
> You hear nor care of love and pain.
> My tears are but a cloud of rain;
> My passion like a foolish wind
> Lifts them a little way above.
> But you, so spherèd, see no more –
> You see but with a holier mind –
> You hear and alter'd do not hear
> Being a stoled apparell'd star.[13]

Christina's biographer W. MacKenzie Bell presumed that 'The Convent Threshold' referred to an Italian vendetta, and William did not contradict him, merely reiterating that it did not refer to any actual incident. Dante Gabriel called it a 'splendid piece of feminine ascetic passion'.[14] Alice Meynell in the *New Review* claimed that it was a masterpiece 'without imagery, without beauty, except that which is inevitable (and what beauty is more costly); without grace, except the inevitable grace of impassioned poetry; without music, except the ultimate music of the communicating word,' and yet without any of these things, 'an immortal song of love and . . . cry of more than earthly fear'.[15]

PART THREE

Just a Fairy Story

They tell but dreams – a lonely spirit's dreams:
Yet ever through their fleeting imagery
Wanders a vein of melancholy love,
An aimless thought of home; as in the song
Of the caged skylark ye may deem there dwells
A passionate memory of blue skies and flowers,
And living streams, far off.

FELICIA HEMANS
'Songs of the Affections'
Poetical Works 1879

CHAPTER EIGHT

On the 27 April 1859, six months after 'The Convent Threshold', Christina completed her most celebrated and mysterious poem 'Goblin Market'. Its combination of the grotesque, the fairytale, the erotic and the moral is unique. It is a disturbing poem to read; the reader is constantly aware that something is going on subliminally that works against a straightforward moral reading of the text. Just as you have decided what the poem is about, it shifts ground beneath you, operating on three levels – the narrative, the allegorical and the psychological. On the simplest level it is a poem about two sisters, one of whom redeems the other by a courageous act. But what does she redeem her sister from? And the act of redemption seems open to almost endless interpretation.

Christina herself insisted that it was 'just a fairytale', but her first readers were aware of the vast psychological landscape opening out behind it. William Rossetti wrote in his notes to the poem

> I have more than once heard Christina say that she did not mean anything profound by this fairy tale – it is not a moral apologue consistently carried out in detail. Still, the incidents are such as to be at any rate suggestive, and different minds may be likely to read different messages into them.[1]

C.M. Bowra in *The Romantic Imagination* thought that what Christina wrote was 'not a direct account of her conscious thoughts, but dreams and longings which did not normally break into her life but lay locked in unexplored corners of her soul'. This is true of any writer, but it was particularly important in Christina's work, because so much of herself was repressed and locked away. She could only become free when 'her genius took command of her and made her write poems which her conscious self would have repudiated as false records of her feelings, but which none the less reflected her true self.'[2]

This other self had passionate sexual feelings awakened by her love affair with Collinson, which were denied any outlet – even masturbation was forbidden. Christina in 'Goblin Market' draws first a picture of two sisters living and sleeping together in happy innocence – the parallel with herself and Maria like 'two turtle doves in the nest of love' is irresistible.

> Golden head by golden head
> Like two pigeons in one nest
> Folded in each other's wings,
> They lay down in their curtained bed:

But after Laura succumbs to the Goblin's temptation it is quite another matter. She creeps to bed and lies

> Silent till Lizzie slept;
> Then sat up in a passionate yearning,
> And gnashed her teeth for baulked desire, and wept
> As if her heart would break.

Christina draws a similar contrast in a small lyric written before 1863. In 'Song' the two sisters are 'Two doves upon the self-same branch', apparently innocent, wandering hand in hand 'flushed in the rosy summer light' like 'two lilies on a single stem'. It is possible to be taken in by this daylight image 'And never give a thought to night'. A great deal of Christina's poetry concerns the night, and the things usually concealed by darkness.

In form and content 'Goblin Market' is totally original – a metrical helter skelter sweeping its ambiguous subject matter headlong from page to page. Edmund Gosse in his *Life of Swinburne* wrote that British poetry in the eighteen-fifties had become a

> beautiful guarded park, in which, over smoothly shaven lawns where gentle herds of fallow deer were grazing, thrushes sang very discreetly from the boughs of ancestral trees, and where there was not a single object to be seen or heard which could offer the smallest discomfort to the feelings of the most refined mid-Victorian gentlewoman.[3]

Into this atmosphere tumbled Christina's goblins, half men, half beast, with their seductive cries and their panniers of exotic, forbidden fruit.

One had a cat's face,
One whisked a tail,
One tramped at a rat's pace
One crawled like a snail,
One like a wombat prowled obtuse and furry,
One like a ratel tumbled hurry-skurry.

Christina may have been inspired by William Allingham's poem

Up the airy mountain,
Down the rushy glen,
We dare not go a-hunting
For fear of little men.

But 'Goblin Market' has its roots deep in the female gothic conscious-ness, springing from the same imagination that produced *Frankenstein*, *Wuthering Heights*, and *The Mysteries of Udolpho* – what the *Athenaeum* in 1847 referred to as the 'eccentricities of women's fantasy'; their gothic creations drawing on all the anger and repressed violence and passion buried within them.

The Goblins are brothers, set up in opposition to the sisters, but whereas Allingham's 'little men' are never explicitly described, Chris-tina used her visits to Regents Park Zoo to provide details for her creations, writing in her letters of weasel-faced armadilloes and tree frogs like tin toys. She was particularly fascinated by a blind wombat which had a cage next to a porcupine and waged intermittent hostilities. Her delight in wombats led her brother Gabriel to buy one, which sat on the epergne during dinner and devoured a box of cigars.

It was Dante Gabriel's pictorial representations of the goblins as beasts with human hands that formed the public's ideas of what they should look like. In the text, and in Christina's own watercolours done in the margins of a copy of the 1862 edition, the goblins are much more varied and humanesque, slim athletic figures dressed in blue, part human, part beast. Their horror lies in their simultaneous likeness and unlikeness, with all its possibilities of deception.

The fruit the goblins sell is a similar combination of the normal and abnormal. They offer the usual greengrocer's fare

Apples and quinces,
Lemons and oranges,
Plump unpecked cherries,
Melons and raspberries,

as well as fruit from the exotic south

> Our grapes fresh from the vine,
> Pomegranates full and fine,
> Dates and sharp bullaces,
> Rare pears and greengages,
> Damsons and bilberries,
> Taste them and try:

But these are no ordinary fruit – they are larger, more succulent, 'odorous and sugar-sweet', with the larger than life, too-beautiful-to-be-true properties of the apple offered by the witch to Snow White.

Christina was fully aware of the link between fruit and sex, established when Eve ate the first apple in paradise and fell from a state of innocence to one of guilty knowledge. The parallel between the consumption of fruit and the sexual act is explicit in the poem.

Christina's choice of sisterhood as the central theme for her poem is also important. Several of her poems at this time are pre-occupied with the relationship of sisters. In the ballad 'Noble Sisters' one jealous sister cheats the other of her lover. 'Sister Maude' betrays hers by telling their parents of her 'shame'. 'In The Lowest Room', completed three years earlier, one sister – the I of the poem – learns humility from the other and accepts a 'subordinate and bedimmed position' in lines embodying the supreme philosophy of Christina's life and faith.

In these poems the two sisters, like and unlike, may represent two halves of one character – a daytime face and a night-time face. The poems also seem to reflect the problems of sibling rivalry – Maria's jealousy of her brilliant and more attractive sister, as well as the closeness and physicality of nursery relationships, sharing not only a room but also a bed. Christina had great admiration for her older sister, but was slightly in awe of her. Edmund Gosse, observing them together thought, like William Rossetti, that Maria's influence was not always beneficial for Christina. Gosse writes that Maria

left upon me the impression of stronger character, though of narrower intellect and infinitely poorer imagination. I formed the idea, I know not whether with justice, that the pronounced high church views of Maria, who throve on ritual, starved the less pietistic, but painfully conscientious nature of Christina. The influence of Maria on her sister seemed to be like that of Newton upon Cowper, a species of police surveillance exercised by a hard, convinced mind over a softer and more fanciful one.[5]

In 'Goblin Market' the two sisters Laura and Lizzie go down to the river each evening for water. Laura cautions Lizzie not to listen to the cries of the goblin men who tramp through the rushes inviting them to come and buy.

> 'Lie Close,' Laura said,
> Pricking up her golden head:
> 'We must not look at goblin men,
> We must not buy their fruits:
> Who knows upon what soil they fed
> Their hungry thirsty roots?'

But Laura is unable to resist the temptation of raising her own 'glossy head' to watch the goblins' progress. Immediately she is surrounded by the pack

> When they reached where Laura was
> They stood stock still upon the moss,
> Leering at each other,
> Brother with queer brother;
> Signalling each other,
> Brother with sly brother.

Laura longs for the 'golden weight' of fruit they offer, but has no money. The goblins invite her to buy with a 'golden curl'. As in Pope's *Rape of the Lock*, the transaction with the hair is sexually significant. Maureen Duffy goes one step further and writes that 'by the usual transposition we know it is pubic hair'.[6] Laura gorges herself on fruit in an orgy of oral eroticism.

> She sucked and sucked and sucked the more
> Fruits which that unknown orchard bore;
> She sucked until her lips were sore;

Dizzy with surfeit, she does not know whether it is night or day. Her sister Lizzie awaits her late return anxiously, reminding her of Jeanie 'in her grave'

> Who should have been a bride;
> But who for joys brides hope to have
> Fell sick and died

She makes explicit the connection between unsanctioned sex and what the goblins offer, for Jeanie too had 'met them in the moonlight . . . Ate their fruits and wore their flowers.' Afterwards she had dwindled and died.

Laura, at first sated by her feast, discovers that sexual gratification only breeds desire for further pleasure of the same kind. Like 'a leaping flame' she goes with her sister to the river eager to taste more goblin fruit, only to discover that having once eaten, she is incapable of seeing them and deaf forever to their cries. As Marion Erle finds out in *Aurora Leigh*, men have no further interest in fallen women.

> Day after day, night after night,
> Laura kept watch in vain
> In sullen silence of exceeding pain.
> She never caught again the goblin cry,
> 'Come buy, come buy;'–
> She never spied the goblin men
> Hawking their fruits along the glen:

Her hair turns grey, she can't eat sleep or work and rapidly declines. A kernel stone she had saved from the fruit fails to germinate though she plants it facing south and waters it with her tears.

> While with sunk eyes and faded mouth
> She dreamed of melons, as a traveller sees
> False waves in desert drouth

Lizzie fears that her sister will die, just as Jeanie died, and she resolves to traffic with the goblins for Laura's sake, though we are not told how she knows that a further meal of the golden fruit will cure her. The moral, as William Rossetti observed, is not consistently carried out. Laura puts a silver penny in her purse and goes down to the river at twilight. The laughing goblins come towards her in a macabre pack

> Flying, running, leaping,
> Puffing and blowing,
> Chuckling, clapping, crowing,
> Clucking and gobbling,

Lizzie stands her ground, tosses them her penny and asks to buy the fruit. The goblins invite her to sit down with them and eat. They offer elaborate reasons why they cannot give it to her to take away.

> Such fruits as these
> No man can carry;
> Half their bloom would fly,
> Half their dew would dry,
> Half their flavour would pass by.

Lizzie refuses to eat the fruit and asks for the return of her money. The goblins cease to be pleasant and persuasive and resort to violence.

> They trod and hustled her,
> Elbowed and jostled her,
> Clawed with their nails,
> Barking, mewing, hissing, mocking,
> Tore her gown and soiled her stocking,
> Twitched her hair out by the roots,
> Stamped upon her tender feet,
> Held her hands and squeezed their fruits
> Against her mouth to make her eat.

The parallel with rape is reinforced by the description of Lizzie resisting this invasion of her person 'Like a royal virgin town'. She will not open 'lip from lip', to allow the goblins to force their fruit into her mouth. At last the goblins abandon the assault and vanish mysteriously. Bruised and beaten Lizzie goes home daubed with the pulp and juice of the fruit, but delighted with her victory.

> She cried 'Laura,' up the garden,
> 'Did you miss me?
> Come and kiss me.
> Never mind my bruises,
> Hug me, kiss me, suck my juices
> Squeezed from goblin fruits for you,
> Goblin pulp and goblin dew.
> Eat me, drink me, love me;
> Laura, make much of me;
> For your sake I have braved the glen
> And had to do with goblin merchant men.'

Although Lizzie's invitation has sexual connotations, and what transpires between the girls is even more disturbingly erotic than the episodes with the goblins, there is also a religious interpretation which is important. Jesus Christ in the Gospel according to St John says that 'Whoso eateth my flesh, and drinketh my blood, hath eternal life'[7] and this has become the basis of the Christian sacrament. So Lizzie, by inviting her sister to eat her flesh and 'suck her juices' promises Laura new life. In the Bible the opposition of Eve who eats the apple and dooms mankind, and Christ whose consumption of a far bitterer fruit redeems them, seems to parallel Christina's opposition of Laura, who eats, and Lizzie who offers to sacrifice herself for Laura's redemption.

Laura starts from her chair and begins to kiss and kiss her sister 'with a hungry mouth'. The goblin juice scorches her lips like wormwood as she gorges, not on sweetness this time but 'on bitterness without a name', ingesting a different kind of knowledge, until she falls to the floor in a kind of orgasm delineated by a series of phallic similes.

> Like the watch-tower of a town
> Which an earthquake shatters down,
> Like a lightning-stricken mast,
> Like a wind-uprooted tree
> Spun about,
> Like a foam-topped waterspout
> Cast headlong down in the sea,
> She fell at last;
> Pleasure past and anguish past,
> Is it death or is it life?

It is a perfect synthesis of religious and sexual ecstasy.

When the waterlilies open their flowers at daybreak, Laura wakes from a long sleep, laughing 'in the innocent old way', restored and made whole again.

The moral of the story, if it is strong enough to be called a moral, is contained in the last stanza. As a grown woman, married with children of her own, Laura calls the children to her to tell them of the goblins in the haunted glen and how 'her sister stood . . .

> In deadly peril to do her good,
> And win the fiery antidote:
> Then joining hands to little hands
> Would bid them cling together, –
> 'For there is no friend like a sister
> In calm or stormy weather;
> To cheer one on the tedious way,
> To fetch one if one goes astray,
> To lift one if one totters down,
> To strengthen whilst one stands.'

The weakness of the last lines, with their metrical sense of anti-climax, stimulates a similar sense of anti-climax in the reader. Is this what the poem has been about? A celebration of sisterly love? And the traditional fairy tale ending of marriage and motherhood 'Their lives bound up in tender lives' may also seem rather tame and inadequate to a late twentieth-century public.

For Christina the ending of the poem had special significance. Originally titled A Peep at the Goblins, she dedicated the poem to her sister Maria. William Rossetti wrote to Christina's biographer MacKenzie Bell that the closing lines of the poem indicated 'something', though he could remember 'no personal circumstances of a marked kind'. Apparently 'Christina considered herself to be chargeable with some sort of spiritual backsliding, against which Maria's influence had been exercised beneficially.'[8] But he refused to speculate further. Others have speculated freely. Violet Hunt (mistress of Christina's nephew) in the *Wife of Rossetti*, told a tale of Maria crouching on the doormat night after night to prevent Christina from running away with a married man. However this apocryphal story has never been corroborated and Miss Hunt's book has been proved totally inaccurate in a number of important respects.

Christina was no happier in 1859 than she had been the year before. In August she was writing 'No hope in life; yet there is hope/In death', and the two poems which immediately precede 'Goblin Market' are the desolate 'L.E.L.' and 'Winter Rain'. The latter poem has been described as referring to pointless menstruation, but it can just as easily be seen as the fruitless pursuit of creative art. Christina was increasingly conscious that she was not only childless, but that her artistic children were all still-born.

> Every valley drinks
> Every dell and hollow;
> Where the kind rain sinks and sinks,
> Green of Spring will follow.

The saturated landscape with its promise of spring is contrasted with her own internal desert

> But miles of barren sand,
> With never a son or daughter;
> Not a lily on the land,
> Or lily on the water.

It seems possible that in this morass of depression her faith wavered and she turned to Maria for support. It is even possible that her desire for death became a tangible wish for self-destruction – hence the tale of Maria barring the doorway to prevent her leaving the house. The notion of Christina eloping with a married man – Collinson and W.B. Scott have been advanced as likely candidates – will not hold together. Even had Christina entertained the notion, W.B. Scott had been entangled first with Pauline Trevelyan and then in March 1859 he had begun a liaison with Alice Boyd, who subsequently joined the circle of Christina's friends. Collinson had not been part of the Rossettis' social circle since he left the PRB and there is no record of any kind to suggest contact of even the most fleeting variety with Christina.

Sometimes Christina's passionate longing for earthly love was transmuted into a longing to be 'ravished by Christ' – a mingling of the erotic and religious evident in much medieval religious poetry and devotional prose, and which occurs frequently in Christina's work. In 'The Heart Knoweth Its Own Bitterness' she writes of her longing

> To give, to give, not to receive!
>   I long to pour myself, my soul,
> Not to keep back or count or leave,
>   But king with king to give the whole.
> I long for one to stir my deep –
>   I have had enough of help and gift –
>   I long for one to search and sift
> Myself, to take myself and keep.

She taunts her cold lover

> You scratch my surface with your pin,
>   You stroke me smooth with hushing breath:-
> Nay pierce, nay probe, nay dig within,
>   Probe my quick core and sound my depth.
> You call me with a puny call,
>   You talk, you smile, you nothing do:
>   How should I spend my heart on you,
> My heart that so outweighs you all?

The only ray of hope available to Christina in 1859 was the inclusion of her poem 'An End' in an anthology called *Nightingale Valley* edited by William Allingham. She filled her time working with 'fallen women', unmarried mothers and prostitutes at the St Mary Magdalen home at

Highgate – an institution for 'the reclamation and protection of women leading a vicious life'. At some time in the late eighteen-fifties she became an associate of the order, staying for a few days at a time and wearing a uniform of dark cloth with white collar and cuffs and a white lace cap and veil. W.B. Scott's wife Laetitia visited Christina there and remarked upon how well the habit suited her – 'like a nun'. In October Christina travelled up to Newcastle with Pauline Trevelyan to stay with Laetitia and William came up a few weeks later with W.B. Scott to escort Christina back to London.

CHAPTER NINE

1860 opened in a similar vein of depression. In *Time Flies*, written almost thirty years later, Christina recalled sitting on a bench for a long time, feeling absolutely wretched. But as she sat the wild creatures came up out of the water close to her and the experience produced a bubble of pleasure 'lit by a dancing rainbow'.[1]

There were lighter moments. Her confidence was given a boost by the marked attentions of another suitor. William thought that it must have been the painter John Brett, and dated his interest in Christina as far back as 1852, though the poem is dated 1860. William's memory – he was seventy-five when he wrote the notes to her poems – may have been at fault. The anonymous John's persistence was the source of some amusement in the Rossetti household, as the playful, 'No, Thank You, John' records. The poem was eventually included in the 1875 edition of her collected *Poems* and she wrote in the margin of her own copy 'The original John was obnoxious because he never gave scope for "No, thank you"'. Later in a letter to Gabriel she denied that the John of the poem was a real person at all. William tried to justify these tergiversations with a series of complex literary and moral arguments, but the explanation is probably simpler – that the man's real name had not been John at all and she wished to spare him the knowledge that he had been publicly made fun of by her.

For Christina, 1859 was a year of participation in other people's lives. Lizzie Siddal was extremely ill again, with sickness and diarrhoea, headaches and general malaise. At times she appeared to be dying, at other times she was well enough to get up and go out. She was sent to the south coast for her health. Dante Gabriel, after procrastinating for years, impulsively bought a marriage licence and went to Hastings to join her. He wrote to his mother that he did not deserve that Lizzie should still consent to marry him. 'Like all the important things I ever meant to do – to fulfil duty or secure happiness – this one has been deferred almost beyond possibility.'[2] They were married on 23 May.

Whether it was the pursuit of duty or happiness that motivated Gabriel remained unclear. His friend Thomas Hall Caine was convinced that he had only married Lizzie 'out of a mistaken sense of loyalty and fear of giving pain'.[3] He also seemed to have believed that Lizzie did not have long to live, writing to Madox Brown that 'Lizzie seemed ready to die daily'. It was the worst possible basis for a successful relationship.

The couple had intended to go to France with Edward Burne-Jones and his new wife Georgina; but Burne-Jones fell ill and was unable to accompany them, and so they set out alone. On their return they moved into Dante Gabriel's lodgings, which they enlarged by knocking through into the apartment next door. For a time they also rented a house in Highgate so that Lizzie could spend the winters above the level of the London smogs. Georgie Burne-Jones visited them shortly afterwards and wrote of an atmosphere of romance and tragedy.

The Rossettis welcomed Lizzie into the family, but were pessimistic about the future, often referring to her as 'poor Lizzie'. William observed that Gabriel's 'propensity for doing whatever he liked simply because he liked it, and without any self-accommodation to what other people might like instead' made it improbable that he would make a good husband.[4] Almost immediately Lizzie became pregnant, and the sickly young woman's fecundity threw Christina's own barrenness into stark relief.

William went to Italy in the autumn and took up the Brownings' casual invitiation to visit them at Marciano, near Siena. Unfortunately he chose a bad time to arrive. Elizabeth's son Pen had contracted sunstroke that day and was very ill. William and Browning held a distracted conversation while Elizabeth wandered in and out, totally preoccupied with her son's condition. William and his companion had to stay with neighbours. He arrived back in England to discover that Henrietta Rintoul's mother had died, leaving her free from the strict parental control she had previously been subjected to and which had prevented their marriage. Henrietta's father had died in 1859 and William expected that their marriage would now take place straight away. He was devastated when Henrietta told him that their four-year-old engagement was at an end. She told William that she loved him, but after the death of her parents felt unable to form 'any new ties'. William thought that her attitude was unreasonable, and totally inexplicable.

He failed to understand that having been suffocated by her parents she needed her independence and the thought of marrying into another kind of emotional and physical bondage was repugnant. There were also other considerations – namely William's continued support of his female relatives.

Christina, who was very fond of Henrietta, became their intermediary. She wrote to William on 30 November that she had been to see Henrietta to return some books and had been subjected to scenes of hysterical grief.

> I never saw anything like her misery. She held me fast kissing me and crying, and I could feel how thin she is and how she trembled in my arms. It seemed some relief to her to tell me a great deal about what is past and what now is; poor dear, I pity her beyond what words can express . . .[5]

Christina writes puzzlingly of being prepared to make a sacrifice to secure Henrietta's happiness, if she could only be sure that Henrietta's happiness was compatible with William's. Possibly Henrietta was not prepared to join a household which included William's mother and two sisters, but the details are not spelled out in the letter.

Christina approached her thirtieth birthday with apprehension. Even as an old woman she could still remember the feeling of relief and exhilaration she had when she consulted the mirror on the morning of her birthday and found her appearance unaltered. But she felt that it was a landmark, signalling that her youth was over. Using quotations from L.E.L.'s 'Verses on the Death of Mrs Hemans', and the Song of Songs, she wrote what many people consider to be her finest poem. Included in collections under the heading of 'Old and New Year Ditties' it is usually referred to as 'Passing Away'. Swinburne wrote with typical hyperbole that he thought 'nothing more glorious in poetry has ever been written'.[6] Other critics regard it as one of the great poems in the English language.

Its theme is mutability, the passage from earthly corruption to eternal life. It begins in depression as Christina reviews her lack of fruitfulness, and the absence of tangible achievement.

> Passing away, saith the World, passing away:
> Chances, beauty, and youth, sapped day by day:
> Thy life never continueth in one stay.
> Is the eye waxen dim, is the dark hair changing to grey
> That hath won neither laurel nor bay?

> I shall clothe myself in Spring and bud in May:
> Thou, root-stricken, shalt not rebuild thy decay
> On my bosom for aye.
> Then I answered: Yea.

In the second stanza she observes her own decline and the hollowness of worldly things.

> Passing away, saith my Soul, passing away:
> With its burden of fear and hope, of labour and play,
> Hearken what the past doth witness and say:
> Rust in thy gold, a moth is in thine array,
> A canker is in thy bud, thy leaf must decay.
> At midnight, at cockcrow, at morning, one certain day
> Lo the Bridegroom shall come and shall not delay;
> Watch thou and pray.
> Then I answered: Yea.

But through faith and prayer, depression is transformed into triumph.

> Passing away, saith my God, passing away:
> Winter passeth after the long delay:
> New grapes on the vine, new figs on the tender spray,
> Turtle calleth turtle in Heaven's May.
> Though I tarry, wait for Me, trust Me, watch and pray:
> Arise, come away, night is past and lo it is day,
> My love, My sister, My spouse, thou shalt hear Me say.
> Then I answered: Yea.

The poem is written in strict metrical form using only one rhyme throughout. It is a supreme example of her craftmanship that the tight structure of the poem does not in any way inhibit the content or its powerful expression. In L.E.L.'s poetry the reader is almost always conscious of the dictates of rhyme and metre which sometimes call attention to a poverty of vocabulary. In Christina's poetry this never happens. Her technical skill, and her ear for the music of words, means that the structural elements of the poem are as unobtrusive and organic a part of the whole as the structural supports of a beautifully designed building. What Ruskin described as her metrical recklessness, her innovatory skill, presents the reader with constant variations of pace and emphasis so that the pattern never becomes monotonous.

The turning of the year also marked the turning point in Christina's life. Dante Gabriel sent some of Christina's poems to the publisher Alexander Macmillan. At the same time John Ruskin, primed by Gabriel, asked to see her work and was given 'Goblin Market' and 'Folio Q', a story about a man 'whose destiny it was not to get reflected in a looking glass'.[7] This was apparently the best story she had ever written, but she destroyed it on being told by Gabriel that it raised 'dangerous moral questions'.

Alexander Macmillan was very enthusiastic about Christina's poems, particularly her 'lively little song of the tomb' (possibly 'When I am dead, my dearest') which he had read aloud at dinner. He asked to see 'Goblin Market' after Ruskin had returned it.

On 25 January, Gabriel wrote to Christina enclosing Ruskin's comments with 'regret and disgust'. They were 'senseless'. Ruskin had decided ideas on art and poetry but was less discerning about the latter. He had sat up all night reading Christina's poems before penning his rather patronising response. They were 'full of beauty and power. But no publisher – I am deeply grieved to know this – would take them, so full are they of quaintnesses and offences. Irregular measure . . . is the calamity of modern poetry.' Ruskin goes on to admire Spenser, Milton (Christina detested Milton) and Keats, and writes that 'your sister should exercise herself in the severest commonplace of metre until she can write as the public like. Then, if she puts in her observation and passion, all will become precious. But she must have the Form first.'[8]

Christina had no intention of writing for an undiscriminating public – the kind of poetry written by the popular nineteenth-century 'lady poets' such as Caroline Norton and Eliza Cook was just the sort of mediocrity she despised, reducing poetry to the level of a ladylike accomplishment. 'Call me Eliza Cook at once and be happy', she wrote sarcastically to Gabriel. According to Christina's nephew Ford Madox Ford, Ruskin had other motives for his dislike of Christina's poetry. He apparently considered that she had damaged Gabriel by publication. There was no room for 'two Rossettis' and she ought to have given way to Gabriel's superior talent.

Fortunately, Alexander Macmillan thought differently and published 'Up-Hill' in the February edition of *Macmillan's Magazine*. Contrary to Ruskin's prediction the public liked it very much. The poem's themes reflected the Victorian ethic of redemption by hard work and self denial as well as the basic tenet of Christianity – suffering now in the hope of reward to come. Following its success Macmillan published 'A Birthday' in April and 'An Apple Gathering' in August.

According to Ford Madox Ford, Christina was 'if not a genie in the form of a cloud of smoke, at least a subtle essence that was bound not only to escape [Ruskin's] embalming, but to survive him'.[9]

On 2 May Lizzie Siddal gave birth to a still-born daughter. She and Gabriel had suspected for two weeks that the baby might be dead, but it was still a terrible blow. Given the state of her health it would have been very surprising if Lizzie had given birth to a healthy baby. She had got into the habit of taking laudanum and brandy alternately in order to cope with the pressures of her life, and it was a lethal mixture to the unborn child. Elizabeth Barrett Browning only succeeded in carrying a full-term baby when she reduced her intake of laudanum on the advice of doctors and with Robert Browning's help and encouragement. There is no record of Lizzie having received the same kind of support.

Although Lizzie recovered physically very quickly she remained deeply depressed. Georgie Burne Jones visited her and found her sitting beside the empty, beribboned cradle rocking it to and fro. Lizzie told Georgie and her husband to speak quietly so as not to wake the baby. She was still very fragile when Gabriel went up to Yorkshire in the autumn to paint a portrait for a commission. He left Lizzie with the Morrises 'in a very delicate state'. However, something upset her and she left hurriedly without explanation. Dante wrote a desperate letter to his mother asking her to find out if Lizzie was all right and to give her some money as he had left her without any. Gabriel had to borrow his own expenses from William and Madox Brown.

It was at this point that Christina wrote 'Too late for Love. Too late for Joy', a poem Gabriel later persuaded her to incorporate into 'The Prince's Progress'. If, as critics have speculated, the poem relates to Gabriel and Lizzie Siddal, it is strangely prophetic.

> Too late for love, too late for joy,
>   Too late, too late!
> You loitered on the road too long,
>   You trifled at the gate:
> The enchanted dove upon her branch
>   Died without a mate;
> The enchanted princess in her tower
>   Slept, died, behind the grate;
> Her heart was starving all this while
>   You made it wait.

Ten years ago, five years ago,
  One year ago,
Even then you had arrived in time,
  Though somewhat slow;
Then you had known her living face
  Which now you cannot know:
The frozen fountain would have leaped,
  The buds gone on to blow,
The warm south wind would have awaked
  To melt the snow.

In the summer of 1861 Christina went abroad. She and her mother, accompanied by William, went to Paris and Normandy, staying mainly at Coutances. Christina thoroughly enjoyed her first experience of foreign travel. Back in London she attended a lecture on France and was elated to discover that many of the places under discussion were those she had visited. 'Boulogne, Rouen and Paris are realities now for me instead of mere names'.[10] The lecturer won Christina's support because he had been a member of a deputation to Napoleon III to end the use of horses in vivisection. Christina was a fierce opponent of the use of animals in experiments.

In October, while Gabriel was in Yorkshire, Alexander Macmillan wrote to him that he had read Christina's 'Goblin Market' aloud to a working men's society. Although at first they had wondered 'whether it was making fun of them: by degrees they got as still as death, and when I finished there was a tremendous burst of applause.' Macmillan thought that a selection of Christina's poems 'would have a chance' with some omissions, and was prepared to run the risk of a 'small edition'. 'My idea is to make an exceedingly pretty little volume, and to bring it out as a small Christmas book. This would give it every chance of coming right to the public.'[11] He asked Gabriel to do the illustrations.

Christina went off to spend some time at the Magdalen Home in Highgate on the understanding that she could work on proofs for the edition while she was there. Before she left she had a social call from Charles Cayley's two sisters. Henrietta appears to have been already known to the family, but it was the first time she had met Sophie. She recorded that she was 'handsome and striking, ready and amusing in conversation', in contrast to the more stolid Henrietta. This is one of the first references to a growing acquaintance with the Cayley family, and this formal visit appears to represent their acknowledgement of a possible relationship between Christina and Charles Cayley.

A poem, 'Winter: My Secret', written in November 1857 seems to suggest the possibility of romantic involvement. Although the secret is unrevealed, the inference is that it is love, and it may indicate the first stirring of her interest in Cayley. This happy poem comes just before the series of desolate poems she wrote in 1859 and 1860 which includes 'Autumn', 'Up-Hill' and 'The Convent Threshold'. L.M. Packer connects 'My Secret' with W.B. Scott, but a reference to 'Russian snows' in the poem would more easily refer to the Russian-born Charles Cayley, whose initial shy ignorance of Christina's affection for him is described in 'A Sketch'. Dante Gabriel thought 'My Secret' too personal for inclusion in her *Collected Poems*, and Christina herself thought that it was 'open to comment'.

Christina had first met Cayley as a pupil of her father's, and he had visited her brothers occasionally over the years, though Gabriel was unenthusiastic about his company. In 'Monna Innominata', the sonnet sequence she wrote to Cayley, Christina regretted not being able to remember their first meeting.

> I wish I could remember that first day,
>   First hour, first moment of your meeting me,
>   If bright or dim the season, it might be
> Summer or Winter for aught I can say;
> So unrecorded did it slip away,
>   So blind was I to see and to foresee,
>   So dull to mark the budding of my tree
> That would not blossom yet for many a May.
> If only I could recollect it, such
>   A day of days! I let it come and go
>   As traceless as a thaw of bygone snow;
> It seemed to mean so little, meant so much;
> If only now I could recall that touch,
>   First touch of hand in hand – Did one but know!

Charles Cayley was an Englishman who had been born in Russia. He had an exceptionally large head with dark unruly hair and dark eyes. He was very shy and absent minded, thoughtful and slow to reply in conversation – so much so that some people were apt to assume he was not going to reply at all. He was satirised in a novel by Oliver Madox Brown as an absent-minded scholarly clergyman. But Cayley was not as stuffy as many people believed. His rather quaint, old-fashioned manners were offset by a twinkle in the eye as if 'enjoying a secret joke', that revealed a keen sense of humour, which Christina shared. Few of his letters to her have survived – she destroyed them – but the ones that remain show his quirky style.

> What can I say of Saturday except that the Museum was quite
> spifflicaiting (I have a cousin in the North country who emphasises her
> words by putting as many letters as possible into them and I suppose
> would not stick at *creighture* or *Wraddicall*)

In another he sent Christina a ridiculous article he had found on the
wombat having once been intended 'to supply a particular want – that,
namely, of an animal available for ordinary food, and conveniently
intermediate in size between a pig and a rabbit.' Cayley comments 'let
us hope that by being eaten they will multiply and earn a livelihood.'[12]

The Cayley family had lost their money in the railway advertising
crash of 1855. The older brother Arthur was Cambridge Professor of
Mathematics, and Charles wrote scholarly books, publishing a metrical
version of the *Psalms* in 1860 (described by William as unreadable), and
in 1861 a translation of an unpublished Italian novel *Filippo Malincontri*.
Christina sent Gabriel a copy and he thanked her for it, remarking that
Cayley seemed 'lower in the scale of creation than ever.'[13]

Christina wrote very little in the winter of 1861/2 except some turgid
verses on the death of Prince Albert. This was partly due to the pressures
of getting *Goblin Market and Other Poems* ready for the press. Gabriel was
very slow to finish the illustrations and the Christmas deadline had to be
pushed back. He was working on a volume of his own early translations
from the Italian poets, made before he was twenty. His life with Lizzie
Siddal was bleak. Lizzie was living in a haze of laudanum and had
despaired of ever having a living child. She tried to give away the
carefully worked layette, and Gabriel had to write to friends and ask
them to refuse it. He still hoped for a child. The only person Lizzie
seemed to confide in was Swinburne, who had come to London from
Cambridge in 1860 and become a close friend of both the Rossettis, as
well as Christina and her mother.

On 10 February Swinburne dined – as he often did – with Gabriel
and Lizzie at the Sabloniere Hotel in Leicester Square. Lizzie was
unwell and rather drowsy, but insisted on coming out with them. After
dinner Gabriel went off to the Working Men's Institute where he took
an art class, and Lizzie went home to bed. When Gabriel came home
around 11 o'clock, she was unconscious, an empty bottle of laudanum
on the table and a note pinned to her nightgown. Gabriel tore it off, read
it and thrust it into a pocket, before summoning the housekeeper and the
doctor. A stomach pump was used, but the laudanum had been in her
system for too long.

At four o'clock in the morning Gabriel dashed round to Madox
Brown's and got him out of bed to show him the note and ask him what

he should do. Madox Brown immediately burnt the piece of paper, and there has been speculation ever since about what it contained. William Rossetti's daughter (Madox Brown's grand-daughter) said that her mother had said that it read simply 'Take care of Harry'[14] – Lizzie's retarded brother – but Gabriel told his friend Hall Caine that what was in the note 'had left such a scar on his heart as could never be healed.'[15]

Madox Brown accompanied Gabriel back to his lodgings and they were there when Lizzie died. The Rossetti family were not told at this point. William knew nothing until midday when Gabriel sent his housekeeper to Somerset House.

Gabriel's grief was at times theatrical. At one point over the next two days he insisted that Lizzie was not dead but only in an opiate coma. The doctors had to be summoned again to recertify her death. His grief was intensified by guilt. He felt responsible for her death, confiding in Hall Caine that Lizzie had lost 'all joy and interest in life' because she had realised that when he married her he had been in love with someone else.[16] This could have been either Fanny Cornforth or Jane Morris, but there were several other 'stunners' in his life at the time. One, an actress called Ruth Herbert, had largely replaced Lizzie's face on canvas by the late eighteen-fifties. Gabriel was totally unable to cope with life on his own after Lizzie's death. William brought him home to Albany Street, where his mother and sisters nursed him through the worst of his grief. He buried himself in work, finding 'the inactive moments the most unbearable.'[17]

At the inquest family and friends told a carefully edited story – the question of the suicide note was never raised – and the verdict of Accidental Death enabled Lizzie to be buried in consecrated ground. Anne Gilchrist, a friend of the Rossettis whose husband had recently died from scarlet fever, wrote to Gabriel quoting Christina's poem 'Up-Hill' – ' "Up-Hill all the way", which for both of us the journey of life has with terrible reality become'.[18]

On the day of the funeral, before the coffin lid was screwed down, Gabriel picked up his manuscript book of poems and in a wild gesture of remorse – possibly inspired by Christina's *Maude* – placed them in the coffin amidst Lizzie's red-gold hair. Gabriel told William that he had often been working on them when Lizzie was ill and suffering and he might have been attending to her. Madox Brown wanted to remove them secretly, guessing that Gabriel would later regret his impulse, but William refused to allow it, because he felt that the action 'did him honour'. Lizzie was buried at Highgate cemetery in the Rossetti family grave with Christina's father Gabriele.

Lizzie's death coincided with the final stages of production of Dante Gabriel's *Italian Poets* and Christina's *Goblin Market and Other Poems*. The volumes came out within a month of each other – Gabriel's scarcely noticed, but *Goblin Market* was a modest sensation, described as 'her brilliant, fantastic and profoundly original volume.'[17] The influence of Tennyson on the poetry being published at the time had come to be regarded by many as 'a kind of Upas Tree' – the mythical plant which killed all who came within its radius. W.B. Scott wrote to Pauline Trevelyan that 'Gardener's daughters and sixteen-year-old Maud's with murdering lovers as well as consumptive music masters and donkey poets making mannerless love to proud ladies, are very closely allied to things silly.'[18] Critics like Gosse agreed with him. Christina's technical innovations such as the short, irregularly rhymed lines and simplicity of expression were seen as a refreshing departure. She, rather than Dante Gabriel, was seen as the leader of the Pre-Raphaelite poetry movement, and Swinburne described her as 'the Jael who led our host to victory'.

Caroline Norton reviewed *Goblin Market* for *Macmillan's Magazine*, contrasting it, oddly, with Allingham's *Angel in the House*. She observed that 'Goblin Market' was a work 'to defy criticism . . . Is it a fable – or a mere fairy story – or an allegory against the pleasures of sinful love – or what is it?' She admired 'the versatility, as well as the originality of genius', and concluded that it was a poem 'to ponder over, as we do with poems written in a foreign language which we only half understand.'

The *British Quarterly* reviewed *Goblin Market* in July and was equally enthusiastic. All the pieces, wrote the reviewer 'are marked by beauty and tenderness. They are frequently quaint and sometimes a little capricious . . .' Gabriel's illustrations were also praised. 'No Goblins could be better or more laughable than these; nor could we imagine anything more felicitous than the mixed longing and hesitation portrayed in the face and action of the damsel'. The title poem was singled out for particular praise, being 'the wealthiest in expression of any in the volume, as it is also the one which is most purely and completely a work of art; but the devotional pieces are those we have liked best . . .'[21]

Christina's religious poetry continued to be elevated. Before Gerard Manley Hopkin's work was published she was regarded as the greatest religious poet of the nineteenth century, and is still considered to be one of the finest in the English language. But as poetry with a religious theme has fallen out of fashion, so her supposedly secular poetry has come back into focus. But this division of her work (originally urged by Gabriel and continued by William when he edited her *Collected Poems*) is artificial and reductive, because her faith was organic and pervaded the whole of her poetic output.

Copies of *Goblin Market* found their way to America even before its publication there in 1866. It got a mixed reception. Emerson, in common with most American readers, admired only the religious poetry. Emily Dickinson, who read the output of other women poets avidly, never commented directly on Christina's work, but her own poetry in the period between 1862 and 1863 is littered with references to goblins which appear nowhere else. Lines such as 'A Goblin drank my Dew', 'Sip, Goblin, from the very lips', and 'No Goblin on the Bloom' are too frequent, and too close a reference to be coincidental.[22] Poem No. 691 written possibly in 1863 also has echoes of Christina's poem.

> Would you like summer? Taste of ours.
> Spices? Buy here!
> Ill! We have berries for the parching!
> Weary? Furloughs of down!
> Perplexed! Estates of violet trouble ne'er looked on!
> Captive! We bring reprieve of roses!
> Fainting! Flasks of air!
> Even for Death, a fairy medicine.
> But, what is it, Sir?

Emily Dickinson's goblins become more explicitly symbols of the hinterland of gothic horror Christina only barely suggested. In Poem No. 414 the boiling wheel of agony 'like a Maelstrom with a notch' draws 'nearer, every Day'

> As if a Goblin with a Gauge –
> Kept measuring the Hours –
> Until you felt your Second
> Weigh, helpless, in his Paws –

The Goblins are associated with isolation – both Lizzie and Laura had to face them alone. So, too in poem No. 590, Emily Dickinson has to face hers.

> Did you ever stand in a Cavern's Mouth –
> Widths out of the Sun –
> And look – and shudder, and block your breath
> And deem to be alone

> In such a place, what horror,
> How Goblin it would be –
> And fly, as 'twere pursuing you?
> Then Loneliness – looks so –

It was no coincidence that Emily Dickinson chose similar subject matter for her poetry, for her experience of life was very close to Christina's. Both had their hopes of love dashed, both lived within a close and restrictive family atmosphere, both were shy and reclusive, religion played a large part in their lives, and both admired Elizabeth Barrett Browning. However, Emily understood better than Christina the terrible consequences of introspection and the impossibility of reconciling the divided self.

> Me from Myself – to banish –
> Had I Art –
> Impregnable my Fortress
> Until All Heart –
>
> But since Myself – assault Me –
> How have I place
> Except by subjugating
> Consciousness?
>
> And since We're mutual Monarch
> How this be
> Except by Abdication –
> Me – of Me?

In 1863 Christina wrote a poem which parallels Emily's, called 'Who Shall Deliver Me', which begins 'God strengthen me to bear myself'. In the poem 'the others' are locked on the outside.

> I lock my door upon myself
> And bar them out: but who shall wall
> Self from myself, most loathed of all?
>
> Myself arch traitor to myself;
> My hollowest friend, my deadliest foe,
> My clog, whatever road I go.

Christina's lines, like Emily Dickinson's, describe the struggle between conformity and 'difference' that seems at times to have stretched Christina's sanity to breaking point. Georgina Battiscombe subtitled her biography of Christina *A Divided Life*, identifying the conflicting influences on her personality – Italian versus English, God versus Self. England, God and Conformity eventually won, but the cost was enormous.

In 1862, for the first time, Christina found great fulfilment and joy in the publication of her poetry and its reception by the public. On 31 March she wrote the sonnet 'In Progress', ostensibly about an unidentified friend (possibly Laetitia Scott), but her family saw a clear parallel between the poem and her own state of mind at the time.

> Ten years ago it seemed impossible
>   That she should ever grow so calm as this,
>   With self-remembrance in her warmest kiss
> And dim dried eyes like an exhausted well.
> Slow-speaking when she has some fact to tell,
>   Silent with long-unbroken silences,
>   Centred in self yet not unpleased to please,
> Gravely monotonous like a passing bell.
> Mindful of drudging daily common things,
>   Patient at pastime, patient at her work,
>   Wearied perhaps but strenuous certainly.
>   Sometimes I fancy we may one day see
>   Her head shoot forth seven stars from where they lurk
> And her eyes lightnings and her shoulders wings.

CHAPTER TEN

It was no coincidence that the years 1861 to 1864 were the healthiest of Christina's life, for they were also the happiest. After a long literary apprenticeship her poetry was published and appreciated, and her personal life was no longer so bleak, as the warm affection between herself and Charles Cayley grew. This time the relationship was rooted in friendship and mutual interests, a growing together of like minds.

Towards the end of 1862 she wrote the first of her *Il Rosseggiar Dell' Oriente* poems – lines so personal that they were written in Italian and locked in her desk until she died. The first was called 'Amor Dormente?' (Is Love Sleeping?) in which the poet bids the lover goodbye in this world with promises of a reunion in heaven. The second was called 'Amor Si Sveglia?' (Is Love Awake?) and it begins

> *In nuova primavera*
> *Rinasce il genio antico;*
> *Amor t'insinua 'Spera' –*
> *Pur io nol dico.*

> In the new spring
> Old feelings are reborn.
> Love whispers "Hope" –
> But I say nothing.

The Italian poems are paralleled in English by Christina's 'Monna Innominata' sonnets, concealed behind the fiction of a female troubador writing to a man she cannot have. No. 4 in the sequence also describes the initial stages of love and the unspoken exploration of each other's feelings.

I loved you first: but afterwards your love,
  Outsoaring mine, sang such a loftier song
As drowned the friendly cooings of my dove.
  Which owes the other most? My love was long,
  And yours one moment seemed to wax more strong;
I loved and guessed at you, you construed me
And loved me for what might or might not be –
  Nay, weights and measures do us both a wrong.
For verily love knows not 'mine' or 'thine';
  With separate 'I' and 'thou' free love has done,
  For one is both and both are one in love:
Rich love knows nought of 'thine that is not mine;'
  Both have the strength and both the length thereof,
Both of us, of the love which makes us one.

The idea that she loved Cayley first and encouraged his intentions is hinted at in letters and other poems such as 'A Sketch', written in 1864, in which, despite the fact that the poet 'might show facts as plain as day', the lover

> Sees not what's within his reach,
> Misreads the part, ignores the whole;

Christina's 'Monna Innominata' sonnet sequence, published in 1882, is one of the most neglected of her works. Its ambitious structure is derived from her own experience of Dante's celebration of Beatrice, and Petrarch's canzoniere dedicated to the elusive Laura. Influenced by Elizabeth Barret Browning's *Sonnets from the Portuguese*, Christina wrote her own 'sonnet of sonnets' from the lady's point of view rather than the man's. The difference is that while Barrett Browning's are a celebration of love, Christina's echo the hopelessness of Petrarch and Dante – exhibiting what Gosse called 'that *desiderium*, that obstinate longing for something lost out of life' which was characteristic of Christina's poetry.[1]

The death of Elizabeth Barrett Browning in 1861 ensured that her work was prominent in Christina's mind, though the sonnets are not a memorial. In her headnote to the sequence Christina acknowledges her debt to her and refers to the different approaches that had been chosen for them.

Had the Great Poetess of our own day and nation only been unhappy instead of happy, her circumstances would have invited her to bequeath to us, in lieu of 'Portuguese Sonnets', an inimitable 'Donna innominata' drawn not from fancy but from feeling, and worthy to occupy a niche beside Beatrice and Laura.[2]

Each sonnet is prefaced by a quotation from Dante and Petrarch, and Christina, like Elizabeth Barrett Browning, altered the masculine tradition to suit her own circumstances. Her reversal of the tradition – making an unnamed man the centre of the sonnets and allowing the lady to speak for herself – is justified in the headnote.

> . . . in that land and that period which gave simultaneous birth to Catholics, to Albigenses, and to Troubadors, one can imagine many a lady as sharing her lover's poetic aptitude, while the barrier between them might be one held sacred by both, yet not such as to render mutual love incompatible with mutual honour.

The romantic legends surrounding the troubadors were very popular at the time – and not just with the Pre-Raphaelites. Two of Laetitia Landon's volumes of poetry – *The Troubador* and *The Venetian Bracelet* were expositions of the legend of courtly love and Dora Greenwell also found herself attracted to it, writing to a friend that 'It had its ideal, however it might transgress it; – one of love, and faith and self-devotion; and as such, falling in strangely and sweetly, with that of everyday Christian life.'[3] This is something that Christina would have agreed with and her sonnets are firmly rooted in the Christian faith.

The main problem for Christina was one of concealment, and the reference to the troubador, her identification with some anonymous medieval female poet, gave her a mask to hide behind. Elizabeth Barrett Browning had done the same thing, choosing the title *Sonnets from the Portuguese* to hide the fact that they were personal expressions of affection, referring the reader back to the *Portuguese Letters* from Caterina to Camoens, purporting to be from a Portuguese nun to a soldier. Christina's headnote draws a similar 'cloud' over her own sonnets, directing the reader to the unnamed lover of a medieval lady and hiding the fact that their inspiration was Charles Cayley, a shy, untidy, middle-aged, and thoroughly unlikely figure, but one whom Christina loved dearly.

> Come back to me, who wait and watch for you:-
> Or come not yet, for it is over then,
> And long it is before you come again,
> So far between my pleasures are and few.
> While, when you come not, what I do I do
> Thinking 'Now when he comes,' my sweetest 'when':
> For one man is my world of all the men

This wide world holds; O love, my world is you.
Howbeit, to meet you grows almost a pang
  Because the pang of parting comes so soon;
  My hope hangs waning, waxing, like a moon
  Between the heavenly days on which we meet:
Ah me, but where are now the songs I sang
  When life was sweet because you called them sweet?

In her Italian poems she envies his mother and his sisters, because they share his life and she looks forward to the day in Paradise when they will feast together.

*   *   *

Dante Gabriel was determined not to go back to his old lodgings and in March began negotiations to lease Tudor House in Cheyne Walk, Chelsea – part of a larger dwelling that had once belonged to Queen Katherine Parr after the death of Henry VIII. The original proposal was that Gabriel's mother, Maria and Christina would come to live there with him, and this would have relieved William of the responsibility of providing for them, which he had patiently done ever since his father died. However, the house was too far out of central London for Maria to have continued her private teaching, and Gabriel, after his initial generous impulse, seems to have realised that that kind of domestic existence would be too restricting. He would be unable to entertain friends such as Fanny Cornforth and be expected to live a much more regulated life. So the scheme was dropped and Gabriel leased Tudor House with Swinburne and Meredith. William was also nominally a co-tenant and for two or three nights a week would stay there, enjoying a respite from undiluted female company.

It was very convivial. W.B. Scott, William Allingham, and John Ruskin were frequent visitors as well as Fanny – the Dear Elephant – who hosted bachelor dinner parties. Despite a housekeeper the domestic arrangements were somewhat erratic. Gabriel's nephew recalled that his dustbins were full of the priceless china he used for everyday and which the servants broke in the kitchen. Allingham made an excursion into the basement kitchen one evening in search of supper, only to find a mouse on the table eating a haddock. On another occasion a raccoon was inadvertently shut in a drawer and ate a large quantity of papers.

Gabriel kept a small zoo in the garden, which was allowed to revert to wilderness. At one time or another there were owls, rabbits, dormice, hedgehogs, two wombats, a wallaby, deer, armadilloes, chameleons, peacocks and parakeets, as well as several large dogs and a small Brahmin bull. The menagerie offended the neighbours who complained about the screeching of the peacocks, and the animals weren't properly cared for and died, were lost, or had to be given away.

Christina, in 'The House of D.G.R.' written for a magazine after her brother's death, draws an affectionate portrait of his life there. She wrote of friendly family parties. 'Gloom and eccentricity' were not the whole story at Tudor House. Gabriel 'when he chose' became 'the sunshine of his circle . . . His ready wit and fun amused us; his good nature and kindness of heart endeared him to us'.[4]

He was very good to Swinburne, introducing him to publishers and other people likely to be helpful in ensuring the success of *Atalanta in Calydon*. But Swinburne proved to be an impossible companion. He was noisy and excitable, with a habit of jumping on and off the furniture when he was talking. His excesses alarmed both William and Dante Gabriel, who feared that he would kill himself with drink. Gabriel complained that he drove him crazy 'dancing all over the studio like a wild cat' and found it difficult to work with him in the house.[5] There were also rumours of homosexuality, and sliding naked down the bannisters at a party. His outrageous behaviour made him many enemies.

In these circumstances it was strange that, after Lizzie's death, Swinburne should have become so very close to Christina. His friendship with Pauline Trevelyan had cooled as he grew tired of her moral strictures, and it was Christina who received a copy of *Atalanta in Calydon* from the poet – Pauline had to buy hers. Christina, usually so scrupulous, was undeterred by Swinburne's atheism. She pasted strips of paper over the parts of the poem that offended her and responded with genuine admiration for Swinburne's gifts. They shared a liking for Carlyle's *Frederick*, published in 1862, Swinburne writing of its 'cold purity of pluck', while Christina thought it 'majesty stripped of its externals'.[6] Swinburne dedicated *A Century of Roundels* to Christina and she later sent him one of her religious prose works, commenting humorously on the inappropriateness of her gift.

Through Gabriel Christina made another friend. Anne Gilchrist was the widow of Alexander Gilchrist, author of the *Life of Etty*, who had died in 1861 while working on a *Life of William Blake* – then relatively unknown and neglected. Alexander had been a close friend of Gabriel's and they were neighbours. However, in 1862 Anne decided to leave London with her children and live at Brookbank, near Haslemere in Surrey. There, with William and Gabriel's assistance, she finished the

Life of Blake. Later she wrote a biography of Mary Lamb. She was a great admirer of Walt Whitman's poetry – her letters to William on *Leaves of Grass* were published as a pamphlet. She corresponded with Whitman, eventually visiting him in America where her proposals of marriage were, understandably, rejected. She also knew George Eliot, who rented Brookbank from Anne in order to write part two of *Middlemarch* in a quiet location.

In June 1863, although they had never met, Anne invited Christina to come down with William and stay with her in Surrey. Christina accepted, and Anne's daughter Grace remembered a

> dark-eyed, slender lady, in the plenitude of her poetic powers ... In appearance she was Italian, with olive complexion and deep hazel eyes. She possessed, too, the beautiful Italian voice all the Rossettis were gifted with – a voice made up of strange, sweet inflexions, which rippled into silvery modulations in sustained conversation, making ordinary English words and phrases fall upon the ear with a soft, foreign musical intonation, though she pronounced the words themselves with the purest of English accents.

Christina was overcome with shyness on this first visit and, after being shown to her room on arrival to prepare for supper, she was too afraid to leave it again. Grace recorded that

> My mother, finding after the lapse of some time that she did not appear in the drawing room circle, went upstairs in search of her, and tapping at her door, found Miss Rossetti ready, but waiting in some trepidation, too shy to venture down alone.

She got on well with the children, playing ball with them under the apple trees in the garden, and finding them frogs and caterpillars. Grace was dazzled by her. 'To my child's eyes she appeared like some fairy princess who had come from the sunny south to play with me.'[7]

In the sunny quiet of Brookbank Christine wrote 'Maiden Song', a ballad about three sisters – Margaret, the fairest of the three is gifted with a voice sweeter than the nightingale. Her sisters win only a herdsman and a shepherd with their inferior notes, but Margaret sings herself a golden-bearded king.

> So Margaret sang her sisters home
> In their marriage mirth;
> Sang free birds out of the sky,
> Beasts along the earth,
> Sang up fishes of the deep –
> All breathing things that move –
> Sang from far and sang from near
> To her lovely love;
> Sang together friend and foe;
>
> Sang a golden-bearded king
> Straightway to her feet,
> Sang him silent where he knelt
> In eager anguish sweet . . .

'Maiden Song', born out of pure felicity, proved one of Christina's most popular poems. Gladstone apparently knew it by heart, and Lady Waterford – an accomplished artist and friend of Gabriel's – painted illustrations in watercolour for the poem.

After Lizzie Siddal's death, Gabriel turned his attention back to Christina. He wanted her to bring out another volume of poetry to capitalise on the success of *Goblin Market*. But Christina was not going to be pushed into early publication. 'Why rush before the public with an immature volume?' she wrote. She wanted to wait until she had 'sufficiency of quality as well as quantity.'[8]

However, Gabriel bullied her into enlarging her elegiac 'Too late for love' into a longer narrative poem, initially called The Alchemist, which became eventually 'The Prince's Progress'. It tells the story of a Prince who sets out to claim his bride but is delayed on the journey, first by a woman, and then by an ancient alchemist in a cave. He arrives only after the bride is dead. Like Cathy in *Wuthering Heights*, like Laetitia Landon and Lizzie in real life, she dies from lack of love.

Christina was an inspirational poet and always had difficulty, despite her bouts-rimés practice, in writing to order. The results were likely to be flat and pedestrian. 'The Prince's Progress' was no exception. It lacked what Christina called 'the special felicity' of 'Goblin Market' and she had trouble with the meter. When Gabriel complained about the 'metrical jolt', she insisted that she couldn't have written the poem without it, but proceeded to 'file and polish' the poem until it had been eradicated. With it, went some of the spontaneity and originality.

The subject of a second volume remained under discussion, and throughout 1863 and 1864 Christina corresponded with Gabriel about the selection of material. Christina wanted to include her poem 'Under the Rose', later retitled 'The Iniquity of the Fathers upon the Children', one of her rare 'political pieces'. It deals with a subject of great concern to Christina – the plight of the unmarried mother, and in particular the fate of the child. It is written from the child's point of view.

> I do not guess his name
> Who wrought my Mother's shame,
> And gave me life forlorn;
> But my Mother, Mother, Mother,
> I know her from all other.
> My Mother pale and mild,
> Fair as ever was seen,
> She was but scarce sixteen,
> Little more than a child,
> When I was born
> To work her scorn.
> With secret bitter throes,
> In a passion of secret woes,
> She bore me under the rose.

It ends with a triumphant declaration of selfhood.

> I think my mind is fixed
> On one point and made up:
> To accept my lot unmixed;
> Never to drug the cup
> But drink it by myself.
> I'll not be wooed for pelf;
> I'll not blot out my shame
> With any man's good name;
> But nameless as I stand,
> My hand is my own hand,
> And nameless as I came
> I go to the dark land.

Gabriel objected to the poem on the grounds that the subject matter was unsuitable for a woman, complaining in another letter that the 'modern vicious taint' of Elizabeth Barrett Browning is discernible in Christina's work, referring presumably to her treatment of similar themes – the unmarried Marion Erle in *Aurora Leigh* – and her love of polemics. Elizabeth Barrett Browning had attracted similar criticism from Edmund Gosse for her use of poetry to put forward political ideas.

'Where she strove to be passionate she was too often hysterical; a sort of scream spoils the effect of all her full tirades.' Gosse's opinion – shared by many other male critics was that women 'in order to succeed in poetry must be brief, personal and concentrated.'[9] Women's poetry should be 'all roses', and what Gabriel called the 'falsetto muscularity' of Barrett Browning had to be avoided at all costs.

Christina defended what she referred to at one point as 'that screech', in her letters to Gabriel. 'Whilst . . . unless white could be black and Heaven Hell, my experience (thank God) precludes me from hers, I yet don't see why 'the Poet mind' should be less able to construct her from its own inner consciousness than a hundred other unknown quantities.' She did however, endorse Gabriel's opinion 'of the unavoidable and indeed much to be desired unreality of women's work on many social matters', but she insisted on her right 'to include within the female range such an attempt as this.'[10]

Christina was also prepared to allow her poetry to be used for other political purposes. In 1863 she donated 'A Royal Princess' and 'Dream Love' to anthologies published for the relief of Lancashire cotton workers laid off because the American Civil War had cut off the supply of cotton to the mills. The extent of the hardship was widely reported in newspapers and Dora Greenwell, also involved in the anthology, alludes to it in her letters. *The Times* described how 'on every side, giant factories, which were the support of thousands, stand mute and motionless, giving no sign of life, save here and there, a streamlet of vapour . . . telling of "half-time" and wages reduced just short of starvation point.'[11]

Christina wrote other, more specifically 'political' pieces. In 1882 she published a satire inspired by a newspaper article which castigated one cabinet minister for resigning from the cabinet and the prime minister – Gladstone – for continuing in office over the same issue. Christina's reply was called 'Counterblast on a Penny Trumpet', published in the *St James Gazette*.

> When rages the conflict fierce and hot,
> If Mr Bright retiring does not please
> And Mr Gladstone staying gives offence,
> What can man do which is not one of these?
> Use your own commonsense.[12]

When it was suggested that Christina should write more poetry in a political vein she declined vigorously. 'It is impossible to go on singing out loud to one's one-stringed lyre. It is not in me, and therefore it will never come out of me, to turn to politics or philanthropy with Mrs Browning; such many-sidedness I leave to a greater than I, and having said my say, may well sit silent.'[13]

In the autumn of 1863 Christina saw a review of a volume of poetry by a new poet called Jean Ingelow, and on 31 December she wrote to Dora Greenwell

What think you of Jean Ingelow, the wonderful poet? I have not yet read the volume, but reviews with copious extracts have made me aware of a new eminent name having risen amongst us. I want to know who she is, what she is like, where she lives. All I have heard is an uncertain rumour that she is aged twenty one and is one of three sisters resident with their mother. A proud mother, I should think.[14]

Jean was actually forty-three, had been born in Lincolnshire but was now living with her family in Kensington. Her collection of *Poems* which included the still popular 'High Tide on the Coast of Lincolnshire', was well reviewed. Alice Meynell, more perceptively, regarded the poems as metrically unskilful and reckless, though 'quite good enough to be difficult to praise'. She commented incisively that 'Her poems . . . have often a single resonance without error, and without indecision; and they leave in the mind the charming memory less of a song than a call.'[15]

Anne Gilchrist sent Christina Jean Ingelow's new volume, and later, after she had met Jean, Christina wrote to Anne that 'she appears as unaffected as her verses, though not their equal in regular beauty; however I fancy hers is one of those variable faces in which the variety is not the least charm.'[16]

Both Christina and Jean Ingelow contributed work to the Portfolio Society, a literary group founded with others by Barbara Leigh-Smith. Christina confessed to pangs of jealousy when Jean's *Poems* went into its eighth edition when *Goblin Market* was only in its second. It was inevitable that reviewers would begin to compare Christina's work with Dora Greenwell and Jean Ingelow, and some of the comparisons were extremely reductive, revealing the kind of criticism the female poet had to endure. The *Athenaeum* in August 1897 published letters from Christina and Jean to Dora Greenwell in which their rivalry was reduced to the level of a sewing contest.

> I must premise that these ladies lived in the days when the cry 'Go spin, ye jades, go spin!' was still not infrequently heard if a woman wished to devote herself to any branch of Art, and all three were anxious to show that though they wrote poetry they were none the less proficient in the usual womanly crafts.[17]

Christina however, despite her representation by Dante Gabriel as the meek Virgin sewing, was hopeless with a needle and had long ago abandoned anything other than essential sewing. In the letters quoted by the author of the article, Dora Greenwell had made Christina the present of a workbag and 'challenged Miss Rossetti to produce a creditable example of skilled needlework'. Christina's letter thanks Dora for the gift, apologising for the lateness of the reply due to pressure of work on *The Prince's Progress*. She ignored the challenge – happy to exchange verses but not embroidery.

The *Athenaeum* quotes a letter from Jean Ingelow to Dora enclosing a workbag with garlands of flowers delicately shaded on a black background. 'The pattern is of my own invention! Is the kettle holder worked yet? I shall be so proud of it. When I next see Miss Rossetti I shall ask for proof that she can do hemming and sewing.' The publication of such light-hearted chaff, mocked the very real craftsmanship of words exercised by the three women, and at the same time pointed up the pressures under which they worked – anxious to prove that poetry did not detract from 'normal' womanly duties. Christina's failure to respond says much for her self possession and singleness of purpose. Perhaps she agreed with Elizabeth Barrett Browning in *Aurora Leigh* that

> The works of women are symbolical.
> We sew, sew, prick our fingers, dull our sight,
> Producing what?

An article in *Fraser's Magazine* must have cheered Christina. She was compared to Jean Ingelow, Adelaide Proctor and Elizabeth Barrett Browning and in Gabriel's words 'given the palm'.[19]

Christina found the early months of 1864 very trying and became ill again. She suffered terribly from the cold, like thousands of others in large unheated houses where the warmth of the fire failed to reach the other side of the room. And the winter smogs brought back a recurrence of the chest problems endemic in industrial areas. Christina hated winter – her southern blood only warming to the summer season.

Winter is cold hearted,
Spring is yea or nay,
Autumn is a weathercock
Blown every way.
Summer days for me
When every leaf is on its tree;

Her Christmas carol 'In the Bleak Midwinter', written sometime in the eighteen-sixties, is a chilling evocation of winter's iron grip on flesh and mind. The traditional coupling of winter with depression and sterility was always at the forefront of Christina's thoughts. The birth of Christ, coming in the middle of winter, signalling new life and pointing towards spring, was therefore doubly important to her. In *Seek and Find* she wrote that 'we behold as in a parable how Grace reverses the decrees of Nature; for we see Winter bestow and Summer take away' (in the form of the Ascension). Christina's symbolism was based wholly on the Bible.

Christina's love affair with Cayley had reached an important stage where both were aware of each other's feelings. There is considerable argument among biographers as to the date of Cayley's proposal of marriage, variously ascribed to 1864, 1865 and 1866, and Christina is sometimes accused of keeping him dangling for two years. Even her brother William didn't know when the subject of marriage was first discussed. The truth is probably that in such a close and slowly deepening relationship there may not have been a formal proposal; simply the growing recognition between them of a permanent attachment. The subject of marriage is never mentioned in Christina's letters until 1866 and in the two years before that she seems simply happy to love and be loved.

But in 1864 the future seemed more precarious than ever. During the winter her health deteriorated and she began to spit blood. Although this was probably due only to severe bronchitis, it was also a symptom of tuberculosis. Her doctors feared the worst and she was sent to Hastings to recuperate with her cousin Henrietta Polydore, whom she called Lalla.

Henrietta had had a rather exotic life. Her father had given up his unsuccessful attempts to establish himself as a solicitor and gone to America some years earlier, renting out his home to Coventry Patmore. Once there, however, his wife left him, taking Henrietta with her, and she was discovered a couple of years later living with the Mormons in Salt Lake City. Henry Polydore brought Henrietta back to England, and she was now a devout Catholic. Occasionally Christina had to alter travel arrangements to ensure that Henrietta would be able to attend Mass. Henrietta had also been diagnosed as tubercular, and died in 1874.

Christina did not mind her exile in Hastings. She wrote in her collection of stories, *Commonplace*, that it was

> a pretty sight in brilliant holiday weather to watch the many parties of health and pleasure seekers which throng the beach. Boys and girls picking up shells, pebbles, and star-fishes, or raising with hands and wooden spades a sand fortress, encircled by a moat full of seawater and crowned by a twig of seaweed as a flag; mothers and elder sisters reading or working beneath the shady hats, whilst after bathing their long hair dries in the sun and wind. Hard-by rock at their moorings bannered pleasure boats with blue-jerseyed oarsmen or white sails . . .

Christina was an observer rather than a participant. She loved the sea, and her favourite pastime was to wander along the beach, alone, picking through the tidal debris. In a letter to William she declared that she could 'plod indefinitely along shingle' with her eyes 'pretty well glued to the ground'.[20]

The Cayleys also had connections with Hastings – Charles Cayley eventually chose to be buried there – so it is possible that he visited her during her long convalescence. They certainly wrote to each other, on one occasion Cayley sent her a 'sea-mouse' he had found on the beach which she treasured, writing a poem which addressed it as 'Part hope . . . Part memory, part anything/You please'.

Christina's cousin Teodorico Pietrocolo Rossetti, a trained homoeopath, protested strongly at the treatment she was receiving. A change of air was the worst thing possible in the second stages of tubercular disease, but his recommendations, which included mercury and aconite, were ignored. Teodorico had begun to translate 'Goblin Market' into Italian, and this was published in 1867. Aguilar, the composer, was also setting it to music, composing a cantata. Christina's reputation was burgeoning while she faced the possibility of death. Her recovery depended on sea air and the daily intake of sherry prescribed by Dr William Jenner.

Dante Gabriel and William sent her a nest of crocodiles drawn by the French artist Griset, for Christmas. 'The Prudent Crocodile' had become part of the family network of jokes. Gabriel wrote that there was another drawing which much resembled the Prudent which he would like to buy for her. Christina wrote back:

I am so happy in my nest of crocodiles that I beg you will on no account purchase the Prudent to lord it over them; indeed amongst their own number, by a careful study of expression one may detect latent greatness, and point out the predominant tail of the future.[21]

Gabriel was, however, unable to resist buying the drawing for his sister.

1864 saw the development of a new acquaintance – the Rev. Charles Dodgson, who, as Lewis Carroll, wrote *Alice in Wonderland*. He was a frequent visitor at Cheyne Walk and at Euston Square, and took several photographs of the Rossetti family. He offered to show Christina and her mother the sights of Oxford. She wrote back, asking for copies of photographs and thanked him for his invitation. 'We tremble in the balance, though I fear the leaden element preponderates. It is characteristic of us to miss opportunities. A year or two ago I had a chance of seeing Cambridge, and of course missed it.'[22] Christina's life was completely circumscribed by her health, her dependence upon her relatives and upon convention.

CHAPTER ELEVEN

Over the winter of 1864 the alchemist episode of 'The Prince's Progress'
still shivered 'in the blank of mere possibility', though Christina hoped
to have the proofs of her next volume ready before a projected visit to
Italy in May.

In January Christina sent a draft of it to Gabriel. 'Here at last is an
Alchemist reeking from the crucible. He dovetails properly into his
niche.' She apologised for the fact that the result was not entirely what
she had envisaged.

> He's not precisely the Alchemist I prefigured, but thus he came and thus
> he must stay: you know my system of work . . . Please read him if you
> have the energy; then, when you return him to me, I must have a
> thorough look-over to the annotated Prince. Lastly, I do hope Vol. II will
> be possible. One motive for haste with me is the fear lest by indefinite
> delay I should miss the pleasure of thus giving pleasure to our Mother, to
> whom of course I shall dedicate. [It is uncertain whether she was afraid
> of her Mother's death or hers before the book was completed.] . . .
> suppose – but I won't suppose anything so dreadful; only knowing her
> intense pleasures in our performances, I am keenly desirous to give her
> the pleasure *when possible*.[1]

Gabriel was eager that Christina should include a tournament in 'The
Prince's Progress' to provide colour and action. Christina refused. It
would interfere with the structure of the poem 'a certain artistic
congruity of construction not lightly to be despised', and which she
humorously outlined.

> 1st, a prelude and outset; 2nd, an alluring milkmaid; 3rd, a trial of barren
> boredom; 4th, the social element again; 5th, barren boredom in a more

uncompromising form; 6th, a wind-up and conclusion. See how the
subtle elements balance each other, and fuse into a noble conglom!

Besides, she wrote, she didn't have the requisite knowledge. 'Not a
phrase to be relied on, not a correct knowledge on the subject, not the
faintest impulse of inspiration incites me to the tilt, and looming before
me in horrible bugbeardom stand TWO tournaments in Tennyson's
Idylls.' She was also conscious that she must not let her more forceful
brother dominate her literary output.

> You see, were you next to propose my writing a classic epic in
> quantitative hexameters or in the hendecasyllables which might almost
> trip up Tennyson, What could I do? Only what I feel inclined to do in the
> present instance - plead goodwill but inability.[2]

Gabriel bombarded her with suggestions for revisions of her poetry,
some of which caused Christina what she described as 'stamping,
foaming, hair-uprooting' paroxysms. But she endorsed many of them,
deleting lines, altering rhymes and adding stanzas at his direction, not
always with felicity. Christina was aware of this, and in another letter,
struck a more serious note.

> I do seriously question whether I possess the working-power with which
> you credit me: and whether all the painstaking at my command would
> result in work better than - in fact half so good as - what I have actually
> done on the other system.[3]

She felt a sense of inferiority when she compared her work to Gabriel's
- his poetry so much more flashy and spectacular when compared to her
simplicity and precision.

> It is vain comparing my powers(!) with yours . . . However, if the latent
> epic should 'by huge upthrust' come to the surface one day, or if by
> laborious delving I can unearth it, or if by unflagging prodment you can
> cultivate the sensitive plant in question, all the better for me: only please
> remember that 'things which are impossible rarely happen' - and don't
> be too severe on me if the 'impossible' does not come to pass. Sometimes
> I could almost fear that my tendency is rather towards softening of the
> brain (say) than further development of mind.[4]

In contrast to her own sense of unfitness, an article in *The Times* in
January described Christina and Jean Ingelow as the 'two foremost

living poets'. Jean Ingelow was criticised for being 'vague and long-winded', but Christina's work was lauded as 'simpler, firmer, deeper'.

There was talk of including some of Lizzie's poems in the volume and Gabriel sent them to Christina. She returned them saying that she detected a note of 'cool, bitter sarcasm' in their 'painful' beauty. Although she told Gabriel that it would give her the 'sincerest pleasure' to have Lizzie's work grace her own, she tactfully takes up a point in his letter.

> I think with you that, between your volume and mine, their due post of honour is in yours. But do you not think that (at any rate except in your volume), beautiful as they are, they are almost too hopelessly sad for publication *en masse*? Perhaps this is only my overstrained fancy, but their tone is to me even painfully despondent; talk of my bogeyism, is it not by comparison jovial?[5]

The poems eventually appeared with Gabriel's; others were printed in William's memoir of his brother's life.

In February 1865 Christina added a second part to her bitter poem 'Memory' written at the height of her despair after Collinson. Part I records the terrible choice 'I made and broke my heart,/Breaking mine idol.' Part 2 describes a state of mind in which the former lover is enshrined in the memory, - a memory which can now be viewed without pain.

> I have a room whereinto no one enters
>   Save I myself alone:
>   There sits a blessed memory on a throne,
> There my life centres;
>
> While winter comes and goes - oh tedious comer! -
>   And while its nip-wind blows;
>   While bloom the bloodless lily and warm rose
> Of lavish summer.
>
> If any should force entrance he might see there
>   One buried yet not dead,
>   Before whose face I no more bow my head
> Or bend my knee there;

In April it was William's turn for publication with a translation of Dante's *Inferno*. The reviews were kind, but unenthusiastic, and he was criticised for being too literal. The translation reflected the streak of pedantry that always held William's work back. He wanted to dedicate

the book to Henrietta Rintoul and once more Christina was his
intermediary. Henrietta was still far from indifferent to William, and the
turmoil of her feelings sometimes made her want to 'drop the
acquaintance of the entire family'. She did in the end consent to the
dedication.[6]

On 22 May Christina and her mother left for Italy with William. She
wrote to Anne Gilchrist that William had invited her to accompany him
primarily for the sake of her health, but though she longed to see Italy
she worried that with herself and her mother in tow he wouldn't be able
to fulfil his ambition to visit Naples. However, William would not let her
refuse the opportunity. They travelled in easy stages, first to Paris where
Mrs Rossetti and Christina bought silk and visited the French
Exhibition, the Louvre and Notre-Dame. A family friend Mrs Adolf
Heimann was also staying in Paris with her children and there were
invitations to tea.

From Paris they travelled to Lucerne in Switzerland via Langres and
Basle, staying in a comfortable hotel overlooking Lake Lucerne.
Although William kept a meticulous daily diary, Christina recorded her
impression only in fragments of poetry and prose – some written long
after she had come back to England. In one of the sonnets in *Later Life*
she remembers how

> The mountains in their overwhelming might
> Moved me to sadness when I saw them first,
> And afterwards they moved me to delight;
> Struck harmonies from silent chords which burst
> Out into song, a song by memory nursed;[7]

They travelled to Andermatt in a hired carriage, staying overnight to
view the Devil's Bridge, and on 1 June crossed the Alps via the St
Gotthard Pass into Italy. Christina's excitement at the thought of seeing
what she considered to be her native land was heightened by an
experience which she later related in *Time Flies* with all the significance
of a divine revelation. The pass suddenly opened on a field of forget-me-
nots.

> All Switzerland behind us on the ascent,
> All Italy before us, we plunged down
> St. Gotthard, garden of forget-me-nots:
> Yet why should such a flower choose such a spot!
> Could we forget that way which once we went
> Though not one flower had bloomed to weave its crown?

All her life she remembered 'that lovely, lavish efflorescence which made earth as cerulean as the sky.'[8]

Christina felt that she had come home. William Rossetti recorded 'the intense relief and pleasure with which she saw lovable Italian faces, and heard musical Italian speech . . .'[9] Fortunately the Rossettis' stay in Italy was not long enough for those first emotionally charged romantic impressions to be tarnished by reality. Everything cooperated to make Christina's visit memorable and her nature expanded in the warmth of the Italian sun. When she heard a nightingale sing during an evening row on Lake Como, her joy seemed complete.

> A host of things I take on trust: I take
> The nightingales on trust, for few and far
> Between those actual summer moments are
> When I have heard what melody they make.
> So chanced it once at Como on the Lake;
> But all things then waxed musical; each star
> Sang on its course, each breeze sang on its car,
> All harmonies sang to senses wide awake.
> All things in tune, myself not out of tune,
> Those nightingales were nightingales indeed:
> Yet truly an owl had satisfied my need,
> And wrought a rapture underneath that moon,
> Or simple sparrow chirping from a reed;
> For June that night glowed like a doubled June.[10]

The following day they went on to Milan where they looked at pictures and walked so far that Christina was forced to spend a day resting at the hotel before travelling on to Pavia. Here for the first time they were disappointed. They were taken aback by the shabbiness of the hotel and lack of cleanliness in the city generally. William described it as being very depressed. They quickly moved on to Brescia where by a strange coincidence their guide was an ex-soldier who claimed to have known Gabriele Rossetti.

Time and limited financial resources pressed them to make Verona their most southerly point, and they turned reluctantly north again via Bergamo, Lecco and Chiavenna. Christina's regret drove her to write bathetic verses on their departure, which begin 'Wherefore art thou strange and not my mother?' It was published by William after her death.

Farewell, land of love, Italy,
Sister-land of Paradise:
With mine own feet I have trodden thee,
Have seen with mine own eyes:
I remember, thou forgettest me,
I remember thee.

Blessed be the land that warms my heart,
And the kindly clime that cheers,
And the cordial faces clear from art,
And the tongue sweet in mine ears:
Take my heart, its truest tenderest part,
Dear land, take my tears.

Their return journey took a slightly different route, past the Rhine falls at Schaffhausen, where Christina just missed seeing a foambow.

In all my life, I do not recollect to have seen one, except perhaps in artificial fountains, but such omission seems a matter of course, and therefore a simple matter of indifference. That single natural foambow which I might have beheld and espied not, is the one to which may attach a tinge of regret, because in a certain sense, it depended upon myself to look at it, yet I did not look.

I might have done so, and I did not; such is the sting today in petty matters . . .

It was typical of Christina to take a small incident like this and twist it into a weighty moral. She adds 'And what else will be the sting in matters all important on the last day?'[11]

Grey, cloudy weather greeted their return to England in July, increasing Christina's sense of loss. She was well aware that she might never see Italy again and was ill for two or three days after their return with exhaustion and depression. William observed sadly in his diary that the trip had not produced the hoped for improvement in her health and spirits. Sometime in July she wrote 'Italia, Io Ti Saluto' which she judged good enough to include in her collected *Poems*. Its keynote is renunciation.

To come back from the sweet South, to the North,
    Where I was born, bred, look to die;
Come back to do my day's work in its day,
    Play out my play –
    Amen, amen, say I.

> To see no more the country half my own,
>   Nor hear the half familiar speech,
> Amen, I say; I turn to that bleak North
>   Whence I came forth –
>   The South lies out of reach.
>
> But when our swallows fly back to the South,
>   To the sweet South, to the sweet South,
> The tears may come again into my eyes
>   On the old wise,
>   And the sweet name to my mouth.

William regretted the fact that Christina could not have spent the rest of her life in Italy where 'the Italian amenity, naturalness and freedom from self-centred stiffness, struck a chord in her sympathies, to which a good deal of what she was used to in England, offered no response.'[12] But even if the idea was discussed, it came to nothing. Christina had no independent income to live on, and circumstances meant that her mother, who was completely English in her outlook and sympathies, was unable to contemplate leaving other members of her family in England.

Christina wrote to Anne Gilchrist that the trip had been

a pleasure in one's life never to be forgotten. My mother throve abroad, and not one drawback worth dwelling upon occurred to mar our contentment. Such unimaginable beauties and grandeur of nature as we beheld no pen could put on paper; so I obviously need not exert myself to tell you what Lucerne was like, or what the lovely majesty of St. Gothard, or what the Lake of Como, with its nightingale accompaniment, or what as much of Italy as we saw to our half-Italian hearts. Its people are a noble people and its very cattle are of high-born aspect. I am glad of my Italian blood.[13]

Her prolonged absence from Charles Cayley, first at Hastings and then abroad, only seems to have heightened their feelings for each other, and at this point matrimony seems to have been seriously discussed. The poetry Christina wrote in the second half of 1865 is low-keyed, with the melancholy notes of previous years, and includes 'An Immurata Sister'.

> Men work and think, but women feel;
>   And so (for I'm a woman, I)
>   And so I should be glad to die,
> And cease from impotence of zeal,

And cease from hope, and cease from dread,
    And cease from yearnings without gain,
    And cease from all this world of pain,
And be at peace among the dead.

          *   *   *

Why should I seek and never find
    That something which I have not had?
    Fair and unutterably sad
The world hath sought time out of mind;
The world hath sought and I have sought, -
    Ah empty world and empty I!
For we have spent our strength for nought,
    And soon it will be time to die.

Sparks fly upward toward their fount of fire,
    Kindling, flashing, hovering:-
Kindle, flash, my soul; mount higher and higher,
    Thou whole burnt-offering!

She was involved in last preparations for the publication of *The Prince's Progress*, now held up by Gabriel's failure to complete the illustrations. When he finished them Christina had to ask tactfully that they be altered to comply with the text: 'to wit, the Prince's "curly black beard" and the Bride's "veiled face"; all else seems of minor moment.'[14]

By Christmas Christina had to write to Macmillan. 'I hardly know how to ask you to keep back P.P. after your 'few days' advertisement; yet if you agree with me in thinking Gabriel's designs too desirable to forego, I will try to follow your example of patience under disappointment.'[15] Gabriel's health was poor. He had minor surgery for hydrocele (the accumulation of fluid around the testes), was plagued with boils, and had begun to take opiates in an effort to suppress insomnia. His mental state was also depressed, and he went to séances in an attempt to make contact with Lizzie.

In the summer Christina had conflicting invitations. Having accepted one from her new friend Alice Boyd to spend six weeks at Penkill Castle with the Scotts, Anne Gilchrist invited her to Brookbank again, and an invitation arrived to stay on the Isle of Wight and meet Tennyson. Christina wrote immediately to Anne explaining the situation.

If the end of my Penkill sojourn deprives me of seeing you its beginning mulcts me of a visit to the Isle of Wight, in which I was promised to meet

Tennyson – poor me! This invitation was only given me yesterday, too late to be closed with; however I am not certain that in any case I should have screwed myself up to accept it, as I am shy among strangers and think things formidable.[16]

Penkill Castle was the Scottish home of W.B. Scott's mistress Alice Boyd, a woman in her late thirties who had walked into Scott's studio a few years earlier, after the death of her mother, in search of a new life. She took painting lessons from Scott and they were soon in love. Alice got on well with Scott's wife Laetitia and by 1865 they had got into the habit of spending the summers in Penkill and the winters at Scott's house in London. Christina maintained her friendship with all three of them, though she must have been aware of the relationships. It was perhaps this knowledge that motivated her withdrawal of 'A Triad' from her published collections. George Chapman had begun to paint the poem and William thought that 'something may have been said by him, or in his set, which impressed Christina with this notion of contingent misconstruction.'[17] William thought her wrong to suppress the poem but, in view of her situation as friend to both Alice and the Scotts, it was probably wiser. Gabriel, too, was involved in a triad with mutual friends Janey and William Morris, and the Madox Brown household expanded to include the eccentric German poet Mathilde Blinde. Christina was always careful not to publish anything that would hurt or offend those around her.

At Penkill she was given lavish hospitality by Alice, who had inherited a very comfortable legacy from her parents. Christina complained jokingly to Anne Gilchrist after her visit that as a result of her hostesses ministrations she was 'positively *fat*'. Christina's letters to Alice show the gradual deepening of their friendship. In 1867 the style is formal and a little stilted, but over the next two years they become warm and affectionate. After one visit – possibly this one – Christina wrote a note of thanks for hospitality.

... substantial shadows and authentic fragments of your kindness accompanied us in a tin box and received cheerful recognition ... being mainly consumed by myself as you probably foresaw ... Yet only think of my humiliation at Killochan: an inexorable railway official defined Mrs Scott as nearly one and a half stone lighter than poor me! Let us hope, as in your case, that the over plus is brain ...

What are you doing, I wonder, as I write (between 9 and 10 o'clock) knitting perhaps, or reading aloud, not snoozing let us hope after Mr Scott's strictures.[18]

Another letter addresses Alice as 'You who are lady of castle and lands and deal justice not only to man and maid but likewise to fish and fowl'. And it was to Alice that Christina confided how much of a burden she found the 'painstaking responsibility and toil' of keeping house.[19]

The Scotts took her for carriage drives and picnics, and she was fascinated by the castle – a converted fifteenth century peel tower with many later additions in the medieval style. Alice gave her a room at the top of the tower with a view of the sea. Alice told Arthur Hughes that it had a 'little four-cornered window . . . which commanded a view over an old fashioned garden . . .' where Christina stood leaning on the sill for hours at a time 'meditating and composing'.[20] Or so Alice Boyd thought. It was more than likely that Cayley was the object of her thoughts. At Penkill she wrote another haunting, allusive lyric

> Oh what comes over the sea,
>   Shoals and quicksands past;
> And what comes home to me,
>   Sailing slow, sailing fast?
>
> A wind comes over the sea
>   With a moan in its blast;
> But nothing comes home to me,
>   Sailing slow, sailing fast.
>
> Let me be, let me be,
>   For my lot is cast:
> Land or sea all's one to me,
>   And sail it slow or fast.[21]

Scott used Christina as his model for some of the murals he painted on the staircase at Penkill, which have since disintegrated. He complained that the women, when they were together, talked of nothing but their health and religious beliefs. Scott's own health was anything but good at the time, and he had taken to wearing a wig to conceal hair loss. The death of Pauline Trevelyan from ovarian cancer also helped to subdue the mood of the holiday.

The Prince's Progress finally emerged from the press in June and was sent to Christina at Penkill, arriving as she was having breakfast. Her delight was marred by a series of misprints in the text.

Swinburne also published a volume of *Poems and Ballads* that summer, though there is no record of his having sent Christina a copy – perhaps he realised that this time he had overstepped the mark of public tolerance. His poems, which are frankly erotic, were withdrawn by his publishers after accusations of obscenity.

By the time Christina came back to London she seems to have come to a decision about Cayley. Although she loved him deeply, she found that she couldn't contemplate marriage with an agnostic. Charles Cayley had no religious faith of any kind – while Christina's was passionate and organic. The idea of physical and spiritual union – the mystical one flesh – with someone who differed on such a fundamental question was anathema to Christina, as it is to many committed Christians today.

Her views on the relationship of the husband and wife were extremely conservative. She wrote in *Seek and Find* that

> in many points the feminine lot copies very closely the voluntarily assumed position of our Lord and Pattern. Woman must obey: . . . She by natural constitution is adapted not to assert herself, but to be subordinate . . . Her office is to be man's helpmeet . . . The man is the head of the woman, the woman the glory of the man.[22]

The fact that Christina's decision was so difficult, and took so long to make, indicates the depths of her affection for Cayley. Her Italian poems include a line which translates 'she who says no, meaning yes'. She describes the pain of such a decision in No. 6 of her 'Monna Innominata' sonnets.

> Trust me, I have not earned your dear rebuke, –
>   I love, as you would have me, God the most;
>   Would lose not Him, but you, must one be lost,
> Nor with Lot's wife cast back a faithless look,
> Unready to forego what I forsook;
>   This say I, having counted up the cost,
>   This, though I be the feeblest of God's host,
> The sorriest sheep Christ shepherds with His crook.
> Yet while I love my God the most, I deem
>   That I can never love you overmuch;
>   I love Him more, so let me love you too;
>   Yea as I apprehend it, love is such
> I cannot love you if I love not Him,
>   I cannot love Him if I love not you.

When Christina's mind was made up she was implacable. William wrote to her offering – if money was the only bar – to support both her and Cayley under his own roof until their means improved. Christina's reply is scribbled anxiously in pencil.

I am writing as I walk along the road with a party. I can't tell you what I feel at your most more than brotherly letter. Of course I am not *merely* the happier for what has occurred, but I gain much in knowing how much I am loved beyond my deserts. As to money, I might be selfish enough to wish that were the only bar, but you see from my point of view it is not. Now I am at least unselfish enough altogether to deprecate seeing C.B.C. continually (with nothing but mere feeling to offer) to his hamper and discomfort: but, if he likes to see me, God knows I like to see him, and any kindness you will show him will only be additional kindness loaded on me.

I prefer writing before we meet, though you're not very formidable.[23]

On 6 September, a few days before this letter was written, a poem by Charles Cayley appeared in *The Nation*. It was called '*Noli me Tangere*' (Touch me Not).

> Luscious and sorrowful bird o'the roses,
> To the vexed March winds prematurely singing.
> Would that a warm hand I could have held thee;
> Kept from a withering chill thy timid heart.
>
> Now have I terrified, now have I pained thee
> Now with stiffening blood have I tangled
> All thy bosom's tremulous plumage,
> For a thorn, for a thorn was against it.[24]

Christina found that reference sufficiently personal to write a reply to it called 'Luscious and Sorrowful', which begins 'Beautiful, tender, wasting away for sorrow'. She continued to see Charles Cayley as a friend and after a short, awkward gap they corresponded again. Some of Cayley's gentle, precisely mannered but humorous letters have survived, but Christina ordered that her letters to him be destroyed after his death. She seemed determined to leave no record of her own intensely private struggle, only – like the 'unnamed lady' – her poetry.

> Many in aftertimes will say of you
>   'He loved her' – while of me what will they say?
>   Not that I loved you more than just in play,
> For fashion's sake as idle women do.
> Even let them prate; who know not what we knew
>   Of love and parting in exceeding pain,
>   Of parting hopeless here to meet again,
> Hopeless on earth, and heaven is out of view.

> But by my heart of love laid bare to you,
>   My love that you can make not void nor vain,
> Love that foregoes you but to claim anew
> Beyond this passage of the gate of death,
>   I charge you at the Judgement make it plain
> My love of you was life and not a breath.[25]

However, Christina was not quite ruthless enough to destroy everything relating to her love affair. In 1867 Cayley sent her a poem which begins 'Methought we met again,'

> And from between our hearts a sword
> Was lifted, when a light supreme had stream'd in around us
> And long we talked of mysteries
> And no laws o' the world or flesh presumed any longer
> To sunder or to mingle us.[26]

Christina not only kept it, but recorded the date on which she received it. Similarly translations of Shakespeare's sonnets 29, 30 and 31 – highly applicable to their situation – which he sent to her, were marked by her '19th May 1870 – but written earlier – I know not under what circumstances.' This was a deliberate flagging of the text for posterity.

William thought that she regretted her decision, and this is probably true. The last sonnet of the 'Monna Innominata' sequence is one of her bleakest productions.

> Youth gone, and beauty gone if ever there
>   Dwelt beauty in so poor a face as this;
>   Youth gone and beauty, what remains of bliss?
> I will not bind fresh roses in my hair,
> To shame a cheek at best but little fair, –
>   Leave youth his roses, who can bear a thorn, –
> I will not seek for blossoms anywhere,
>   Except such common flowers as blow with corn.
> Youth gone and beauty gone, what doth remain?
>   The longing of a heart pent up forlorn,
>   A silent heart whose silence loves and longs;
>   The silence of a heart which sang its songs
>   While youth and beauty made a summer morn,
> Silence of love that cannot sing again.

CHAPTER TWELVE

After she had rejected marriage, Christina's life became centred around her mother, who was approaching seventy and needed care. By 1870 Mrs Rossetti's handwriting had become very shaky and she was plagued by minor ailments – colds, coughs, sore feet and nose bleeds. Although Maria and the Aunts were attentive, it was Christina who looked after her, wrote letters for her and dealt with business matters as her proxy. The mother/daughter role was in the process of being reversed. William Allingham, whom Mrs Rossetti regarded as Gabriel's closest friend and mentor, described her in 1867 as 'looking strong still, with her handsome full-coloured face and rich-toned voice of sincere and touching intonations. She says nothing clever, but it's always a pleasure to be near her'.[1]

Frances Rossetti was the matriarch of the family, Gabriel's 'dear Antique' or 'Teaksicunculum'. Her influence on her children had always been greater than that of her husband, and one should not underestimate its effects on Christina. As the baby of the family, and often ill, Christina had been very dependent on her mother. She dedicated all her poetry to her, and destroyed without hesitation anything that offended Frances Rossetti's strict evangelical principles. Naturally submissive, strictly brought up by Anna Pierce, Mrs Rossetti had been content with her position as wife and mother and had accepted self-abnegation as her duty. Christina strove to be like her, and, driven by devotion, suppressed her own – much more passionate – feelings and personality. Just as William's loyalty and sense of duty to his mother and sisters acted against his own interests (he would have made a fine physician) so Christina's love for her mother had led her into a life of self-sacrifice and repression.

There is, however, no record of the kind of oppression endured by

Dora Greenwell, whose mother exacted more than mere affection and dutiful attendance. Mrs Greenwell became unable to allow the vivid and sociable Dora to leave her side, and if she planned to go out would bribe her to stay in.

> "Dora, I'll give you a shilling if you'll not go to that place this evening but stop at home with me." Dora would refuse – making it a kind of game. "Oh, dear, no mother, I couldn't think of stopping away for a shilling. I'm asked to meet the Dean, and all sorts of fashionable people; . . . I refuse to come to terms under anything less than half a crown." And a polite refusal would be sent . . .[2]

It was expected that a child, particularly a daughter, would make these kind of sacrifices for a parent, whether motivated by love or duty, whether reasonable or not. On one occasion Dora wrote humorously of having to 'beg for the Royal Worcester cups' to entertain a guest. Christina, like Dora, would have felt bound by duty, if she had not been bound by love.

No one can estimate the extent of Frances Rossetti's influence over Christina's decision to end her relationship with Charles Cayley. The views of Frances and Maria have never been recorded, and William kept a discreet silence on the subject. But it is possible that her mother's experience of marriage was one of the weights in the scale against Christina's own. When, years later, William remarked what a peaceful, happy life their mother had had, Christina was unable to agree. On the contrary, she told him, her mother's life had been often unhappy and fraught with disappointment.

Early in 1867 Margaret Polidori died and was interred in the same grave as Lizzie Siddal and Gabriele Rossetti. In June the family moved to a new house at 56 Euston Square (subsequently renamed Endsleigh Gardens to commemorate a notorious murder). They were joined for a while by Aunt Eliza until she set up a separate establishment at 12 Bloomsbury Square with her sister Charlotte. There was a tentative proposal that Aunt Charlotte buy the lease of 56 Euston Square which was due for renewal and after protracted negotiations she succeeded in purchasing it for £1,000 in 1871. The house was settled first on Eliza then on Frances and finally William.

Christina, on the recommendation of Jean Ingelow, acquired herself an American publisher – Roberts Brothers of Boston. At Jean's instigation she sent a copy of the newly published *Prince's Progress* together with *Goblin Market* round to their representative, who was staying in London and a combined American edition appeared shortly afterwards.

Christina was once more ill during the winter months, but this time the doctor pronounced it nothing worse than congestion of the lungs. She was now, after the publication of her second volume of poems on both sides of the Atlantic, an established figure, and the invitations she received reflect the change of status. Unfortunately she was neither well enough, nor confident enough, to accept many of them. Her brother's friend George F. Watts lived at Little Holland House and there Christina met the Prinseps – Thoby, his son Val, and Julia Cameron, who called at Euston Square to photograph Christina and her mother. Christina also met the beautiful Mrs Jackson, Virginia Woolf's grandmother.

Robert Browning had returned to live in London after Elizabeth's death, and was invited to dinner at the Rossettis. There was also a certain amount of contact with Barbara Leigh Smith, who was now married to a French army physician she had met in North Africa called Bodichon who was extremely eccentric and kept a jackal instead of a dog. Barbara was campaigning for money to establish what eventually became Girton College. Christina seems to have found Barbara rather overpowering and preferred the company of Enrica Filopanti, an Italian married to the revolutionary Barile who refused to support his wife and left her to earn her own living as a teacher.

Edmund Gosse first met Christina at one of Ford Madox Brown's regular gatherings. Though she generally shrank from large social functions, Madox Brown's house was very much a home from home, and most of the members of her family and their close friends were there. Swinburne – now dubbed the 'libidinous laureate' for his *Poems and Ballads* – Jane Morris, dressed in a trailing gown of ivory velvet; Dante Gabriel, who had put on a great deal of weight, squatting on floor cushions at her feet, and William – now romantically interested in Madox Brown's eldest daughter Lucy. In the middle of this informal, lively group Gosse saw Christina 'sitting alone . . . like a pillar of cloud, a Sibyl whom no one had the audacity to approach.'[3] Her appearance was severe. Christina had never taken much thought to the manner of her dress and became more indifferent as she grew older. A cartoon by Max Beerbohm shows Gabriel pressing a variety of 'stunning' fabrics on her and saying 'What *is* the use, Christina of having a heart like a singing bird and a water-shoot and all the rest of it, if you insist on getting yourself up like a pew-opener?'[4] Gosse recorded that

Her dark hair was streaked across her olive forehead, and turned up in a chignon; the high stiff dress ended in a hard collar and plain brooch, the extraordinarily ordinary skirt sank over a belated crinoline, and these were inflictions hard to bear from the High-Priestess of Pre-Raphaelitism.[5]

Women were expected to be ornamental. Christina's disregard for dress had much in common with Emily Brontë and Emily Dickinson. Emily Dickinson adopted dresses of plain white cotton; Emily Brontë's dress was described by Mrs Gaskell as 'ugly and preposterous'. Another friend described her as an 'ungainly, ill-dressed figure'. Fashion controls women – the corsets and crinolines of the eighteen-seventies and eighties restrained them physically as well as socially. There is an element of conformity, an implication of seeking approval in 'dressing up'. By opting out of fashion these three women declared their 'difference'.

For Christina there was an additional dimension. It was part of her regime of self-denial. In *Letter and Spirit* she wrote that 'It cannot be much of a hardship to dress modestly and at small cost rather than richly and fashionable, if with vivid conviction we are awaiting the "white robes" of the redeemed.'[6]

Gosse found Christina's personality equally daunting.

When it is added that her manner, from shyness, was of a portentous solemnity, that she had no small talk whatever, and that the common topics of the day appeared to be entirely unknown to her, it will be understood that she was considered highly formidable by the young and flighty.[7]

However, when Gosse talked to her about religion and poetry he was rewarded with a glimpse of the other side of her personality, and she became warm and animated. Few guessed at her sense of humour. She wrote laughingly to Gabriel that 'a human being' had written to ask permission to put one of her songs to music and had for once chosen not 'When I am dead, my dearest', but 'Grown and Flown' instead.

Christina poured this lighter side of her personality into her children's poems and had begun to think of getting together a collection. She was also experimenting with prose and polishing up short stories written over the previous fifteen years.

Maria was extremely busy, outside her teaching schedule, researching and writing *The Shadow of Dante*, intended to be an introduction to the works of the poet. William, too, was working on an edition of Walt Whitman's poetry, from which he omitted many of the poems that had appeared in *Leaves of Grass* because of his prudish aversion to a certain quality 'of downrightness and crudity or even a coarseness of expression which is rightly resented on the grounds not only of decorum and delicacy, but also of literary art.'[8] In spite of the problems of censorship, William wrote ecstatically on Whitman's gifts, in a letter to Anne Gilchrist. 'That glorious man Whitman will one day be known as one of the greatest sons of Earth, a few steps below Shakespeare on the throne of immortality. What a tearing away of the obscuring veil of use and wont from the visage of man and life.'[9]

Not only Whitman's poetry, but Shelley's was being quoted and read in the Rossetti household. William was working on an edition of Shelley's poems with accompanying memoir. In this, too, he was criticised for his alteration of the text. Although he only amended what he called 'absolute blunders' he regretted his actions later. He also regretted suppressing some details from the memoir at the request of Claire Clairmont, whom he visited in Italy. William's actions as the editor of others call into question his reliability as an editor of Christina's work after her death. His integrity would not allow him to falsify, but he often omitted and occasionally amended, without feeling it necessary to acknowledge his alterations.

In 'A Nightmare', different words were substituted by William to tone down what is a rather erotic poem. The manuscript reads:

> I have a *love* in ghostland –
> Early found, ah me how early lost! –
> Blood-red seaweeds drip along that coastland
> By the strong sea wrenched and tost.
>
>   *   *   *
>
> If I wake he *rides* me like a nightmare:
> I feel my hair stand up, my body creep:
> Without a light I see a blasting sight there,
> See a secret I must keep.[10]

William, publishing the poem after her death as 'a fragment', substituted 'friend' for love, and 'hunts' for rides, reducing the power of the poem and subtly altering its meaning. There is also a whole page missing from the manuscript between the first verse and the last. William mentions this in his footnote to the poem, but not his alteration of her words.

All three Rossettis read and criticised each other's manuscripts. It may well have been their household that prompted W.B. Scott's sarcastic remarks in his autobiography

> I know whole households competing with each other . . . A pretty sight,
> but not so safe as bezique to short tempers, nor so economical if the desire
> to appeal to the public supervenes as it generally does, keeping up the
> large annual amount of money thrown to the printer's devil.[11]

Dante Gabriel was also feeling the pace of competition. He had begun
to write poetry again and, as Madox Brown had predicted, to regret his
decision to make painting his sole vocation. At times he declared to
friends that he should after all have been a poet. The manuscripts he had
buried in Lizzie's grave began to haunt him, and eventually became an
obsession. He suffered from insomnia and disturbance of vision, and
feared that he might be going blind like his father. Rest cures at the
houses of various friends, including Barbara Bodichon, failed to effect
much of an improvement. He was drinking heavily – mainly whisky –
and taking laudanum to quell the pain of various physical ailments. In
1870 he began to take chloral on the advice of his friend William
Stillman, believing it to be less harmful.

Gabriel began to suffer from delusions, perhaps stimulated by the
séances he attended in an attempt to contact Lizzie, and the mixture of
alcohol and opiates. When he stayed with the Scotts in 1869 at Penkill
he was in a highly emotional state and firmly believed that a half tame
chaffinch that flew to his feet and allowed him to pick it up was the spirit
of his dead wife. When Alice Boyd told a story of the house bell having
been rung mysteriously while they were out, it confirmed Gabriel's
feeling tht he had had a visit from Lizzie. He talked of suicide daily at
Penkill, and the Scotts were convinced that he had been going to throw
himself from the top of the waterfall at Lady's Green, only stepping back
at the last moment to clutch W.B. Scott's hand convulsively.

Not only was Gabriel coping with unexorcised guilt about Lizzie's
suicide, but he was also in love with a married woman – Jane Morris.
William, spending three nights a week at Tudor House, was well aware
of Gabriel's problems and the seriousness of his condition, but he tried
to keep it from his mother and sisters for as long as possible.

In 1869 Gabriel made the decision to have Lizzie's body exhumed
and the volume of poetry removed. The incident at Penkill had
convinced him that Lizzie approved. Official permission had to be given
and there were complex legal formalities to be gone through. It was
further complicated by the fact that Margaret Polidori had been buried
after Lizzie and so Frances Rossetti's permission might have been

required (she was the legal owner of the grave). However, this was circumscribed and complete secrecy was maintained; not even William was told until afterwards. Gabriel was not present at the exhumation, which took place at night, and friends reported to him that Lizzie's glorious hair was still as beautiful as ever – unchanged since her death. The poems were disinfected and returned to him, so that he could prepare them for publication.

Gabriel was anxious that Christina should join his own publisher F.S. Ellis. Both he and William had been dissatisfied for some time at the amount of money she was paid by Macmillan. William did his best to persuade Macmillan to increase his advances to her, though he still had quite a number of copies of both *Goblin Market* and the *Prince's Progress* on his hands. At the same time Gabriel was negotiating with Ellis on her behalf. Christina, caught in the middle, maintained a friendly correspondence with both publishers. Ellis was invited to tea to meet Alice Boyd. 'I do not know whether it is monstrous to imagine you wasting 4 o'clock next Tuesday afternoon on a kettledrum; but I should like our acquaintance to get beyond knowing each other's handwriting by sight ... If I blunder in asking you, pray pardon.'[12] Christina was trying to persuade Ellis to let Alice illustrate *Sing-Song*, her collection of children's poems. Ellis agreed, but subsequently regretted the decision when Alice's drawings did not reach the required professional standard. This put Christina in a difficult position.

Ellis also accepted *Commonplace*, a collection of short stories written by Christina between 1852 and 1870. The pedestrian title did little to promote the book, but Christina couldn't think of anything more suitable. Maria suggested 'Births, Deaths and Marriages', but that was too similar to another volume in print, and scarcely more interesting. Ellis asked for another story to add bulk to the six offered, and Christina eventually managed to find him two more – one newly-written and one rescued from the wastepaper basket. The title story was specially written to provide bulk for the volume, and went backwards and forwards between them as Christina rewrote it in accordance with Ellis's revisions.

The story has a good opening in a modern, journalistic style.

> Brompton on sea – any name not in Bradshaw will do – Brompton on sea in April.
> The air keen and sunny; the sea blue and rippling, not rolling; everything green, in sight and out of sight, coming on merrily.

There are three women in the story, Catherine, Lucy and Jane, and there are elements of Christina in all three. Lucy, like Christina, feels 'a sensible relief to feel and look at thirty very much as she felt and looked at twenty-nine. Her mirror bore witness to no glaring accession of age having come upon her in a single night.' Catherine's sacrifice of herself, in order to look after her younger sisters, also owes something to Christina, and Jane is a projection of the worldliness Christina so feared and guarded against in herself. A man 'might fall in love with Jane, but no one could make a friend of her'.

Some of Christina's biographers have used this story as part of the evidence for the Christina/W.B. Scott theory, i.e. that it is a story about a girl – Lucy – in love with a married man. But the facts of the story are that Lucy has fallen in love with a man after a brief acquaintance and he has subsequently married someone else, while she cherished hopes of his engagement to her. It is much more applicable to Collinson than to Scott.

The structure of the story is disjointed – broken into several short parts or 'chapters', not continuous in time and awkwardly connected. Chapter three begins 'The last chapter was parenthetical, this takes up the broken thread of the story.' Christina's technique had scarcely advanced since *Maude*, but there is nothing that more rigorous editing could not have remedied. Odd touches lift the story from banality. A description of London 'dingy and glaring' . . .

> London-Bridge station with its whirl of traffic seems no bad emblem of London itself, vast, confused, busy, orderly, more or less dirty . . . soiled by thousands of feet passing to and fro: on a drizzling day each foot deposits mud in its passage, takes and gives mud, leaves its impress in mud . . . not attractive to persons fresh from the unfailing cleanliness of sea coast and inland country.

One of the most powerful passages in the story is a description of the twenty-nine-year-old Lucy in the throes of unrequited love.

> Alone in her room she might suffer visibly and keenly, but with any eye upon her she would not give way. Sometimes it felt as if the next moment the strain on her nerves might wax unendurable; but such a next moment never came, and she endured still . . . By day she could forbid her thoughts to shape themselves, even mentally into words, although no effort could banish the vague, dull sorrow which was all that might remain to her of remembrance. But by night, when sleep paralysed self-restraint, then her dreams were haunted by distorted spectres of the past;

never alluring or endearing – for this she was thankful – but sometimes monstrous, and always impossible to escape from. Night after night she would wake from such dreams, struggling and sobbing, with less and less conscious strength to resume daily warfare.

There are far too many characters for a short story, but the dialogue is mostly convincing. Christina had a very good ear for the eccentricities of speech.

After her initial disappointment Lucy makes a happy marriage with a caring, unworldly man. Jane marries for money, describing her husband as 'the habitation tax' to be paid on her country mansion. Catherine resigns herself to spinsterhood, waiting for a future 'further off' – the implication being that it is life after death.

The best stories in the book are 'Nick', a gothic fairy tale very succinctly told, 'Vanna's Twins', a moral tale where a woman's hesitation over a charitable donation results in the deaths of two children (Christina commented to Alice Boyd on the story that 'I used not to be very tenderhearted over babies'), and 'The Lost Titian', in which the painter loses his masterpiece on the throw of a dice and it is painted over and lost. Christina disclaimed that this story was based on fact. It remains one of her most distinguished pieces of prose writing.

> Nothing remained to be added. The orange drapery was perfect in its fruit-like intensity of hue; each vine-leaf was curved, each tendril twisted, as if fanned by the soft south wind; the sunshine brooded drowsily upon every dell and swelling upland; but a tenfold drowsiness slept in the cedar shadows. Look a moment, and those cymbals must clash, that panther bound forward; draw nearer, and the songs of these ripe, winy lips must become audible.

Christina struggled to complete the proofs against increasingly poor health. For the past year she had been suffering from lethargy – 'a persistent weariness' and general feeling of malaise, but throughout 1870 her symptoms became more specific and alarming, though no diagnosis was made until 1871. To Alice Boyd she wrote that she didn't know 'exactly what the matter with me amounts to, but I am all out of sorts and lazy.'[12] In May she was sent to Gloucester for a month to stay with Henry Polydore and his daughter Henrietta, and then to the seaside for her usual summer 'prescription' which failed to have the desired effect.

Gabriel's *Poems* came out in April to ecstatic reviews, partly orchestrated by Gabriel himself. Though William had urged him not to 'diplomatise' and to let the book take its chance, the contents were too important for him to do so. He drew up a list of periodicals likely to be sympathetic to it, or where friends of his were reviewers and asked Ellis to send it only to those on the list. The first edition of 1,000 copies sold out in a week and Gabriel made £300 – a substantial amount for poetry even by today's standards.

Blackwood's Magazine was not one of those on his list, and their review, when they eventually got hold of a copy, was less eulogistic than the others. It described the poems as 'interesting and pleasantly readable', but maintained that they laid 'no hold on the imagination', the ear or the memory, and it used the words 'fleshly' and 'unbearable' with reference to the *Blessed Damozel* – written when he was eighteen, but connected in his mind with Lizzie.[13] Gabriel took it badly, writing to his friend Frederick Shields that the 'unpleasantness' of it had lingered longer than he would have thought possible. Some of his friends also had reservations. Madox Brown thought it less original than Christina's poetry. It embodied the 'thoughts of Dante in the language of Shakespeare' rather than expressing his own thoughts in the language of his own time.[14]

Christina's *Commonplace*, in contrast to her brother's success, met with a cool response from the public. Initially she was optimistic, writing to Anne Gilchrist that 'as yet I don't know of any severe handling of me and mine. And my health at present is so very tolerable that I may be all the braver to undergo the lash.'[15] *The Times* wrote perceptively that 'The tragic element in human life saves the humblest existence from absolute Commonplace', and the review, although not hostile, was not calculated to tempt the public to buy the volume. Another reviewer talked of 'painting with moral greys', but as he also compared the book to Mrs Gaskell's *Cranford* – Christina's favourite novel – presumably she was pleased. Gabriel was unenthusiastic, though he tried to be encouraging. He described *Commonplace* as 'certainly not dangerously exciting to the nervous system', and added a postscript 'Of course, I think your proper business is to write poetry and not Commonplaces.'[16]

The edition sold so few copies that Christina wrote to Ellis releasing him from his obligation to publish *Sing-Song* – 'I am so sorry for all the money you have spent on *Sing-Song*, which may well hide its diminished head for one while . . . I fear my poor little book is troublesome to you (nearly) even as it were in its grave.'[17] Ellis sent her £35 in compensation which she returned. As a result, she was without a publisher again. It did, however, get her out of a difficult situation with Alice Boyd, since the idea of the illustrations could simply be dropped. Both Christina and her brothers had been afraid that W.B. Scott would insist on stepping into the gap left by Alice's inadequacy, and they had already decided that Arthur Hughes would be the best person to do the illustrations. There was never any talk of Christina illustrating her own work, though she drew or watercoloured in the margins of her own manuscripts. Like Emily Brontë, she had talent, but she was too untutored to draw well enough to use it professionally. Gabriel sent one of her designs – an apple motif – to William Morris and she hoped that he would be able to use it, but that too was turned down.

William was also having a difficult time with the critics. His edition of Shelley, with accompanying memoir, attracted severe criticism from the Shelley family as well as the reviewers. One paper called it the worst edition of Shelley's work ever published. Someone sent William a fragment of Shelley's charred skull, and he wore the macabre relic in a locket around his neck.

In April 1871, Christina became 'wretchedly ill' and was only capable of lying on a sofa during the day, exhausted even by that. She had pain and fever and Dr William Jenner – physician to Queen Victoria and the Prince of Wales – was summoned. He ordered her to bed, where she remained for several weeks unable to eat. By June the fever had gone down and Dr Jenner recommended that she be taken out in the open air as soon as possible. It was unfortunately the 'most miserably chilly and lightless June' that William could remember, and fires were lit in the hearth every evening and sometimes during the day too. Christina was taken out in a Bath chair and immediately contracted a cold and had to be kept in again. Further bad news came about Henrietta Polydore, who was in the final stages of tubercular decline and not expected to survive the summer.

The family were also approached about a project to exhume Gabriele's body and rebury it in Italy with suitable honours. This produced a strong family reaction and the proposal was turned down. Spirits in the Rossetti household were very low, and not even the success of Maria's book on Dante could raise them very far. In October an attack on Dante Gabriel's *Poems* appeared in the *Contemporary Review* entitled 'The Fleshly School of Poetry' written by Thomas Maitland – a pseudonym for Robert Buchanan.

The review identified 'morbid deviation from healthy forms of life' in Gabriel's poetry, 'stupendous pre-ponderance of sensuality and sickly animalism . . . no gleam of nature, not a sign of humanity . . . formally slovenly and laboriously limp . . . frivolous, absurd, reckless.'[18] Insult was piled upon insult. The attack was apparently motivated by a desire for personal revenge against Gabriel for a supposed slight to Buchanan's beloved friend David Grey, who had died some years earlier. Though urged to ignore it by his friends, Gabriel could not put it out of his mind. W.B. Scott wrote that shortly after it appeared Gabriel arrived late for dinner in a state of considerable agitation and kept shouting out 'Robert Buchanan' at intervals all evening.

A forceful reply 'The Stealthy School of Criticism' failed to exorcise Gabriel's feelings of resentment and it continued to fuel his depression. His consumption of chloral had gradually increased as the drug had less and less effect on his insomnia and he was officially taking in excess of 100 grains in a dose. William believed that the chemist diluted it on the secret instructions of the doctor, but even half that amount would have been substantial.

Shortly after publication of the 'Fleshly School of Poetry', Christina's condition again deteriorated. Dr Jenner was in attendance on the royal family and so it was his deputy, Dr Wilson Fox who saw her. She felt faint, suffered from headaches, and her hands were shaking – making it almost impossible to write. A swelling in her throat prevented her from swallowing properly and her heartbeat was irregular. William described her as 'a total wreck'. Dr Fox prescribed digitalis for her heart, but appeared mystified as to the cause of her illness. Dr Jenner, when he returned, told the family that she was suffering from something so rare that he had only seen one or two cases in his lifetime. It was left to a surgical friend of Maria's to explain that Christina had exopthalmic bronchocele, or Graves' disease, an illness which causes overactivity of the thyroid gland.

Christina's skin turned brown, her hair fell out and she lost a great deal of weight. She had trouble swallowing anything but liquids with frequent choking attacks. The doctors told her that this was 'nervous constriction' only and nothing to do with her swollen thyroid. William wrote that she seemed 'more scared and upset than I think I ever before saw her at any moment of pain or distress'.[19] She was very conscious of her physical degeneration and would see no one but family and close friends. She wrote to William that she was 'less ornamental than society may justly demand,' adding a postscript, that 'habitual ugliness has overtaken even my letters. Pardon.'[20]

In January she had what was described as a heart attack and was confined to one floor of the house. Her bed was moved into her mother's room, behind the drawing room on the first floor. The difficulty in swallowing persisted, and was complicated by bouts of vomiting.

Dante Gabriel's condition had also worsened. He told William that the maids at Cheyne Walk had seen a figure in white at the doorway of the bedroom. On another occasion he complained of supernatural visitations in the form of a child whimpering. How much these were projections of his own mind it is difficult to assess. He was seriously disturbed, and beginning to see conspiracies against him even among friends. Swinburne was one of those who drifted away, according to him Gabriel 'died to me by his own act and wish', sometime in 1872. The breach probably had something to do with stories which Swinburne was spreading, that Gabriel had told him he was guilty of murdering his own unborn children. Whether this was a reference to abortions procured by his mistresses (which some people believed) or, more likely, to something Lizzie had said about Gabriel causing the death of her still-born daughter, is impossible to clarify. It was all rumour and counter rumour, but it preyed on Gabriel's feelings of guilt and grief towards Lizzie and her dead child. The reissue of Buchanan's article as a pamphlet was seen by Gabriel as yet another part of the conspiracy.

On 2 June 1872 William was summoned to Cheyne Walk and spent 'one of the most miserable days of my life, not to speak of his,' with Gabriel, who was 'past question, not entirely sane'.[21] He was suffering from delusions, hallucinations and nervous excitability. William summoned W.B. Scott and his physicians Mr Marshall and Dr Hake were sent for. They prescribed sedatives and rest and it was hoped that the symptoms would subside.

Mrs Rossetti and her daughters were not told of the severity of his illness. Christina's condition was causing 'grave anxiety' at the time and Jenner thought that her life was in jeopardy. The doctors were attending three times a day. Both Frances and Maria were exhausted, having been ill themselves with a particularly virulent type of influenza.

A few days after Gabriel's collapse, Robert Browning published *Fifine at the Fair* and sent him a copy. Unfortunately when Gabriel read it, he thought it was yet another attack on him. He became very agitated and Dr Maudsley, the eminent psychiatrist, was called in. Absolute quiet was recommended and Gabriel was taken to Dr Hake's house in Roehampton by cab. During the journey he heard bells ringing and on arrival thought that a gypsy encampment was 'a demonstration got up in his disparagement'. During the night he heard voices abusing him and swallowed an entire bottle of laudanum he had managed to conceal. A suicide attempt – if that is what it was – was not suspected until the following afternoon when he failed to respond to attempts to rouse him and the empty bottle was found in a drawer.

William went immediately to fetch Mrs Rossetti and Maria, calling at Madox Brown's on the way to ask him to summon Mr Marshall. Christina was too ill to come and Aunt Eliza agreed to stay with her. They were not told at the time of the bottle of laudanum. Spirits of ammonia were held under Gabriel's nose and Mr Marshall administered strong black coffee – the only antidotes they had – but Gabriel remained unconscious for two days. Only his large body-weight and his in-built tolerance to opiates saved him from following Lizzie Siddal's example. Gabriel had once joked about suicide in a letter to William.

> Apropos of death, Hunt and I are going to get up among our acquaintance a Mutual Suicide Association, by the regulations whereof any member, being weary of life, may call at any time upon another to cut his throat for him. It is all of course to be done very quietly, without weeping or gnashing of teeth. I, for instance, am to go in and say, "I say Hunt, just stop painting that head for a minute and cut my throat." To which he will respond by telling the model to keep the position, as he shall only be a moment, and having done his duty, will proceed with the painting. [22]

When Gabriel was finally roused, he was in a severe depressive state and partially paralysed in one leg. He was clearly unfit to go home and could not even be safely left alone. Ford Madox Brown offered a room until something more permanent could be arranged. Gabriel's paintings were removed from Tudor House and stored at W.B. Scott's and Madox Brown and William took over management of his finances. Anticipating the fact that he would be unable to work for some months, they sold off a quantity of porcelain.

On 20 June he went to Scotland, accompanied by Madox Brown and Dr Hake – the latter in the capacity of both friend and physician. He had written a book called *Vates* or *The Philosophy of Madness*, which Gabriel had much admired. Gabriel lent some of Dr Hake's poetry to Christina, but she was unimpressed. Her comments were incisive. 'Deadly Nightshade' was 'startling in its awfulness', and 'Madeline' was only marginally better – 'I altogether lost myself in its mazes and perished in its quag'. Of the whole, she asked Gabriel 'I recognise beauty – but how about meaning?'[23]

While Gabriel was in Scotland, Christina went to Barbara Bodichon's house in Sussex. She had begun, very slowly, to improve, though some of the more marked physical features of the disease remained. Her skin was still sallow and her eyes protruded. Charles Cayley was one of the few people she would see. The last part of her poem 'By Way of

Remembrance' was dedicated to him in manuscript. It was never published in her lifetime, though she used the sestet as part of the less personal tenth sonnet in her 'Monna Innominata' sequence.

> I love you and you know it - this at least,
>   This comfort is mine own in all my pain:
>   You know it, and can never doubt again,
> And love's mere self is a continual feast:
> Not oath of mine nor blessing-word of priest
>   Could make my love more certain or more plain.
>   Life as a rolling moon doth wax and wane -
> O weary moon, still rounding, still decreased!
> Life wanes: and when Love folds his wings above
>   Tired joy, and less we feel his conscious pulse,
>   Let us go fall asleep, dear Friend, in peace:-
>   A little while, and age and sorrow cease;
>   A little while, and love reborn annuls
> Loss and decay and death - and all is love.

Christina worried that her mind had been affected, because she still suffered from lack of concentration. The illness and the closeness of death - she had written to William at one point that she accepted the fact of death as the will of Almighty God - altered her almost as much as her adolescent crisis had done. She became more serious, and narrower in her outlook. She began to read factual books, devotional works, biography and history - Southey's *Life of Nelson* and Goldsmith's *History of Greece*. She began to retreat, more and more, behind the barriers of her religious faith.

CHAPTER THIRTEEN

While Christina convalesced, first at Hampstead and then at Folkestone, she managed to find a new publisher for her collection of children's poems. *Sing-Song* was published in 1872 by Routledges, with illustrations by Arthur Hughes, and this time Christina negotiated a deal whereby she was paid a ten per cent royalty on each copy sold, rather than a lump sum. It was dedicated to Charles Cayley's small nephew – 'the baby who suggested them'. Although many of the rhymes are sentimental enough to embarrass modern tastes, several have survived into contemporary anthologies because their simplicity and honesty have rendered them timeless.

Isobel Armstrong, in *Women Reading Women's Writing*, recalls the moment of recognition which came for her at the age of nine reading 'Who has seen the wind?' She writes of 'crystal, limpid simplicity' which 'did not infantilise'.[1] The language catches the mystery of the wind, with its subtle suggestions of sound.

> Who has seen the wind?
> Neither I nor you:
> But when the leaves hang trembling
> The wind is passing thro'.
>
> Who has seen the wind?
> Neither you nor I:
> But when the trees bow down their heads
> The wind is passing by.

The poem employs a question and answer technique that Christina often used in her poetry and which is particularly effective in her children's verses.

What are heavy?   Sea sand and sorrow:
What are brief?   Today and tomorrow:
What are frail?   Spring blossoms and youth:
What are deep?   The ocean and truth.

Some of the poems are variations of nursery rhymes – others press home
a moral. *Sing-Song* also includes references to the deaths of children –
poems about 'A baby's cradle with no baby in it', or a baby who fell
asleep and could not be woken except in heaven, or more explicitly:

Why did baby die
Making Father sigh,
Mother cry?
Flowers that bloom to die,
Make no reply
Of 'why?'
But bow and die.

Twentieth-century critics, squeamish about death rather than sex, have
questioned Christina's frank attitude. In *The Pelican Guide to English
Literature*, Volume Six, G.D. Klingopulos writes that her children's
poems 'contain too much talk of death and transcience to be useful in the
nursery'.[2] For us the deaths of children have become less common, but
in the middle of the nineteenth century it was rare to find a family that
had not been touched by such bereavement. The proliferation of the
subject in art and literature, which seems morbid to us, was a kind of
public mourning for individual and almost universal sorrow.

What is unusual about *Sing-Song* is its celebration of childhood – its
directness of address, from someone who claimed that she didn't like, or
get on well with children, and had no maternal feelings at all that she
would admit. Yet *Sing-Song* communicates the physicality of motherhood in verse after verse.

My baby has a mottled fist
My baby has a neck in creases
My baby kisses and is kissed
For he's the very thing for kisses.

Anne Gilchrist wrote to William that the 'melody' of *Sing-Song* was as
'sweet and spontaneous as a robin's song'. The reviewers and the public
liked it too and it remained in print until early in the twentieth century,
becoming one of Christina's rare commercial successes. Children's

writing was a new departure for her, and perhaps may have been inspired by her friends Dora Greenwell and Jean Ingelow who had both successfully published verses and stories for children. Jean Ingelow commented in a letter to Dora that 'writing for children is so completely its own reward; it obliges one to be simple and straightforward, and clears away some of the mystical fancies in which one is apt to indulge, and which are a mere luxury.'[3]

The summer of 1873 was spent convalescing at Kelmscott - the beautiful period house near Lechlade in Oxfordshire which Dante Gabriel had rented jointly with William and Janey Morris since 1871. It was an impressive gabled manor house with mullioned windows set deep in walls several feet thick, and surrounded by a formal garden with sculptured yew hedges. The river Thames had been dammed into a lake which was prone to flooding in winter, making the house damp and uninhabitable. Inside the walls were hung with tapestries and the rooms were rather too dark to be appropriate for painting. The wall hangings, flapping in the draughts, depicted depressing scenes from the Bible and the classics and became for Gabriel 'a persecution'. He was at Kelmscott in the company of Dr Hake's son George, pursuing a regime of rest, fresh air, good food and a steady reduction of chloral. He had begun to paint again and was working on a portrait of Jane Morris as Proserpine, his representation of her perhaps a reference to the six months of the year they were able to spend together at Kelmscott, before Jane went back to London to the house she shared with William Morris.

The writer Theodore Watts-Dunton was also staying at Kelmscott that summer and spent a lot of time with Christina. He remembered wandering along the path beside the weir with her while Gabriel pounded across the meadows 'at the rate of five miles an hour' with George Hake. They discussed Shelley's 'Skylark', which Christina regarded as sublime, and the peculiarities of English pronunciation. They looked at flowers and mosses and Christina impressed Watts-Dunton with her love of the countryside - she reminded him of a 'wondering London child' let loose in the country. He wrote in the *Athenaeum* that 'She loved the beauty of this world, but not entirely for itself; she loved it on account of its symbols of another world beyond.' He also became aware that beneath her spirituality lay 'a rich sensuousness that under other circumstances of life would have made itself manifest, and also a rare potentiality of deep passion.'[4]

William, who was very close to a complete breakdown from the strain of the previous two years, went to Italy for the summer in the company of the Scotts, Alice Boyd and Lucy Madox Brown. Part of the object of the visit was to see Claire Clairmont, living in Florence, about some papers she had relating to Shelley and Byron, which William had a commission to purchase. But Claire was in very poor health after a fall and, though he had some interesting conversations with her, he never saw the papers and after two or three days he came away without them.

During the holiday William and Lucy Madox Brown became engaged. They had known each other since Lucy was a small child, when William had accompanied Gabriel to her father's studios. She had been taught by both Mrs Rossetti and Maria and had been a frequent visitor to the house. Lucy was now thirty, William forty-four and neither wanted to have a long engagement. Lucy hoped to be able to carry on her career as a painter after marriage. She had been taught by her father and was conscious of all that she was capable of doing, and still wanted to do. William wrote that 'she was ambitious of excelling and not indifferent to fame; and she had an exalted idea of art and its potencies'.[5]

Christina initially welcomed Lucy into the family circle, writing to William that Lucy's 'sweetness and amiability and talent make her a grace and honour to us'.[6] To Lucy she addressed a typically generous – if slightly awkward – letter.

I should like to be a dozen years younger and worthier every way of becoming your sister, but, such as I am, be sure of my loving welcome to you, as my dear sister and friend.

Despite the fact that both William and Lucy were agnostics, she ends:

May love, peace and happiness, be yours and his together in this world, and together much more in the next; and when earth is an anteroom to heaven (may it be so, of God's mercy to us all), earth itself is full of beauty and goodness.[7]

Underlying both letters is a sense of unease and uncertainty. William's marriage to Lucy presaged a complete change in their way of life. Mrs Rossetti had been used to running the household in her own way, and lately Christina had run it for her, handling keys and money and instructing the servants. Now Lucy would be in charge and changes were inevitable. Christina wrote long, intricate letters to William about the contents of cupboards, the rearrangements of rooms; inventories of individual possessions had to be made and the spare room cleared of the bits and pieces that Christina and Maria had been in the habit of keeping there. Christina's health was still far from good and occasionally her anxieties about the upheaval broke through her superficial calm. She was betrayed into pettiness.

My Dear William,
I am truly sorry for my ebullition of temper this morning (and for a hundred other faults), and not the less so if it makes what follows seem merely a second and more serious instance.

My sleeping in the library cannot but have made evident to you how improper a person I am to occupy any room next a dining room. My cough (which surprised Lucy, as I found afterwards, the other day at dinner) makes it unseemly for me to be continually and unavoidably within earshot of Lucy and her guests. *You* I do not mention, so completely have you accommodated yourself to the trying circumstances of my health: but, when a "love paramount" reigns amongst us, even you may find such toleration an impossibility. I must tell you that not merely am I labouring under a serious relapse into heart-complaint and consequent throat-enlargement (for which I am again under Sir William Jenner's care), but even that what appeared the source of my first illness has formed again, and may for aught I can warrant once more have serious issues.

The drift of all this is that (through no preference for me over you, as you may well believe, but because of my frail state which lays me open to emergencies requiring help from which may you long be exempt) our Mother, if I am reduced to forego all your brotherly bounty provides for me, will of her own unhesitating choice remove with me. We believe that from all sources we shall have enough between us, and you know that our standard of comfort does not include all the show demanded by modern luxury. I have very little doubt that an arrangement may be entered into which shall lodge us under one roof with my Aunts; thus securing to us no despicable amount of cheerful companionship, and of ready aid in sickness.

Dear William, I should not wonder if you had been feeling this obvious difficulty very uncomfortably, yet out of filial and brotherly goodness had not chosen to start it: if so, I cannot rejoice enough that my perceptions have woken up to some purpose.

I do not know whether any possible modification (compatible with all our interests, and not least with Lucy's) may occur to you as to arrangements; to me, I confess, there scarcely seems any way out of the difficulty short of a separation. Perhaps in a day or so you will let Mama or me know what you judge best.

Of course Mamma is in grief and anxiety; her tender heart receives all stabs from every side. – If you wonder at my writing instead of speaking, please remember my nerves and other weak points.[8]

Other things were also gnawing at Christina. Partly as a result of illness and exhaustion she had been unable to write poetry for some time. She wrote to Macmillan in 1875 when he proposed bringing out a combined edition of *Goblin Market* and the *Prince's Progress*, that 'additional matter' for the volume would probably not be forthcoming. 'I fear there will be little indeed to offer you. The fire has died out, it seems; and I know of no bellows to revive dead coals. I wish I did.'[9] The little poetry that she was able to write records her suffering. In 'A Martyr', the young woman prays to God

> Let not the waters close above my head,
> Uphold me that I sink not in this mire:
> For flesh and blood are frail and sore afraid:
> And young I am, unsatisfied and young,
> With memories, hopes, with cravings all unfed,
> My song half sung, its sweetest notes unsung . . .

Her growing religious zeal also put curbs on her imagination. In *Letter and Spirit* she quoted the Beatitudes, ' "Blessed are the pure in heart", but how shall a heart preserve its purity if once the rein be given to imagination; if vivid pictures be conjured up, and stormy or melting emotions indulged? This surely were to commit sin already in the heart, and to act in direct defiance of God . . .'[10] By limiting her imagination, she began slowly, systematically, but unknowingly, to kill the source of her creative inspiration.

William's engagement prompted Maria to make the long-deferred decision to join the Anglican Sisterhood at All Saints. Her health had been far from good in the past two years – she was already suffering from the cancer which eventually killed her – and Christina and her mother were very worried about the lack of comfort in the convent, the cold rooms and uncarpeted floors. Maria was resolute and, once the decision had been made, radiantly happy.

The modest commercial success of *Sing-Song* prompted Christina to try her hand at a children's story, originally called *Nowhere*. In February she wrote to her old publisher Macmillan, bypassing Ellis and Routledges.

> I have tried to write a little prose story, such as might, I think, do for a child's Xmas volume, and if you would allow me to send it you to be looked at, you would truly oblige me. Properly speaking, it consists of three short stories in a common framework – but the whole is not long.[11]

To Gabriel she wrote that it was 'in the *Alice* style with an eye to the market'. The first that Christina knew of its acceptance by Macmillan was an advertisement in the *Athenaeum*. She wrote to Macmillan recommending Arthur Hughes as illustrator. She was also delighted to receive £5.9s accumulated royalties from *Goblin Market* which was still selling, though very slowly. Christina was glad of the money, she told Macmillan, because she had a wedding present to buy.

William and Lucy were married at a register office on 31 March 1874 and there was a small wedding breakfast afterwards at the Madox Browns. Only the immediate family were there and William and Jane Morris. William Morris apparently resented having to go, but knew that a refusal would have offended both families. He and William Rossetti had never been close and Morris's relationship with Gabriel was under strain, partly because of his love for Jane, and partly because his illness had gradually estranged even Gabriel's closest friends. Gabriel had begun to repudiate the whole concept of Pre-Raphaelitism telling one acquaintance that he was weary of 'the visionary vanities of half a dozen boys' and that the 'banding together under that title was all a joke'.[12] William Morris's firm, in which Madox Brown and Gabriel had been involved with other Pre-Raphaelites, was also in the process of breaking up as Morris sought commercial independence and that further soured their personal relationships.

Gabriel's presence at the wedding breakfast caused a certain amount of anxiety. He was nervous about meeting distant Brown relatives, and was too unwell to attend the large evening reception. William and Lucy left straight afterwards for a honeymoon in France and Italy and William managed to fulfil his ambition to visit Naples.

On their return it was soon obvious to Christina and her mother that they could not live with Lucy. It was not simply the strain of becoming guests in what had been their own home, there was also Lucy's atheism – stronger and more militant than William's own. The rituals of Bible reading, prayer and meditation that formed the framework of Christina's days were anathema to Lucy. Though neither Christina nor Frances would press their beliefs on anyone, there was an atmosphere – in William's words, 'the feeling existed on their side, and on the other side the cognisance of the feeling'.[13]

Lucy was also young and extremely sociable – the Madox Brown's had always held open house for friends – and she now did the same at Euston Square. Christina and her mother were used to a very quiet, almost reclusive life and, although William thoroughly enjoyed the change, they did not. He was, however, saddened that Lucy developed a dislike of old friends of the Rossettis such as Mrs Heimann and William Allingham and discouraged their visits to such an extent that the acquaintance was broken off.

There was additional friction between Christina and Lucy which Christina would have been loathe to admit. William had always been her closest sibling, and she had come to rely on him in many small ways, for advice, for financial support, for male companionship. Now Lucy – the love paramount – held first place in his affections, and although Christina would not have admitted that she was jealous or possessive, she found it difficult to give William up. There was jealousy of a different kind on Lucy's side. She saw Christina in a protected environment (provided by William) which enabled her to write, free from the domestic hindrances which Lucy now encountered. She fought hard to continue to paint after her marriage and as William recorded 'she tried more than once to set resolutely to work again; but the cares of a growing family, delicate health, and the thousand constant interruptions' which are the lot of the housewife and mother 'always impeded her, and very much to her disappointment and vexation, she did not succeed in producing any more work adapted for exhibition'.[14]

Christina and her mother spent the summer at the All Saints Mission Hospital in Eastbourne as paying guests. By September they were staying for weeks at a time in the Bloomsbury Square house rented by Charlotte and Eliza Polidori – giving both families a breathing space from each other.

In the summer Christina's first volume of devotional prose *Annus Domini* came out. This particular direction was perhaps encouraged by her friendship with Dora Greenwell. Dora had been writing devotional works since 1863, regarding the ideal as 'a book contemplating *life as it is* in a Christian spirit, yet from the natural standpoint'. She hoped that her own books would help 'to get the Christian life a little more into the open air'.[15] Christina, too, wanted to put her own small weight into the scales, feeling the need more and more as she grew older to use her skills in the service of her religion. Christina's religious prose follows fairly conventional paths. Dora Greenwell admitted in one of her letters that 'there are doors in one's own mind one does not dare to open:' and Christina, who had unflinchingly stood on the most dangerous thresholds when she was younger, now shut some of those doors firmly behind her. The best way to resist temptation, she explained in *Time Flies*, was to avoid it altogether. In spite of this, the spiritual peace she sought, and which Maria had in such full measure, eluded her. *Annus Domini* is prefaced by her beautiful poem 'Wrestling' which begins

> Alas my Lord,
> How should I wrestle all the live-long night
> With Thee my God, my strength and my delight?
>
> How can it need
> So agonised an effort and a strain
> To make Thy face of mercy shine again.
>
> How can it need
> Such wringing out of breathless prayer to move
> Thee to Thy wonted love, when Thou art Love?

Annus Domini is a tiny book about four inches by three, suitable for carrying about in a pocket for easy reference. It contains a prayer for each day of the year with accompanying scriptural text and was published by James Parker and Co. The prayers illustrate Christina's passionate faith – 'O Lord Jesus Christ, the Second Man, I bless, I adore, I magnify, I love Thee ... O Lord Jesus Christ, to Whom we are espoused, keep us ever, I entreat Thee, virgin souls, faithful in Thy love.' Christina's God, whom she seems tempted now to regard as her heavenly spouse and the focus of her emotional life, is a God of the Old Testament; terrible, yet loving. The holocausts of hell are ever present in her writings – the suffering and the sacrifices of Christ and other biblical figures, saints and martyrs are to be mirrored by our own sufferings and to be purified by fire.

> O Lord Jesus Christ, Whose counsel standeth for ever, let not dust and ashes, a worm, a puff of wind, creatures of a day, let us not, O Lord, ever set our will against Thy Will, or despise our birthright with Esau, or harden our hearts with Pharoah. But today before the night cometh, today in the day of grace, grant us repentance unto amendment of life; that in the last great Day of account Thou sweep us not away with the besom of destruction.

Christina promises to devote her art to God.

> O Lord Jesus Christ, Lord of David, grant I pray Thee, that as he danced before Thine Ark and sang praises upon the harp unto Thee, even so we may gladly devote to Thy service all the talents which Thou hast given us; using them not to puff up our own pride, but to do Thee honour.

In October 1874 Lucy's half-brother Oliver, known in the family as Nolly, died unexpectedly of blood poisoning. Christina and her mother had been very fond of him and felt the loss almost as much as Lucy. He had considerable gifts, publishing his first novel when still only in his teens.

Speaking Likenesses came out, as promised, in November in time for the Christmas market. Christina dedicated it to 'my dearest Mother, in grateful remembrance of the stories with which she used to entertain her children'. Christina didn't like the wording of the title page 'with illustrations *thereof* by Arthur Hughes', or the captions which had been inserted under the illustrations, but her objections were ignored by Macmillan.

The book is written as a 'told' story, rather self-consciously in places, and begins 'Come sit round me, my dear little girls, and I will tell you a story'. They are instructed to pick up their needlework so that their hands are not idle. 'Now I start my knitting and my story together.' It is a story within a story, within a story – like a nest of Chinese boxes, a moral tale of a small girl who is cross on her birthday because it doesn't live up to her expectations. She is punished by a terrible dream in which she is pinched and pummelled, starved of food, and finally walled up in a dream house. It recalls very vividly the sadism small children inflict on each other, and the scenes of physical harassment echo 'Goblin Market'. Other parts of the story are more directly sentimental.

> I tell you from the sad knowledge of my older experience, that to every one of you a day will most likely come when sunshine, hope, presents and pleasure will be worth nothing to you in comparison with the unattainable gift of your mother's kiss.

The moral dimensions of the tale left *The Academy* reviewer somewhat puzzled. 'We have an uncomfortable feeling that a great deal more is meant than appears on the surface, and that every part of it ought to mean something if we only knew what it was.'[16] Christina thought the moral of the story and its connection with the title pretty obvious, writing to Gabriel that the children were constantly meeting 'speaking likenesses' of their own faults and characters. The *Athenaeum* thought, with justification, that the tale would have been more original 'if Alice had never been to Wonderland'.[17]

In August 1875 Christina spent four weeks with her mother at the All Saints Mission House at Clifton in Bristol, where Maria was working. Maria, despite her ill-health, was to take her final vows that autumn. Christina loved Clifton and wrote letters to William full of nostalgia for the country.

> Clifton would I think be too Cheltanamy for you: yet a nice place it appears, refreshingly tree-full, blossoming right and left and suggesting a highly advantageous St. John's Wood. The Downs, however, far excel any feature known to me of that quarter and affords a really good drive . . . On some houses the great white magnolia blooms and on one today I spied the rare sight of a myrtle in blossom.[18]

Christina even tried to persuade Gabriel to rent a house near Bristol.

She spent some time with Dora Greenwell, who was staying with her brother in Clifton and not in good health. Christina commented to William that she was 'a good deal invalided and far more delapidated than myself, poor thing.'[19] Dora, a fervent advocate of anti-vivisection and supporter of the Society for the Prevention of Cruelty to Animals, was probably the originator of the leaflets that Christina sent to family and friends at this time. A friend, she told William, had just informed her that experiments on animals were not carried out under the influence of chloroform, as she had previously been led to believe.

When they returned to London Christina and her mother went to stay with the Aunts in Bloomsbury Square, and Lucy's first baby, a girl, was born on 20 September, and called Olive, (a name she later changed to Olivia). Once Lucy's lying-in period was over, Christina and Frances moved back into the family home, but began to spend longer and longer periods in Bloomsbury Square. Christina was busy with preparations for her volume of *Collected Poems*. Gabriel was still objecting to 'Under the Rose' – now called 'The Iniquity of the Fathers Upon the Children'. Although Christina acknowledged the 'unwieldiness' of the title, she didn't like Gabriel's suggested alternative 'Upon the Children' because she didn't feel it was lucid enough.

Gabriel also objected to the inclusion of 'The Lowest Room' – which exhibited the 'modern vicious taint' of Elizabeth Barrett Browning, and advised her to exclude the taint from all future poetry. He also detected traces of Jean Ingelow's influence. Christina retorted that it had been written before the *Goblin Market* volume and therefore 'before Miss Ingelow misled me any-whither'. She defended the inclusion of the poem as she had done before.

> I am truly sorry if I have judged amiss in including *The Lowest Room* . . . To my thinking it is by no means one of the most morbid or most personal of the group; but I am no good judge in my own cause . . . The whole subject of youthful poems grows anxious in middle age, or may at some moments appear so; *one is so different, and yet so vividly the same.*[20]

Gabriel pressed his point, and a few days later she wrote to him again from Bloomsbury Square.

> After impervious density, I begin to see light (I think) on your objection to *The Lowest Room*; and I already regret having inserted it, *you having scale-dipping weight with me*. Bulk was a seductive element . . . I still don't dislike it myself, but can lay no claim to impartiality.[21]

Despite Gabriel's objections the poem appeared at the end of Christina's volume like a credo.

She still saw Charles Cayley occasionally, and sometimes he called for a game of whist with Christina and her mother and Aunt Eliza. They continued to correspond, and sometime around 1875 Christina wrote 'Cor Mio', a sonnet which she changed and depersonalised to fit into her 'Later Life' sequence. The original may well have been written with Cayley in mind.

> Still sometimes in my secret heart of hearts
>   I say 'Cor mio' when I remember you,
>   And thus I yield us both one tender due,
> Welding one whole of two divided parts.
> Ah Friend, too wise or unwise for such arts,
>   Ah noble Friend, silent and strong and true,
>   Would you have given me roses for the rue
> For which I bartered roses in love's marts?
> So late in autumn one forgets the spring,
>   Forgets the summer with its opulence,
> The callow birds that long have found a wing,
>   The swallows that more lately got them hence:
> Will anything like spring, will anything
>   Like summer, rouse one day the slumbering sense?

In 'Later Life', the personal origins of the poem are disguised by substitution of a contemplation of autumn for the first eight lines, beginning 'So late in Autumn half the world's asleep'. It is a perfect example of the way in which Christina wrote poetry from a personal standpoint, inspired by a particular emotion, or situation, and then masked it for publication.

Throughout the spring of 1876 Maria continued to decline and in July she was sent to the mission hospital at Eastbourne. Christina and Frances made preparations to go to Eastbourne to be near her. Before they left it was finally decided that Christina and her mother should set up home with Charlotte and Eliza Polidori, relieving them of the difficulties of sharing a house with Lucy. Christina wrote to Gabriel that: 'William is cut up, I think, at losing our dearest Mother; but I am entirely unpleasing to Lucy and, could we exchange personalities, I have no doubt I should then feel with her feelings.'[22]

While they were at Eastbourne, Charlotte and Eliza found what seemed to be a suitable house at a rental they could afford. Christina wrote to Lucy, taking all the blame on herself for the failure of their relationship. That this was not entirely the case is vouched for by William, who, though he refused to take sides in the matter, indicated that a good deal remained to be said about Lucy's behaviour towards her sister-in-law.

> Dear Lucy,
> Perhaps you have heard that what promises to be a comfortable residence has been fixed upon for our house-party, in Torrington Square; No. 30. I hope, when two roofs shelter us and when faults which I regret are no longer your daily trial, that we may regain some of that liking which we had as friends, and which I should wish to be only the more tender and warm now that we are sisters. Don't, please, despair of my doing better.[23]

Maria's condition was 'very grave'. She was sent back to London to obtain specialist advice, and the Order temporarily relieved her of her duties. The specialist ordered that Maria be 'tapped' to remove excess fluid from her body, and on 16 October the process had to be repeated. It became obvious that Maria did not have long to live. William and Lucy were on holiday at Newlyn in Cornwall and Christina wrote to warn them. 'You must already be prepared without my telling you, for *anything* I may have to write.' William decided to come home, though Lucy and the baby remained. Christina wrote to tell Lucy that Maria had endured a second tapping and was being kept absolutely quiet. 'No one can see her without seeing how little strength remains for exhaustion'. Gabriel had called to see his mother 'to grieve with her and comfort her'.[24]

Maria was too weak to be tapped again, and she gradually deteriorated, unable to eat, hardly able to swallow the lemonade prescribed for her. By 12 November Christina told William that Maria's death was 'only a matter of days'. On 24 November at about 1.30 in the afternoon Maria died peacefully and Christina took it upon herself to write the necessary letters. 'Our dearest Mother is bearing her sorrow with that peace which the world neither gives nor takes away'.

The arrangement of the funeral also fell on Christina's shoulders. The service was to be at the All Saints Mission, and it was strictly family only. Christina talked to William about the inadvisability of Gabriel coming to the second service at the graveside. Since Lizzie's death and subsequent exhumation he had had a morbid dread of graveyards and, in his present frail mental condition, the family did not want to expose him to the ordeal.

Maria was buried in Brompton Cemetery, according to the rites of the Sisterhood. She had wanted a cheerful funeral, and as far as possible her wishes were met. In *Time Flies* Christina described the scene:

> Flowers covered her, loving mourners followed her, hymns were sung at her grave, the November day brightened, and the sun (I vividly remember) made a miniature rainbow in my eyelashes. I have often thought of that rainbow since.[25]

Part Four

Tenacious Obscurity

'Each sore defeat of my defeated life
  Faced and outfaced me in that bitter hour;
  And turned to yearning palsy all my power,
  And all my peace to strife,
  Self stabbing self with keen lack-pity knife.'

CHRISTINA ROSSETTI
'An Old-World Thicket'
c. 1882

CHAPTER FOURTEEN

The move to Torrington Square, and the death of Maria, left Christina alone with three elderly ladies for whom she was largely responsible. She ran the household, wrote letters for them, read to them and generally looked after their welfare. It was not a cheerful environment. Visitors to the house spoke of the absolute silence, and the smell of ageing flesh.

In *Letter and Spirit* she wrote of the difficulties of living with one's elders. 'They speak and we wish they would be quiet, their manners are old fashioned, their taste is barbarous, their opinions are obsolete, their standard is childish . . . ' She concluded that it was very hard to reach a position of 'reverence and submission'. There wasn't always universal harmony at Torrington Square. In a letter to Aunt Eliza, who was forthright and somewhat anti-social, Christina refers to arguments over cards, taking the blame for this upon herself. Aunt Charlotte had a more equable temperament – Christina praised her for her patience and tolerance – and she was much easier to live with.

The Torrington Square house had no garden of its own and was very expensive. Gabriel disapproved of their choice, nicknaming the Square 'Torrington Oblong'. The railed communal gardens were soot blackened and uninviting, and the house was rather gloomy, starved of light by the trees outside. On the ground floor was a narrow dark entrance hall and the dining room which became Aunt Eliza's bedroom as her health failed. At the back there was a small room overlooking the yard which Christina used as her 'den', and where she entertained her close friends.

On the first floor across the front of the house was the drawing room which caught the sun during the day. It was sparsely furnished with an odd mixture of items from the Rossetti and Polidori households and the walls displayed a selection of family portraits by Gabriel. It was Gabriel who contributed the beautiful antique chandelier which had previously hung in Cheyne Walk – when the sun shone it threw prisms of light around the room. In one corner was a large terrarium containing the fern garden which was Christina's hobby. She had begun to put on weight, and took to wearing a cap during the day to cover her hair. Christina's days were circumscribed by the needs and physical limitations of her elderly relatives. Her own life had to be fitted into the odd corners of theirs. Her feelings are expressed in a beautiful sonnet called 'Why?' which begins

> Lord, if I love Thee and Thou lovest me,
> Why need I any more these toilsome days?
> Why should I not run singing up Thy ways,
> Straight into heaven, to rest myself with Thee?

There is repressed anger in the poem, not quite assuaged by Christ's response

> Bride whom I love, if thou too lovest Me,
> Thou needs must choose My Likeness for thy dower:
> So wilt thou toil in patience, and abide
> Hungering and thirsting for that blessed hour
> When I My Likeness shall behold in thee,
> And thou therein shalt waken satisfied.'

Mrs Rossetti was too frail to travel easily now and Christina was forced to forego the pleasurable summers spent beside the sea. She wrote to Gabriel

Thank you for a helpful feeler put out in the direction of Felixstowe. But two things (alas!) prevent our profiting thereby. First our Mother very wisely has contracted her radius, and now seeks places not remote from London, thus avoiding the exhaustion of long journeys. Secondly as we are making a sociable family party this year, we must avoid the glaring seaside on account of poor Aunt Eliza's eyes.[1]

Christina missed her annual seaside holiday and the long solitary walks along the beach. Just how much a sacrifice it was is evident from sonnet No. 17 in her 'Later Life' sequence written at some point between her collected poems in 1875 and her *Pageant* volume in 1881.

Something this foggy day, a something which
Is neither of this fog nor of today,
Has set me dreaming of the winds that play
Past certain cliffs, along one certain beach,
And turn the topmost edge of waves to spray:
Ah pleasant pebbly strand so far away,
So out of reach while quite within my reach,
As out of reach as India or Cathay!
I am sick of where I am and where I am not,
I am sick of foresight and of memory,
I am sick of all I have and all I see,
I am sick of self, and there is nothing new;
Oh weary impatient patience of my lot! –
Thus with myself: how fares it, Friends, with you?

In spite of the domestic preoccupations which fenced her in, her poetic
inspiration began to return again – though almost invariably now on a
religious theme. In 1877 she sent Gabriel a poem she had just written in
the old way as a 'genuine lyric cry' which she distinguished from 'skilled
labour'. The poem was called 'Mirrors of Life and Death' and was
published in the *Athenaeum* on 17 March 1877. The theme of the poem
is that Nature is a mirror

> The mystery of Life, the mystery
> Oh Death, I see
> Darkly as in a glass;
> Their shadows pass,
> And talk with me.

Each separate verse is a 'mirror' of some kind.

> As the Sun with glory and grace
> In his face
> Benignantly hot,
> Graciously radiant and keen,
> Ready to rise and to run –
> Not without spot,
> Not even the Sun.

*   *   *

> As a Mole grubbing underground;
> When it comes to the light
> It grubs its way back again,
> Feeling no bias of fur
> To hamper it in its stir,
> Scant of pleasure and pain,
> Sinking itself out of sight
> Without sound.

As usual, she discussed its content with Gabriel.

> Please remark that I have adopted your *omission* of "sun of", and your *re-arrangement*: and wink at my *mouse* and *mole* from whom I cannot wean myself. I have, however, woven in a few fresh "mirrors", and some of these tone down (I hope) any abruptness of the m. and m. Now my little piece satisfies myself, and I shall be very glad if it goes under your auspices to the Athenaeum, though I would have spared you further trouble by acting for myself now that I am old enough and tough enough. The alternative of a declinal I must brave; at the worst it will not be my first experience in the same line. As to my *mole and his fur*, perhaps you have not noticed the fact of his skin having no right-and-wrong way of the grain (as for instance, a cat's has): it grows like the *biasless* nap of velvet, and as a naturalistic fact this is explained as adapting him to his career of grubbing to and fro. I hope this speciality is well enough known for my couplet to convey its drift; at any rate I will run the risk and enlarge the public mind . . .
>
> I overlooked "Benignantly hot" – Do you know, I like it, – and do not want to be exclusively "dreamily sweet", – nor fancy that all the rest is so.[2]

She promised to send Gabriel more of her recent poems if he would promise to 'respect my *thin skin* and do not start the subject in public'. 'Mirrors of Life and Death', which today seems rather trite and unoriginal, attracted a lot of attention. Gerard Manley Hopkins in particular, singled it out for praise. A much more important poem, written around the same time and published in 1882, was 'The Thread of Life' which describes a new feeling of self-hood. Christina sees the human condition as a prison, each individual bound by a 'self-chain'. The second verse ends triumphantly 'But what I was I am, I am even I'. This new self-hood, dedicated to Christ, provides fulfilment and a sense of vocation. Christ bids the poet sing

Therefore myself is that one only thing
I hold to use or waste, to keep or give;
My sole possession every day I live,
And still mine own despite Time's winnowing.
Ever mine own, while moons and seasons bring
From crudeness ripeness mellow and sanative;
Ever mine own, till Death shall ply his sieve;
And still mine own, when saints break grave and sing.
And this myself as king unto my King
I give, to Him Who gave Himself for me;
Who gives Himself to me, and bids me sing
A sweet new song of His redeemed set free;
He bids me sing, O Death, where is thy sting?
And sing, O grave, where is thy victory?

In the *Face of the Deep*, a devotional commentary on the Apocalypse published in 1892, Christina returns to the same theme of acceptance and self knowledge. 'Who I am, I am ... I cannot unself myself' ... 'Rocks may fall on us, mountains cover us; but under mountain and rock remains the unextinguishable I.'[3] This idea of 'selving', that uniqueness of each thing and individual, Christina shared with Gerard Manley Hopkins, whose admiration for her work influenced his own directions. In particular, the braiding of words in patterns of repetition and alliteration which she sometimes employed and which became one of the main characteristics of Hopkins work.

Hopkins was only one of a number of younger poets in the second half of the nineteenth century who saw in Christina Rossetti's poetry a new way forward. Ford Madox Ford in 1911 wrote in *The Critical Attitude* that 'Christina Rossetti seems to us to be the most valuable poet that the Victorian age produced.' He regarded her poetry as a true indicator of the direction of poetry in the twentieth century – her directness and economy, and her use of personal circumstance as legitimate subject matter for poetry. Charles Sisson in the 1984 edition of her works published by Carcanet says that Ford's diagnosis 'has been confirmed by much that has happened since then and is hardly questionable in the nineteen-eighties.'

In 1877 Gabriel was ill again with severe depression following another minor operation to draw fluid from his scrotum. He was attended by Mr Marshall, who had attended him during his previous breakdown. Christina wrote to William that 'Poor Gabriel is so dreadfully depressed as apparently to give himself no chance of rallying'.[4] Marshall recommended convalescence in a quiet location as 'an absolutely essential step', and Christina and Frances prepared to accompany him. One of the main causes for concern was the amount of chloral Gabriel was consuming, accompanied by similar measures of neat spirit, to take away the nauseous taste. On 15 August Christina wrote another bulletin for William

> You may like to know about our visit to Chelsea yesterday before paying yours today. Poor Gabriel was greatly depressed, but in some points better: he walked and sat a little in the garden, and played a game of chess with me. Warmly and gratefully did he speak of Mr Brown, who had sat up reading to him, and very affectionately he made mention of the comfort of seeing you. The special incident however to tell you is that whilst we were there Mr Marshall called and stayed a long time with him. We of course, left him alone with his patient: but after a while he joined us in the drawing room and held an anxious conversation with Mamma, plainly telling us that, though one month of adequate observance of rule would make all the difference in Gabriel's favour, he could not survive many months on the present system. Well: he had spoken, I suppose, very plainly also to Gabriel, who had owned to him a very serious breach of rule; and Gabriel has now consented to be put in charge of a regular nurse, who will enforce that moderation which his very life now requires. Mr Marshall knew of a most eligible nurse just set free from another case; and he has furnished G[abriel] with a written table of diet etc., admitting of no misunderstanding.[5]

A farmhouse was found at Hunter's Forestall near Herne Bay in Kent and Gabriel was installed with the nurse, Mrs Mitchell. Ford Madox Brown stayed with him initially, and when he left the painter Frederick Shields took his place. Christina and her mother went down towards the end of August. For Christina it was the beginning of a long friendship with Shields, whose deeply religious character excited her admiration. As to the rest of his character, Christina was fully aware of his faults, admitting to Gabriel that he walked the world as his 'own wet blanket'. She felt sorry for his wife, who after their marriage when she was only just sixteen had been sent to school according to the strictest religious principles and spent much of the year alone.

Shields made Christina a present of his drawing for the painting *The Good Shepherd* which she hung in the drawing room at Torrington Square. She told her biographer MacKenzie Bell that Shield's philosophy of art and faith was her own ideal. 'You see, he does not treat sacred themes merely as an artist; they are part of his life.'[6] Wholeness, self-hood, a complete integration of the different parts of her personality was Christina's goal.

At Hunter's Forestall Gabriel's condition was slow to improve, and it was proving almost impossible to reduce his intake of chloral. As soon as the dose was reduced his insomnia returned and the nurse was forced to increase it again so that he could get some sleep. Christina wrote regular reports for William.

> Poor dear Gabriel had a somewhat less uneasy night last night; but it seems only shades of difference which are in question, nothing near the contrast between good and bad. His depression is very painful, though sometimes a shadow of the old fun breaks out and lights all up for the moment. Yet some positive advance seems to have been made if we look back a few weeks. The rooms are no longer kept in semi-darkness, he does not now sit in that attitude of dreadful dejection with drooping head, he perspires less, and, if I am not mistaken, the pains in his limbs have lessened. He looks stout, his complexion is florid; only his eyes have a peculiar appearance which cannot, I fear, be favourable. Sometimes he is unable to listen to reading, but very often he listens for a good while with interest. Generally a little whist helps on the evening fairly. He has not even yet attempted to take Mamma's portrait, and his hand is often visibly tremulous.[7]

Just as Branwell Brontë had come to depend on Emily in his final breakdown, so Gabriel became very dependent on Christina emotionally. Like Emily, Christina was able to sympathise without condoning her brother's conduct. She alone seemed to understand his artistic frustrations and the burden of guilt that clouded his consciousness. When William wrote tentatively suggesting that many of his symptoms were imaginary, Christina remonstrated sharply that they were none the less real or painful because of that, and she commented perceptively, 'It is trying to have to do with him at times, but what must it be *to be* himself.'[8]

In October Christina and her mother were still in Kent, and Theodore Watts-Dunton had replaced Frederick Shields. They feared that if Gabriel's intake of opiate was reduced too much he would simply 'order chloral direct for himself from the chemist'. Christina confided her fears to William

> All I thus repeat to you is in strictest confidence, but *you* ought to be informed of what is and of what threatens. He has spoken of not continuing here beyond about the end of this month, but has not so said it that I feel any certainty as to our breaking up at any given moment; if he ceases to conform to rule, I know not what to look forward to, whether we stay or whether we leave. God help us.[9]

In November Gabriel was well enough to be moved into the Euston Square house with William and Lucy. He was still too ill to work, except in a desultory kind of way, though he executed the beautiful chalk portrait of Christina and her mother, now in the National Gallery. William thought the portrait 'markedly like a certain aspect of Christina's face . . . Whenever I set my eyes upon it, the lines from her poem, *From House to Home* come into my mind –

> Therefore in patience I possess my soul;
> Yea therefore as a flint I set my face.[10]

There was unpleasantness over Augustus Howell, an unscrupulous picture dealer who had been forging paintings in collaboration with his mistress, and selling them as Gabriel's own work. There was confusion over paintings which Gabriel had given him to sell, and several things had gone missing. Gabriel was clearly not in a condition to manage his own affairs.

In February Lucy's second child, a boy they named Arthur, was born. It was a source of great concern to Christina and her mother that Lucy and William did not have the children baptised. Although relations between the two households had improved, the children were a renewed source of friction. There was trouble between Christina and Lucy over a visit made by Olive, who was almost three, and her nurse to Torrington Square. Christina appears to have complained that Olive had been 'making herself more than sufficiently "at home",' and Lucy threatened to curtail her visits. Christina wrote to Lucy to try to clear up the misunderstanding.

My Dear Lucy,

I am heartily glad you have written, because it gives me a chance of doing away with an impression I never meant to create. I quite admire our clever little Olive, and am really glad she should be imbued with *Sing Songs*; and the more at her ease she is among us, some of her nearest relations, the better; and, if some day she comes to love me as well as to be familiar with me, that will be better still, – only I do not count on such a happy consummation, as I know myself to be deficient in the nice motherly ways which win and ought to win a child's heart. You do not know how much pleasure, moreover, you will retrench from Mamma's quiet days if you check Olive's coming here or her perfect freedom when she is here. *That* is a truly motherly heart, full of warm nooks for children and children's children: and she could not bear *her* gratification in seeing and hearing your little ones to be doubted or misunderstood. This with her love to you and to them. And mine too, please, to all three: not a crocodile love!

"Kiss and be friends" is a very sound old exhortation: get Olive to be my proxy, and I shall not fear to miss the result. Need I?[11]

Christina's collected *Poems* were selling reasonably well, but she was disturbed to find, when enquiring what had happened to her royalty payments, that Macmillan, without consulting her, had been applying them to offset the deficit he had incurred on the *Prince's Progress*. He had also printed a second edition without telling Christina. She would have let the matter rest, but both Gabriel and William thought that something further ought to be done. They extracted Christina's permission to allow Watts-Dunton (who was also a qualified solicitor) to act on her behalf in negotiations with Macmillan, and she agreed on condition that there would be no legal proceedings.

... If he will kindly take it without my involving myself in heavy law-expenses I will accept your opinion that it is advisable ... But only and absolutely in the most amicable manner; as being quite certain that no wrong has either been done or dreamt of, as knowing that I am satisfied with actual arrangements, and as bearing in mind that I stick to my position of cordial personal friendship with my friendly publisher ... Nothing however, not proof positive that I had been pillaged! would make me have recourse to law: This is a statement at once preliminary and final. Moreover I am hugging hopes of getting together before long enough verse for a *small* fresh volume: so least of all at this moment am I in the mood to alienate the staunch Mac ... [12]

The projected volume did not come to fruition until 1881. However, in 1879 she published another prose work with SPCK called *Seek and Find*. It is a series of studies on the Benedicte. Christina wrote to Gabriel apologising for the lack of poetry, 'yet I flatter myself that some of it is that prose which I fancy our Italian half inclines us to indite'.[13] Her brothers felt that the mass of references included in the text rather than set out as footnotes, swamped the beauty and simplicity of the prose.

Gabriel's health continued to fluctuate, though the trend was consistently downhill. In the summer he quarrelled with Madox Brown, one of the staunchest of his friends and allies. Gabriel's violent mood swings, irritability and delusions, exaggerated, if not actually caused by the drugs he was taking, had gradually eroded all but a few of his many friendships. Even Jane Morris was forced to tell him, gently, that his conduct towards other people was intolerable. He was no longer able to visit the Morris household and could only see Jane at Cheyne Walk. His letters to her are loving and thoughtful and she continued to write affectionately, though not as often as Gabriel would have liked. He told her that the 'removal of her long interest' in him would be unbearable.[14]

Early in October Gabriel took an overdose of chloral, and once more had to be nursed back to health. Christina wrote to William

> We spent a long morning with Gabriel yesterday, and found him less depressed than I was prepared for. But what a state his mouth is in, and his voice was wretched. However, he was fairly chatty as to books and people, and showed us some beautiful drawings. I wish you could have heard the tender and grateful warmth with which he mentioned your kindness in illness - "like a woman" - and the sweetness of your disposition.[15]

It had become impossible for Gabriel to live alone, and after various artist's assistants had been tried William found Thomas Hall Caine, a young writer who occupied the roles of mentor and friend for the final years of Gabriel's life.

In July 1880 an article about the Rossetti family appeared in *The Pen*. Christina read it in Eastbourne where she was managing a rare holiday beside the sea with her mother, and she wrote to Gabriel

> How I wish we knew who did write *The Pen* article. Don't think me such a goose as to feel keenly mortified as being put below you, the head of our house in so many ways. I much like the mention of our dear Father, and I like also as far as it goes, the tribute to Maria: William too fares fairly. In your 'non-fit' pun I revel. Who can it be who knows so much about our family and yet in one or two points is positively at fault - as when he leaves us *no* English element, and seems to make you the eldest of the group? If ever you find out, I hope you will enlighten us.[16]

The 'he' of the article was in fact Alice Meynell, struggling to fit her journalism and poetry around the demands of her husband and family. The details were culled from her friends George Meredith and Coventry Patmore, but is is Alice's vivid intelligence that pervades the article. Patmore gave a lovely picture of Alice in domestic life, spilling into her kitchen with her children, 'laughing like many primroses'. She regarded it as inevitable that women's poetry should be 'melancholy and self-conscious', but she was more critical of the attitudes to which Christina gave explicit utterance and accepted without question (if not without struggle). 'It is the lot of us, "love-lorn females"', Christina wrote to

William on the birth of his son Arthur, 'to sing second in life, tho' not in music'.[17]

In August 1880 Lord Henry Somerset wrote to Christina requesting permission to set some of her poetry to music. Christina at first assented, but was then informed by Gabriel and William that because he was involved in a sexual scandal, it would be very damaging of her to allow him to do so. Christina vacillated, anxious not to refuse until she had made up her own mind in the affair. Whether her brothers made her aware of Lord Henry's homosexuality is not known. It could not be explicitly written about at the time; even the name is left blank in Christina's letters to Gabriel. Lord Henry sent her two documents

> One I think any candid person would admit carried great weight, the other goes far with me. But I do not feel it right to let them out of my hands, or even to show them, except to our Mother, who is at least as favourably impressed by them as I am. The practical point to which all this tends is that I am going to send *** back all his letters and papers, so that he may feel sure they neither in my lifetime, nor afterwards pass into other keeping . . . Poor fellow, whatever his case may be, he is infinitely to be pitied.[18]

Lord Henry was angry and disappointed by Christina's response.

> *** has written in answer. He does not say a word about the setting; but asserts himself "an innocent man" (premising that he "will not affect to misunderstand my letter"), and appears what in one case I consider justly hurt, and in the other resentful. I am very much pained: and think I shall write once more – FINALLY – not of course to reconsider the question of the music, but to make myself less uncomfortable in case (however blindly) I have been unjust. No explanations or details or assertions will be needed: and under no possible circumstance can harm ensue. Do not laugh: I am weighed upon by the responsibility of all one does or does not do[19]

Christina's scrupulosity grew more marked as she grew older. A poem of hers called 'Yet A Little While' was published in the *University Magazine*. Christina had not previously read the magazine and was shocked when she saw the kind of articles it contained. She wrote to the editor refusing to contribute again with people who were

> of a school of thought antagonistic to my own. If so, I am sure you will kindly set me free from my quasi-engagement to write on demand for the

Magazine; for I could never be at my ease or happy in literary company with persons who look down upon what I look up to. I have not *played* at Christianity, and therefore I cannot play at unbelief.[20]

She displayed similar prudishness in a letter to Frederick Shields over some fairy drawings, which were much in vogue at the time and usually depicted the female nude form. Christina thought that 'last night in admiring (Miss) – 's work I might better have said less unless I could have managed at the same time to convey more. I do admire the grace and beauty of the designs, but I do not think that to call a figure 'a fairy' settles the right and wrong of such figures.' Her conscience had been troubling her all night because she had not said anything at the time. She disapproved of portrayals of the nude form (as did her brothers and a large part of Victorian society) and she thought that 'women artists should set the example and lead the way'.[21]

CHAPTER FIFTEEN

Towards the end of 1880 Christina finally found a home for a work completed some years earlier, before the death of Maria, and which had previously failed to find a publisher. The SPCK was glad to capitalise on the success of her previous volume and brought out *Called to be Saints* early in 1881. She wrote to Gabriel, who worried that her religious prose would damage her reputation as a poet 'I don't think any harm will accrue from my SPCK books, even to my standing; if it did, I should still be glad to throw my grain of dust into the religious scale.'[1]

Called to be Saints is a series of devotional studies on the saints days of the church calendar, and is dedicated to Maria's memory with an epigraph from Hooker's *Ecclesiastical Polity*. For each saint Christina provides a life story, the full biblical text relating to him, a meticulous botanical description of the flower which is their emblem, an appropriate gem stone, a prayer and a psalm. For the Virgin Mary Christina chooses the Snowdrop, which

seems born of the snow which forbids not its blossoming: for it wears pure white as a garment, and it droops its head as thought it were an icicle . . . The snowdrop has been called Our Lady of February, The Fair Maid of February, and the purification flower: thus its aspect and its names alike turn our minds to purity and piety; and the common soil whence it springs may become for us as a stepping-stone towards heaven.[2]

The text is interspersed with poems of variable quality. The lyric which accompanies the Annunciation is one of her best.

Herself a rose, who bore the Rose,
She bore the Rose and felt its thorn.
All Loveliness new-born
Took on her bosom its repose,
And slept and woke there night and morn.

Lily herself, she bore the one
Fair Lily; sweeter, whiter, far
Than she or others are:
The Sun of Righteousness her Son,
She was His morning star.

On the feast of All Saints she alludes to her sacrifice of human love for divine love, which must come first, and makes a reference to the two important occasions in her life, mentioned in her letters, when she reached some religious crisis point.

Often as I have let slip what cannot be regained, two points of my own experience stand out vividly: once, when little realising how nearly I had despised my last chance, I yet did in bare time do what must shortly have been for ever left undone; and again, when I fulfilled a promise which beyond calculation there remained but scant leisure to fulfil.[3]

These two 'thresholds' in her life, were obviously significant to Christina though she guarded the details closely. Her poem 'Twice', written in 1864, may refer to the same events. The first part of the poem refers to earthly love.

I took my heart in my hand,
    (O my love, O my love),
I said: Let me fall or stand,
    Let me live or die,
But this once hear me speak –
    (O my love, O my love) –
Yet a woman's words are weak;
    You should speak, not I.

You took my heart in your hand
    With a friendly smile
With a critical eye you scanned,
    Then set it down,
And said: It is still unripe,
    Better wait awhile;
Wait while the skylarks pipe,
    Till the corn grows brown.

As you set it down it broke –
 Broke, but I did not wince;
I smiled at the speech you spoke,
 At your judgement that I heard:
But I have not often smiled
 Since then, nor questioned since,
Nor cared for corn-flowers wild,
 Nor sung with the singing bird.

In the second part of the poem, the poet offers her heart – her broken heart – to God, and this time it is not refused.

This contemned of a man,
 This marred one heedless day,
This heart take Thou to scan
 Both within and without:
Refine with fire its gold,
 Purge Thou its dross away –
Yea hold it in Thy hold,
 Whence none can pluck it out.

In January James Collinson died, only three months before his sister Mary, who had once refused to correspond with Christina. Two more deaths, in what William called the 'mortuary catalogue' of the second half of Christina's life. She commemorated Collinson's death by putting one of his sonnets in *Time Flies* on 24 January. It was reproduced 'from memory', and she added tendentiously, 'I think it devotional; perhaps others may think so too'. The sonnet is in the form of a dialogue and begins with a demand countered by an excuse.

"Give me thy heart". I said "Can I not make
Abundant sacrifice to Him who gave
Life, health, possessions, friend of all I have,
All but my heart once given?"

As in Christina's poem 'Twice', earthly love has to be superseded by heavenly love. The central section describes an ideal of one flesh bound up in the love of Christ.

"Give me thy broken heart" Can love enslave?
Must it be forced to look beyond the grave
For its fruition? Lord for Thy love's sake
Let this thing be: as two streams journeying on
Melt into one and widen to the sea
So let two souls love-burdened make but one,
And one full heart rest all its love on Thee.

Once the misunderstanding over royalties had been settled with
Alexander Macmillan, Christina wrote to him offering a new volume
'on the old terms'. Macmillan accepted, without even seeing the poems
and Christina was delighted, though nervous at the prospect of facing
the critics again with new work – her first apart from children's verse
and prose since the *Prince's Progress* in 1866. She wrote to William that
she was 'somewhat in a quake, a fresh volume being a formidable upset
of nerves, but at any rate, it cannot turn out TWINS!' Lucy had
unexpectedly given birth to a boy and a girl on 23 April, named
respectively Michael and Mary. A second daughter, Helen, had been
born in 1879 and Christina now had five nieces and nephews.

Christina took a great deal of trouble over her *Pageant* volume,
meticulously reserving the copyright to herself. 'Copyright is my
hobby:' she wrote to Alexander Macmillan, 'with it, I cannot part. If it
is of any value, I think I have the first claim upon it, and if it is of none,
it may gracefully be left to me.' With the birth of the twins, 'the minutest
prospective gains become of double value, and I cling to my dear
copyright more than ever.'[4] Under the Copyright Act 1842 the author
could only retain copyright for forty-one years during their lifetime and
for seven years after death. There was no international copyright and
pirated editions of works were common. Macmillan was one of those
agitating for reform of the copyright laws during the seventies and
eighties.

The contents of *A Pageant and Other Poems* were not discussed with
Gabriel, whose health was too poor to withstand any great demands on
his concentration. Christina and her mother could not even be sure of a
welcome when they called to see him. In his worst moods, he felt unable
to see anyone. He wrote to Christina, who was staying at Sevenoaks with
her mother for a short holiday, expressing considerable curiosity about
her new volume. She wrote back telling him that a copy was on its way
to him. She explained tactfully that 'William saw the sonnets before
you, merely because calling one day he downright asked to look at the
book – a nervous moment for me, though I braved it out.'[5] She took up

Gabriel's suggesion to send copies to Watts-Dunton and Hall Caine for review, though she 'winced at the prospect'. She was 'well pleased to be away just now from London' and jokes about her appearance; 'If only my figure would shrink somewhat! For a fat poetess is incongruous, especially when seated by the grave of buried hope!'[6]

Christina need not have worried about the reviews. Watts-Dunton in the *Athenaeum*, commented on her 'love of allegory and symbol'. He described her music as 'apparently lawless as a bird's song, yet, like a bird's song, obeying a law too subtle to be recognised.' Her lyrical gift was 'quite apart from intellectual strength'. He singled her sonnets out for particular praise, comparing her to Shakespeare and Matthew Arnold. Apart from the title poem, a rather pedantic and unwieldy children's verse tableau around the months of the year, which has rarely been performed, the centre piece of the volume is Christina's 'Monna Innominata' sonnet sequence, and the less favoured, but beautiful, sonnets from 'Later Life'.[7]

She felt that Hall Caine in the *Academy* had failed to understand her reference to Elizabeth Barrett Browning's *Sonnets from the Portuguese*, and her comments are a good example of hair splitting.

> surely not only what I meant to say, but what I do say is, not that the Lady of those sonnets is surpassable, but that a "Donna Innominata" by the same hand might well have been unsurpassable. The Lady in question, as she actually stands, I was not regarding as an 'innominata' at all – because the latter type, according to the traditional figures I had in view, is surrounded by unlike circumstances. I rather wonder that no one (so far as I know) ever hit on my semi historical argument before for such treatment – it seems to me so full of poetic suggestiveness.[8]

When a Mr Patchett Martin wrote an article in which he declared that Christina was a 'greater literary artist' than Elizabeth Barrett Browning, Christina wrote a letter of protest. 'I doubt whether the woman is born, or for many a long day, if ever, will be born, who will balance, not to say outweigh Mrs Browning'.[9]

Gabriel proved unable to read *A Pageant* when he received it, though he assured Christina that the parts he had looked at were 'full of beauties'. In his letter he drew Christina's attention to a new volume of poetry by Augusta Webster, declaring that it was written 'without vocation', like George Eliot's lyrics. Christina wrote back: 'I am not well versed in George Eliot as a bard, but feel inclined to rate Mrs Webster decidedly higher'.[10] Her antagonism to George Eliot was hardly surprising, since George Lewes had been previously married to the daughter of Swynfen Jarvis MP, whom Christina had coached in Italian. The Rossetti family were entirely on the side of the official Mrs Lewes.

Augusta Webster, seven years younger than Christina, had published several volumes of poetry and verse plays and, though never particularly popular, was admired by Browning. Her intellectual gifts were considerable – she spoke several languages, translated the classics, and wrote for *The Examiner*. Augusta sent Christina copies of her new *Book of Rhyme* and Christina returned the compliment with *A Pageant*. Augusta was a firm advocate of women's suffrage, a subject on which she had already written to Christina, the correspondence being referred to by her as a 'courteous tilt on the strong-minded woman lists'.

The subject of the Strong-minded Woman – contemporary slang for feminist – was very topical. Charlotte Yonge devoted a whole chapter of her book *Womankind*, published in 1876, to it. The strong-minded woman, according to Miss Yonge, was to men

> 'a laughing stock and a terror', for they 'vote her capital fun' and try how far she will go, but they do not respect her . . . When she has no beauty or charm, her pretensions make her merely obnoxious to them, and deprive her of that tender halo of sweet kindness and sympathy that attracts friendship and esteem.

In answer to the argument that 'to please men . . . is one of the most unworthy motives . . . to hold up to woman,' Miss Yonge replies: 'approbation is a standard by which to judge. That which a man could not tolerate in his sister or daughter is not becoming and is unsexing'.

The idea that women might be either physically or mentally superior, or even equal to men, Miss Yonge will not tolerate, and it is sad to find her advancing the old arguments. Physically, 'the man improves as he grows older . . . the woman's bloom is a much more fleeting thing'. And mentally 'where has the woman ever been found who produced any great and permanent work? What woman has written an oratorio, or an epic, or built a cathedral?'[11]

Though Augusta Webster and Barbara Bodichon were able to resist these arguments, Christina, with her mind so firmly rooted in the Bible, could not have done so without questioniong some of the very basic tenets of her faith. Her letters to Augusta on the subject show her struggling to present her feelings in a rational and logical framework.

You express yourself with such cordial openness that I feel encouraged to endeavour also after self-expression – no easy matter sometimes. I write as I am thinking and feeling, but I promise that I have not even to my own apprehension gone deep into the question; at least, not in the sense in which many who *have* studied it would require depth of me. In one sense I feel as if I had gone deep, for my objection seems to myself a fundamental one underlying the whole structure of female claims.

Does it not appear as if the Bible was based upon an understood unalterable distinction between men and women, their position, duties, privileges? Not arrogating to myself but most earnestly desiring to attain to the character of a humble orthodox Xtian, so it does appear to me; not merely under the Old but also under the New Dispensation. The fact of the Priesthood being exclusively man's, leaves me in no doubt that the highest functions are not in this world open to both sexes: and if not all then a selection must be made and a line drawn somewhere . . .

Many who have thought more and done much more than myself share your views, – and yet they are not mine. I do not think the present social movements tend on the whole to uphold Xtianity, or that the influence of some of our most prominent and gifted women is exerted in that direction: and thus thinking I cannot aim at "women's rights".[12]

Christina did not find it easy to contradict 'one I admire', but she refused to apologise for her convictions. It was sad that she could not feel, like Anne Gilchrist, that a new age was dawning for women. Anne wrote to William that 'Today is but the dawning of time for them, I am persuaded – hints of a future of undreamed of beauty and greatness, just beginning to disclose themselves, by and by to unfold into a Life Poem that will beggar all words.'[13]

Perversely, Christina supported the idea of female MPs

Also I take exceptions at the exclusion of married women from the suffrage, – for who so apt as Mothers – all previous arguments allowed for the moment – to protect the interests of themselves and of their offspring? I do think if anything ever does sweep away the barrier of sex, and makes the female not a giantess or a heroine, but at once and full grown a hero and a giant, it is that mighty maternal love which makes little birds and little beasts as well as little women matches for very big adversaries.[14]

In the autumn Gabriel was again deeply depressed and was persuaded to go to the Lake District, to Fisher Ghyll near Keswick in the company of Hall Caine and his mistress Fanny Cornforth. He found the mountains and the solitude unbearably depressing and came back on 17

October worse than before. Shortly after his return he suffered a paralytic attack in his left arm and leg.

His physicians tried to replace the chloral with morphine, and throughout December their notes tell a horrific story of repeated cycles of chloral, whisky and morphine, with intervals of restless sleep, nightmares and delusions. When awake he was haunted by guilt about past actions. The same religious straitjacket in which Christina had been reared acted on Gabriel's sensitive nature in much the same way, fostering a disproportionate sense of guilt. He felt remorse for his behaviour towards his father, his treatment of Lizzie, his mistresses and his adulterous love for Jane Morris (though she said afterwards that she had never 'quite given in' to him). He talked of confessing to a priest, and Christina wrote to him on 2 December

> I write because I cannot but write, for you are continually in my thoughts and always in my heart, much more in our Mother's who sends you her love and dear blessing.
>
> I want to assure you that, however harassed by memory or by anxiety you may be, I have (more or less) heretofore gone through the same ordeal. I have borne myself until I became unbearable to myself, and then I have found help in confession and absolution and spiritual counsel and relief inexpressible. Twice in my life I tried to suffice myself with measures short of this, but nothing would do . . . I ease my own heart by telling you all this, and I hope I do not weary yours. Don't think me merely as the younger sister whose glaring faults are known to you, but as a devoted friend also.[15]

It was rare for Christina to allude to what Gabriel had always humorously referred to as 'the skeletons of Christina's various closets'. In her concern for her brother she offered to send the Rev. Burrows, rector of Christ Church, her friend and religious mentor.

Christmas was very subdued. Christina declined Lucy and William's invitation to Christmas dinner because her mother did not feel up to it. 'Our party of old ladies', she wrote, 'will dine (D.V.) peacefully in company'. She adds that 'Tonight, (21 December) festivities receded into extra impossibility, for we have been seeing Gabriel, and have borne the shock of finding out the state he is in, laid up and partly powerless. God help us, for human help is a very helpless thing.'[16]

On medical advice Gabriel was sent down to Birchington on Sea in Kent where a bungalow had been rented for him. Christina and Mrs Rossetti would have liked to accompany him, but Mrs Rossetti was forbidden by her doctor to go until the weather had become warmer, and it was March before they travelled down. They were both disturbed by the deterioration in his condition since he had left London, and Christina sent William frank reports almost daily.

> This is all grievous for you to read, and I on the spot must write as I hear ... Mrs Abrey (the nurse) seems to fear that some deep-seated mischief may exist in the liver or what not, undermining the possibility of returning to health.[17]

> I think there are grounds to fear that some terrible mischief lurks in his constitution, and is (so to say) burrowing about him and checking any return of strength or revival of sensitiveness ... Pray do not doubt the *reality* of poor dear Gabriel's illness: do not let any theory or any opinion influence you to entertain such a doubt.[18]

Gabriel's friends Watts-Dunton, Hall Caine and Frederick Shields came down from time to time, sharing the burden with Christina and her mother. All tried to preserve as cheerful and normal an atmosphere as possible. Augustus Howell walked in unexpectedly one evening, looking even more rakish than usual, and amused Gabriel by telling him a fantastic story about having a commission to buy horses for the king of Portugal. No one believed him – but he was very entertaining.

Distressing news arrived for Christina from Bristol. Dora Greenwell, who had been much saddened by the recent death of her 'attached friend', died at her brother's home after a fall. She had been very despondent towards the end, summing up her life in a letter to a friend – 'one word would alone tell my story – inadequacy'.

While Christina was in Kent, J.H. Ingram, editor of a series of biographies of *Eminent Women*, approached her through William, to contribute a volume on Adelaide Proctor. Christina was pleased with the idea, but uncertain about the subject.

> Mrs Fry I would gladly try at, nor do I fancy I should find Lady Augusta Stanley insurmountable: I should decline the 2 Georges (Sands and Eliot) and prefer leaving Miss Martineau. Mary Lamb I should think would be both manageable and well worth writing. Meanwhile it strikes me that the very person to write A.A. Proctor would be not myself but Anna Mary Watts, who was in the heart of that social set, instead of (as I was) on its merest outskirts.[19]

Mary Lamb was eventually written by Anne Gilchrist, and Lucy took on Mary Shelley. Christina told Ingram that, although willing, in her present domestic circumstances it was impossible to begin work.

My absence from London puts me out of the way of books of reference such as of course would be essential to any practical attempt to ascertain whether I could meet your requirements: . . .

My response does not, I fear, read very promisingly, and pray feel no scruples at turning elsewhere. How long I shall continue in the country I have no means of foreseeing as my movements do not depend upon myself in this matter.[20]

By the end of March Gabriel was in a 'pitiable state' and a week later his doctor diagnosed kidney failure and advised Christina and her mother that the condition was fatal. William came down briefly on 1 April, returning to London on the following day to honour his commitments at the Inland Revenue. However, on the 6th Gabriel's condition was so alarming that Christina sent telegrams to William and Watts-Dunton. Lucy, who was visiting her father in Manchester, was summoned by William.

Christina sat up with Gabriel every night until dawn, though he was only semi-conscious. On Easter Sunday she missed Holy Communion in order to remain with him. He died at half past nine in the evening, surrounded by his friends and family.

The funeral at Birchington church, on a cold, flinty blue day, was very sparsely attended. Lucy arrived from Manchester only minutes after Gabriel died, and two days later Aunt Charlotte came down from London to keep her sister company. Mrs Rossetti had to be supported to the graveside by Christina and William. Hall Caine, Watts-Dunton and Shields were present, but none of the old Pre-Raphaelite Brotherhood. Hunt and Millais, Madox Brown, W.B. Scott, Edward Burne-Jones and William and Jane Morris, were all unable to attend, and Gabriel's mistress Fanny Cornforth was prevented by propriety from doing so.

Gabriel's grave was on rising ground looking out towards the sea. Christina gathered a bunch of woodspurge and forget-me-nots, and the family returned in the afternoon to pay their private respects and decorate the grave with flowers.

His will, drawn up only weeks earlier, left everything equally divided between William and Christina. However, Christina refused to be a beneficiary, arguing that her mother's name should have been in the will instead of hers. William explained Gabriel's practical reasons for leaving the money to her, but Christina was adamant, and the considerable bequest was paid to Frances Rossetti.

CHAPTER SIXTEEN

The months after Gabriel's death were spent arranging for a suitable memorial. Madox Brown was commissioned to design an Irish cross for the grave with a simple inscription, and Shields was asked to provide two stained glass panels for the church windows at Birchington. The first design submitted – from Gabriel's *Mary Magdalene at the Door of Simon the Pharisee* – was rejected and Shields suggested the Eve of the Passover instead. He worked from a drawing which Ruskin had given to the Ashmolean Museum in Oxford and his research was painstaking. He went to great lengths to discover the exact identity of the bitter herbs eaten at the Passover.

The other panel was to be one of Shields's own designs. Christina wrote in her letters to Shields of the difficulty in finding a subject which would express both 'the man and the work'. She suggested the Raising of the Widow of Nain's Son, which her mother had approved.

> We considered that as Baptism is 'a death unto sin, and a new birth unto righteousness', an instance of Resurrection might be viewed as typically appropriate to a Baptistry: while Gabriel (tho' not an only son) was a beloved, loving, conspicuous son of a widow, who cherishes among her dearest hopes that of receiving him back at the general Resurrection by the overflowing mercy of God.

Christina added, 'I tell you this so freely because you always invite confidence'. She was quick to offer Shields a generous advance and reassure him that the agreed price of £100 was not a fixed limit for the window. She asked him to send in an account straight away for final payment, as her mother, now, eighty-four, 'feels that today's duty had more than ever better be performed today and not postponed till tomorrow.'[1]

William was anxious that a biography of Gabriel should be written as soon as possible by someone close to the family and sympathetic to their wishes. He hoped that Theodore Watts-Dunton would undertake the task. William intended to compile a volume of Gabriel's letters to accompany the memoir. Christina spent hours helping her mother sort through Gabriel's letters, deciding what could be used and what should be suppressed. She wrote to Swinburne that her mother had twice broken down, while looking through the letters, overwhelmed by her loss. Christina carefully copied out those selected and sent the edited versions to William. However, the hoped-for biography from Watts-Dunton never materialised. When William tackled him on the subject he said that he considered it was better to wait until several people – among them Howell and W.B. Scott – were dead. Eventually William wrote the memoir himself.

In January 1883, one of William's twins, Michael, who was almost two, became seriously ill. As it became apparent that he was not going to survive, Christina begged William and Lucy to allow her to baptise him. It was part of her belief that baptism was 'the sole door I know of whereby entrance is promised into the happiness which eye has not seen nor ear heard, neither hath heart of man conceived.'[2] Without baptism, she believed, it was difficult for even a child to enter the kingdom of heaven.

William and Lucy discussed the matter and decided that it could do no harm, and would ease Christina's mind considerably. To her great relief she was able to baptise Michael privately – neither William nor Lucy were present. All three of them sat with the baby until he died. Lucy occupied the last hours making a beautiful, lifelike drawing of her son, which was even recognised by his twin sister. Michael was buried in his grandmother's grave at Highgate.

In February Charles Cayley, who was suffering from a heart condition, decided to put his affairs in order. He wrote to Christina asking if she would act as his literary executrix, and intimating that he would also like to leave his residual estate to her. Christina destroyed his letter, but its content can be deduced from her reply.

My Dear Old Friend,
I will not dwell too much on the sad possibility you hint to me, but rather will put forward – as I sincerely can – the apparently at least equal probability that I may become the leader and not the follower along that path. Nor will I care what are the steps so long as the goal is good. Nor will I despair of the good goal for either of us . . .

But, all else assumed as inevitable, I should value though I should not need a memorial. And three of the translations would be very dear: watching over them, I might in a measure nurse your name and fame. Yet, if you think any of your family could feel hurt, do not do it: very likely there was a moment when – and no wonder – those who loved you best thought very severely of me, and indeed I deserved severity at my own hands, – I never seemed to get much at yours. And some trifle that you had been fond of and perhaps had used would be precious to me.

Now let us suppose the reverse position, and let me explain my own plans. If my dearest Mother outlives me, everything I have (a mere trifle in all) goes to her: perhaps you may recollect my telling you that even now I am not so much as independent, so little indeed have I. Beyond this immediate vista, – William made me a home for so many years that (especially now that he has a young family) I am inclined to rate the money-portion of my debt to him at (say) £100 a year for 20 years: here at once is £2000! and far enough am I from possessing such a sum. Not that William puts forward any such view, but *I* entertain it all by myself. So, to sum up, you see I am an indefinite distance off from having much at my pure disposal. If I live long enough, that is if I survive certain members of my family, I believe I shall be amply provided for: but this is no contingency to count upon. I dare say you will trace, though I certainly have not stated, what sort of train of thought set me upon saying all this.

I hope you will enjoy the Ashburton MSS. If I had a little more energy I might seek to enjoy them too, but that seems too enterprising a possibility. My Dante article proceeds at the pace of a lag-last snail; perhaps it will reach the printing-office some day.[3]

The Dante article was 'Dante Illustrated out of his own Poem', one of two articles that Christina was commissioned to write, and which appeared in *The Century* in May 1884. The other was 'Dante – An English Classic', published in the *Churchman's Shilling Magazine* in 1867. Christina, like other members of her family, had been 'sucked into the Dantesque vortex'.

Early in 1883 John Ingram wrote again to William with a suggestion that Christina should write the life of Elizabeth Barrett Browning for his *Eminent Women* series. This was much more to Christina's taste than earlier proposals and she wrote back directly to Ingram.

My brother has showed me that obliging letter in which you express good will that I rather than some others should undertake a life of Mrs Browning. I should write with enthusiasm of that great poetess and (I believe) lovable woman, whom I was never, however, so fortunate as to meet. But before I could put pen to paper it would be necessary for me to know what would be Mr Browning's wish in the matter – and by his wish, whatever it might be, I should feel bound; both because he as her husband seems to me the one person entitled to decide how much or how little concerning her should during his lifetime be made public, and because having long enjoyed a slight degree of acquaintance with him I could not but defer to his wish.[4]

There seems to have been some reluctance on Browning's part to have details of his wife's private life exposed to public gaze. William doubted that his permission had ever been sought, but Christina's next letter to Ingram implies that it was not forthcoming. The difficulties that this created, and the ethical dilemmas, prompted Christina, after some thought, to refuse.

Do you know, I do not feel courage to embark on the memoir of E.B.B.; it seems to me clear that without Mr Browning's co-operation the thing cannot (at least during his lifetime) be thoroughly executed: besides which, I strongly sympathise with his reticence where one so near and dear to him is concerned.[5]

Ingram was still anxious to secure Christina for his series. He wrote the life of Elizabeth Barrett Browning himself and offered Christina Ann Radcliffe, whose gothic novels she had enjoyed so much when she was young. On 24 April 1883 she wrote to Ingram.

My brother tells me you are kindly thinking of me for Mrs Radcliffe. She takes my fancy more than many, altho' I know next to nothing about her. And I will try my pen upon her, if you please. Are any hopes to be indulged of private letters, journals, what not, becoming accessible to us? or must I depend exclusively on looking up my subject at the British Museum?[6]

The greatest obstacle where Mrs Radcliffe was concerned was the lack of material available. Apart from a short memoir appended to her collected works by Field Talfourd there was little to work from – no letters or journals as Christina had hoped. At Ingram's suggestion she put an advertisement in the *Athenaeum* seeking information, and wrote to Dr Richard Garnett at the British Museum. Despite many hours 'Radcliffising' in the library, Christina's enquiries yielded so little that she felt obliged to write to Ingram, withdrawing from the project.

Returned from the seaside I can only say I have done my best to collect
Radcliffe material and have failed. Someone else, I daresay, will gladly
attempt the memoir, but I despair and withdraw. Pray pardon me for
having kept you so long in suspense.

   Apologising for all that has been disappointment in my doings and not
doings.[7]

Christina carried on with her devotional prose works, putting the
finishing touches to *Letter and Spirit* – a study of the commandments,
dedicated once more to her mother. There were no poems in it.
Christina felt that the slackening of her poetic impulse was part of God's
will for her. 'I am not surprised to find myself unable to summon it at
will and use it according to my own choice'.[8] At this point in her life
God's will seemed to direct her towards prose. In a later work *Time Flies*
she described the difficulty of the task she felt had been set for one whose
work was largely inspirational.

   Supposing our duty of the moment is to write: why do we not write?
   Because we cannot summon up anything original, or striking, or
   picturesque, or eloquent, or brilliant.
   But is a subject set before us? It is.
   Do we understand it? Up to a certain point we do.
   Is it worthy of meditation? Yes and prayerfully.
   Is it worthy of exposition? Yes indeed.
   Why not begin?
   From pride and vainglory, Good Lord, deliver us.[9]

She confessed to Watts-Dunton that she found it difficult. 'I work at
prose and help myself forward with little bits of verse'.[10]

   In *Letter and Spirit*, published by the SPCK in 1883, Christina analyses
in detail the religious creed, essentially Anglo-Catholic, which ruled
every aspect of her life, including her art. It was not a creed of joy or
freedom, but one of restriction and suppression, an accumulation of
negatives

   The exceeding difficulty of laying a finger (so to say) on any distinct
   breach especially of the First Commandment sends us perforce to sift
   motives, gauge tendencies, test not conduct directly, but the standard
   which regulates conduct. Even virtues must be mistrusted; their root as
   well as their shoot must be examined . . .
      The First Commandment, being itself framed upon a Negative, invites
   us to study negatives in our search for perfection.[11]

Christina often found the path to salvation difficult. In *Called to be Saints* she describes how often it seems that

> Our yoke is uneasy and our burden unbearable, because our life is pared down and subdued and repressed to an intolerable level: and so in one moment every instinct of our whole self revolts against our lot . . .

Her reward for such repression and denial was to be in heaven, for there would be 'No lack there, nothing subdued there; no bridle, no curb, no self-sacrifice': only an 'outburst of sympathy, fullness of joy, pleasures for evermore, likeness that satisfieth; beauty for ashes, oil of joy for mourning, the garment of praise for the spirit of heaviness.'[12] She wrote to Frederick Shields that the sacrifice of human love was one of the things that had to be foregone for the love of God.

In June Swinburne sent Christina two copies of his *A Century of Roundels* – one for her and one for her mother – the dedication in the form of a roundel was to Christina. He urged her to visit the Channel Islands. Guernsey, he told her, had 'every loveliness and grandeur packed into it'.[13] Christina's mother was beyond such a long journey, and it was only the desire to revisit Gabriel's grave that enabled her to get as far as Birchington on Sea, where she and Christina spent their summer holiday. A nasty fall on the steps of the lodging house, which had no rail, left Mrs Rossetti badly shaken, and more determined than ever to go out as little as possible. Christina sometimes went out alone, and on at least one occasion she walked past the house where Gabriel had died – renamed Rossetti Bungalow – and stood for a while gazing into the garden.

While at Birchington Christina read the *Memoir of Emily Brontë*, the latest volume brought out by Ingram. Christina found it interesting but commented to William 'does it strike you as being, in the main, a memoir of Emily?' The author had obviously had difficulty collecting sufficient material about so private a character as Emily. The book is primarily about the Brontë family in which she figures as one of the characters. There is admiration for her poetry 'Songs . . . of defiance and mourning', but little sympathy with *Wuthering Heights* which the author presents as arising from a violent imagination and an experience 'limited and perverse', enlarged by Branwell's excesses.[14]

Frederick Shields had brought his wife to Birchington for her health, and Christina spent a lot of time searching out cheap lodgings for them – something she was very good at from long experience. However, they proved very hard to please, and moved to Margate, declaring Birchington was too noisy.

That summer, Christina found that she had reached a new plateau of acceptance and resignation, writing to Lucy that

> . . . it is such a triumph for *me* to attain to philosophic calm that, even if that subdued temper is applied by me without common sense, 'color che sanno' may still congratulate me on some sort of improvement! Ask William, who knew me in my early stormy days; he could a tale unfold – though indeed I am sorry to recollect how much you yourself have undergone from my irritability, and how much there is for you to bury in kind oblivion.[15]

She told another friend, Katharine Tynan Hinkson, that although she had been a very melancholy girl, she was now a very cheerful old woman.

1883 ended as it had begun, with a death. The morning after Christina's fifty-third birthday Charles Cayley was found dead in his bed, having died from heart failure in his sleep. Henrietta and Professor Arthur Cayley were summoned by the doctor and one of their first actions was to tell Christina, as soon as she came back from church where she had gone to hear the litany. She went with them to Cayley's rooms where he still lay as if asleep, and then she turned, as she always did, to her brother William, going straight round to his office at Somerset House to tell him. William said he could never forget 'the look on her face, and the strain of self-command in her voice; she did not break down'.[16] Christina went from the Inland Revenue to Covent Garden, where she bought a wreath of flowers to lay on the sheet that covered him.

Sophie Cayley, summoned by a telegram, telling her only that her brother's condition was very grave, wrote to Christina the following day.

> I came by the next train; but found, as I had dreaded all the way, it was only a preparation, as people kindly think. They found him dead in his bed, and the Doctor says he must have passed away, hours before, in his sleep. He looks beautifully calm and peaceful, and he is in God's all merciful and holy keeping. But it has been a terrible shock. Some time ago we were uneasy about his health, and tried to get him to come for a little change and nursing; but latterly we thought him better again, especially while my sister was in town. He has left you all his own works that are now at his publishers, and a large writing-desk, in which is an envelope with a letter of yours to him, and a ring: there is also a large packet of your letters. Would you like them returned? You were I know *the* friend he valued most.[17]

On 11 December the Cayleys invited Christina to spend the night with them in Hastings and accompany them to the funeral on the following day, but she refused, perhaps because she did not want to parade her grief in public. Mrs Rossetti sent a wreath and Christina a formal cross.

In No. 9 of her *Il Rosseggiar Dell' Oriente* poems, Christina had already faced the moment when death would separate her from the man she loved, and she had always hoped that Cayley would have a change of heart where faith was concerned, hoping that there would be a reunion after death.

> When the time comes for us to part,
> And each of us must go our separate way,
> The moment which must come, the last moment
>   Whenever it may
>
> When one of us must tread an unfamiliar path,
> The other following his usual course,
> Let no reproach suffuse our faces,
>   Let there be no remorse
>
> If you go first, alone and strong
> Or if I go before you on the path,
> Let us remember everything we said:
>   That it was always Truth.
>
> How much I loved you. Oh, how much!
> And could not show you what was in my heart,
> More, so much more than I could tell you
>   I loved with all my heart.
>
> Much more than happiness, much more than hope,
> I cannot say more than life – such a small thing.
> So bitter-sweet you are now to my fearful heart
>   Remembering.
>
> But you preferred integrity to me,
> The truth, my friend; and who can know aright
> Who you will love in the end; the flower blooms only
>   In the sun's light.

Professor Cayley wrote to Christina after the funeral to tell her that Charles had left her the remainder of all his books in print, published by Longman's. The books, which were warehoused, proved more of a liability than an asset; few of them were ever sold. There was also a much more personal bequest. As Sophie Cayley had mentioned, Christina was to have his 'best writing desk' and 'any packet that may be lying therein addressed to her'. The envelope contained a ring, and a letter she had once written to him. Whether it also contained a letter to her from Cayley to be read after his death cannot be determined.

Charles Cayley had kept all Christina's letters to him tied up in separate parcels, and these too were left to Christina 'to reclaim or order to be destroyed'.[18] She asked Professor Cayley to destroy them for her. Christina guarded her privacy very closely. When an application was made to her by the Rev. William Dorling, asking her to contribute to a memoir of Dora Greenwell, she refused, and would not allow her letters to Dora to be quoted, because, Dorling remarked, 'Miss Rossetti does not like accepting in public the very high praise of her own genius and poetry which Dora expresses in these letters.'[19]

Sophie had asked William to write an obituary on Cayley for the *Athenaeum* and he not only obliged, but also persuaded Madox Brown and his brother in law, Francis Hueffer, to contribute similar articles for other periodicals, in which the 'gentle scholar' was remembered with affection. Christina was deeply grateful and she wrote to William straight away to thank him. 'Mama and I are delighting – what a word! – in your article. She thinks it one of the best of the kind, if not the *best* she ever read. *I* cannot write about it.'[20]

In January 1884 she made a trip to Hastings, alone, to visit Cayley's grave, returning in the afternoon to avoid leaving her mother overnight. Shortly afterwards she revised a poem she had written in 1853, taking the best verse and writing another to precede it. The title 'One Sea-Side Grave' has sometimes been taken to refer to Gabriel's, but William connected it specifically with Cayley, and it is true that the timing seems to bear him out.

> Unmindful of the roses,
>   Unmindful of the thorn,
> A reaper tired reposes
>   Among his gathered corn:
>   So might I, till the morn!
>
> Cold as the cold Decembers,
>   Past as the days that set,
> While only one remembers
>   And all the rest forget, –
>   But one remembers yet.

Christina's poetic inspiration had almost completely dried up now, a source of regret to the public as well as to herself. Swinburne sent her a copy of *A Midsummer Holiday* which included a poem entitled 'A Ballad of Appeal', to Christina G. Rossetti. He asked her forgiveness for having taken a liberty 'in addressing you publicly without so much as a "*with* your leave" or "*by* your leave".' The poem begs that Christina produce more 'Sweet water from the well of song', and Swinburne added in his letter that it was 'but very little of all that one would like to say'.[21]

Christina replied, thanking him for 'so kind an estimate of me, however little I may justify it. Pray believe that dumbness is not my *choice*; nor will I attempt to justify it with the parrot who screamed "But I think the more". And perhaps I may safely add that no one is more pleased than I am when by fits and starts I become vocal.'[22] In these last, difficult years the wonder is not that she wrote so little poetry, but that she wrote at all.

Christina's prominence in the public mind as one of the greatest living poets, ranking with Tennyson and Browning, attracted many young admirers who wanted her opinion of their work and her advice. Christina did not welcome this attention and dreaded having to give an appraisal of their poetry. She found it impossible to be anything but honest and was aware how hurtful truth could be. Her nephew Ford Madox Ford told a story of a young poet who called on Christina in the hope of being able to show her his verses, which he had in his pocket. Christina, who knew him by repute, apparently detected the slim volume and subjected him to such an incisive attack on the defects of contemporary poetry that he did not dare to produce it. With William she was less restrained, commenting on another young poet 'I think him clever, but what is the use of *cleverness* in matters poetic.'[23]

In 1885 Katharine Tynan Hinkson a young Irish poet who had just published her first collection, came to see Christina after a short correspondence with William. She had called her book *Louise de la Valliere and Other Poems*, the title poem connecting with a poem of Christina's published in 1881 called 'Soeur Louise de la Misericorde', about Louise de la Valliere, mistress of Louis XIV, who became a nun. She sent a copy to Christina who wrote to Katharine after she had read the poems, expressing her 'sincere admiration of your poetic gift. But beyond all *gifts* I account *graces* and therefore the piety of your work fills me with hopes far beyond any to be raised by music of diction. If you have honoured my form by thinking it worth imitating, much more may I your spirit.'

Katharine was invited to tea – 'only please do not "interview" me. I own I feel this modern fashion highly distasteful, and am tenacious of my obscurity'.[24] After their first meeting, Christina commented that Katharine was 'an agreeable young woman enough, and deferential enough to puff me up like puff paste.'[25]

Katharine was initially disappointed by Christina, who appeared dressed in thick boots and a short grey skirt, 'garments fit for a ten mile walk over ploughed fields', and who was 'so much more brisk and cheerful than I expected'. She felt that Christina 'laid this cheerfulness on herself as a duty, thinking perhaps like Dante, that sadness was one of the sins. Cheerfulness in that house seemed a little discordant. Entering it you felt the presence of very old age, a silence that . . . was heavy and seemed to darken as well as to muffle sound.' The Aunts were not in evidence when she called, confined to their rooms by ill-health, but Mrs Rossetti was there, sitting in a high-backed chair beside the fire, and Katharine remembered the way she turned to her daughter 'laying a fine old hand on hers. "My affectionate Christina," she said.'

Once Mrs Rossetti had retired to her room for her afternoon rest the two women could talk more freely and Katharine was conscious of a lifting of constraint. They talked about Dante Gabriel and Elizabeth Siddal, and then, inevitably about books. Christina was particularly impressed with Alice Meynell's *Preludes*, her first volume of verse published in 1875. She lent Katharine Mrs Gaskell's *Cranford*, and Katharine remembered how she had laughed as she turned the pages over, re-reading 'bits she well knew and loved.' Katharine went away, 'uneasy because of her pretence of robustness, of brusquerie, almost'.[26]

A friendship slowly developed between the two, and they continued to correspond. Katharine described the days on which she received letters from Christina as 'white-stone days'. Christina sent her a copy of *Time Flies*, inscribed simply to Katharine Tynan. 'I have ventured to write in it your name without the formality of "Miss" – an omission I like towards myself often.'[27]

Katharine admired not only Christina's literary skill but also 'the strong spiritual beauty of the face her brother painted as the young Mary, predestined to superhuman sorrow. Her great, heavy-lidded eyes always seemed to me of peculiar significance.' She wanted to write an article about Christina and, although Christina would not refuse her friend permission, Katharine sensed a great reluctance on her behalf. Sitting on the hearthrug one sunny autumn afternoon, Katharine suddenly 'burst out in an assurance that I would write nothing.' Christina's relief was overwhelming. She told Katharine, 'I should not be myself . . . it is like sitting for a photograph, where one puts oneself in unnatural poses. I don't like the custom of interviewing, because it leads to self-consciousness, and the interviewed person is always turning out their best side for the public.' As Katharine was leaving she told her that 'When I am gone will be time enough.'[28] In accordance with her wishes Katharine's article was not published in *The Bookman* until after Christina's death.

In a later article for *The Bookman*, Katharine reveals that Christina had told her that she 'might have married two or three times', corroborating William's account of her love for James Collinson and Charles Cayley. The third party is tantalisingly anonymous, but possibly the 'John' whose attentions Christina found so irritating. Katharine summed up her own thoughts on Christina, who, she observed, was 'not Italian for nothing'.

> What on earth had she to do, this flame-hearted saint, with the grey streets of London, above all with Bloomsbury, more than all, with the Mid-Victorian or Early-Victorian woman she tried to look like? There was nothing at all of England in her way of loving, the mortal love, or the Divine Love.[29]

In the summer of 1884 Christina once more took her mother to Birchington, but the journey was almost too much for Mrs Rossetti. Difficulties with luggage, and the absence of a fly at the station to take them to their lodgings, taxed Christina's organisational abilities to the utmost. She wrote to William that they had thankfully been rescued by a clergyman who had managed everything for them and then come back to visit the following day with his wife and children. They stayed in Birchington long enough to see Shields's long-delayed window erected in the church and make final alterations to Gabriel's grave.

In February 1885 Lucy Rossetti became seriously ill with bronchial pneumonia, apparently caught when she got up in the night and went upstairs in her bare feet to comfort her daughter Helen who was crying. Lucy took a long time to recover, and the cough refused to go away. Doctors recommended sea air, and so she went first to Bournemouth and then to Ventnor on the Isle of Wight for a long holiday.

Christina was at work on *Time Flies*, a Christian reading diary, rather similar in format to the Friendship Books of Francis Gay. There is a thought, a poem or a prayer for each day of the year, sometimes focused on some historical figure – St Perpetua and St Etheldreda are two examples. Incidents in Christina's own life form a large part of the content. On 29 April she remembered going for a walk with a friend (Frederick Shields) at Birchington and discovering a funnel web in the hedgerow. In the early morning sunshine it was 'jewelled with dewdrops, and each of these at sunny moments a spark of light or a section of rainbow. Woven, too, as no man could weave it, fine and flexible, frail and tenacious.' Her meticulous observation leads inevitably to a moral.

> Yet are its beauties of brilliancy and colour no real part of it. The dew evaporates, the tints and sparkle vanish, the tenacity remains, and at the bottom of all lurks a spider.

Christina's didacticism is leavened with humour.

> It was once pointed out to me that in countenance a grey parrot and an elephant resemble each other . . . It is startling to reflect that you and I may be walking about unabashed and jaunty, whilst our fellows observe very queer likenesses amongst us.

The prose is interspersed with poetry, the first Christina had published for ten years. While some poems simply express pious platitudes there are odd lines that recall her earlier skill. 'Better than life's heaving heart is death's heart unheaving' is a line from 'If Love is Not Worth Loving', singled out for special mention by the critics. The dominant sentiment is summed up in the epigraph to 13 April – 'Endure Hardness', and its accompanying verses.

> A cold wind stirs the blackthorn
>   To burgeon and to blow,
> Besprinkling half-green hedges
>   With flakes and sprays of snow.
>
> Thro' coldness and thro' keenness,
>   Dear hearts, take comfort so:
> Somewhere or other doubtless
>   These make the blackthorn blow.

Only by believing this could Christina keep going. She approached Frederick Shields to design the cover for *Time Flies*, but he was too ill to do so. She also solicited his support for a petition against a proposed Institute of Preventive Medicine, where tests and experiments would take place on animals.

Christina took up another cause that summer, signing a petition to raise the age of consent to sixteen. Public feeling had been stirred up by an article in *The Pall Mall Gazette* which described how children of poor or destitute parents were often sold into prostitution. Christina had not been able to visit the Institution at Highgate for some years, because of the weight of her domestic duties, but this was a campaign which had her full support.

W.B. Scott had a heart attack in 1885. Christina went round to the house to comfort Laetitia, but found only Scott and Alice Boyd. Shortly afterwards Alice took Scott to Penkill where she nursed him lovingly until he died. Christina was obviously fond of Scott, writing him playful verses on his birthday – some of them jointly to Scott and Alice Boyd. Though one of them refers to 'My old admiration before I was twenty', none of them exhibit more than Christina's normal expressions of affection to her friends – they are certainly less openly loving than her letters to Frederick Shields.

As Lucy was still at Ventnor, William spent Christmas with his mother and aunts at Torrington Square, and Christina commented in her letters that it had given them all great pleasure to have him back in the family circle in his old familiar place. For William it was less pleasant. He had been separated from his wife and children for months and did not know when they would be reunited.

It was an unusually cold winter and there were riots and civil unrest among the unemployed – some of whom were destitute. Christina wrote to Lucy that 'it is heart sickening to think of the terrible want of work – and want of all things at our very doors – we so comfortable'. Christina saw emigration as the only answer.[30]

In February Mrs Rossetti fell in the bedroom, even though Christina was with her. She hurt her back and had to be confined to bed. Christina tried to get an All Saints nurse but there were none available. However, she was very pleased with Annie Jackson who nursed Mrs Rossetti devotedly. Aunt Charlotte was also in bed, attended by Mrs Abrey who had nursed Gabriel, and William thought she would never get out of bed again. Mrs Rossetti's condition steadily deteriorated. Christina wrote to Shields to thank him for his concern for her mother. She hoped that his wife's health would improve, adding that 'for me there is no earthly hope'.[31] On 8 April, almost four years to the day since Gabriel's death, Mrs Rossetti died peacefully, having been unconscious for some time. Christina recorded the moment in her mother's diary, which she had been keeping ever since her mother became too weak to write. The last entry reads

I Christina G. Rossetti, happy and unhappy daughter of so dear a saint, write the last words. Not till half an hour after noon on April 8 (Thursday) did my dearest mother cease from suffering, though for a considerable time it had (I am assured) been unconscious suffering . . . William, Nurse Annie Jackson, Harriet and I watched by her on and off the last sad night. At the moment of death William, Nurse, Mr Stewart and I were present . . . My beautiful mother looked beautiful after death, so contented as almost to have an expression of pleasure. I had her dressed in the 'widow's cap' she has worn more than 30 years.[32]

CHAPTER SEVENTEEN

Christina wrote to Lucy at Ventnor to inform her of Mrs Rossetti's death, adding sadly, 'It has become a different world since last I wrote to you'. William thought that Christina saw their mother's death as 'the practical close of her own life . . . All that remained for her was religious resignation for a sorrowful interval and a looking forward to the end'.[1] Financially now she was secure, since under Mrs Rossetti's will she inherited around £4,000 – some of it from Gabriel's estate. As she had intimated to Charles Cayley she felt morally obliged to regard £2,000 of that money as William's. She explained her feelings in a letter to Lucy.

> Love and thanks, my dear Sister, for all you have felt and expressed for us: I can still say 'us' and look forward to the end of our separation. But please do not fancy me bearing this bitter trial so much better than I really am bearing it. It has been a comfort to see William, though now I rejoice that he is going to have a reviving time at Ventnor . . .
>
> Did William tell you of a conversation we had? – when I said that I hoped finally to leave at least as much as £2000 to him. I have long felt in his debt for all those years when his munificent affection provided me with a most ungrudged home, and he and we all think that, if we loosely compute this debt as for 20 years at £100 a year, I shall pay the *money* in full; and *love* can only be repaid in kind, – he moreover never till I talked to him viewed it as money-indebtedness. Now I particularly want you to know all this, because, if I were so unhappy as to lose my dear William, I should (so far as I foresee at present) feel that his claim lapses in full to yourself or to the children . . .
>
> Sympathy has flowed in from very different quarters, and I like to see the love and high honour in which my dearest Mother was held. High and low have shown kindness. After speaking separately to each of my Aunts I find it is the preference of both that I should continue to make my home with them, and thus it is settled.[2]

Christina's position was unenviable. She described herself to Watts-Dunton as living 'in a circle of the absent, who inhabit either this world or the next'.[3] Aunt Charlotte was bedridden and required constant nursing. Aunt Eliza, though physically stronger, became increasingly infirm mentally with what appears to have been senile dementia. Aunt Charlotte, whom William summed up as a very ordinary lady in every respect, also became treacherously unreliable in mind towards the end. Something of Christina's restricted existence is reflected in William's diary entry for 4 October 1886. 'Christina dined with us – an incident perhaps unprecedented these four years.'

Her nephew Ford Madox Ford (born Ford Madox Hueffer, the son of Lucy's sister and her husband Francis Hueffer) visited her occasionally and later recalled his impressions.

> I do not know that in her drawing room in the gloomy London square Christina Rossetti found life in any way ennobling or inspiring. She must have found it if not exceedingly tragic, at least so full of pain as to be almost beyond supporting. Her poetry is very full of a passionate yearning for the country, yet there in box-like rooms she lived, her windows brushed by the leaves, her rooms rendered dark by the shade of those black-limbed London trees that are like a grim mockery of their green-boled sisters of the open country.

Ford described her sitting in black, outwardly calm, her hands folded in her lap, her head a little on one side, expressing herself with absolute precision, but inside undergoing 'always a fierce struggle between the pagan desire for life, the light of the sun and love, and an ascetism that in its almost more than Calvanistic restraint, reached also to a point of frenzy.'[4]

She wrote affectionate letters to Ford, addressing him as a relative, though scrupulously pointing out in parenthesis that he was actually only a 'connection' by marriage.

In these circumstances it was not surprising that Christina's health suffered. By January 1887 she was consulting Sir William Jenner again and he diagnosed angina. He sent her to Torquay for a much-needed holiday. She was, she wrote to William 'not conspicuously in bloom, but let us hope I resemble the trampled camomile which "yields more sweets the while".'[5] Christina took her niece Olive with her for the first time, and the experiment does not seem to have been a success. She told William that she was very concerned to see traces of a jealous disposition in Olive, though neither William nor Lucy felt there was any foundation for such a suspicion at all.

Lucy, whose health had also deteriorated as TB invaded her damaged lungs, was at San Remo, where William joined her for a brief visit. Her prolonged convalescence had put a strain not only on their relationship but on William's finances. Christina found herself in the pleasant position of being able to make a gift of £100 to Lucy towards her expenses, tactfully explaining that her mother had intended to leave such a sum to Lucy in her will. While William was there, an earthquake shook the Riviera causing a great deal of damage and loss of life. San Remo escaped lightly, but because of the risk of after shocks William and Lucy had to spend the next day and night out of doors in the chill February weather. Christina was very concerned when she read of the news in England and wrote immediately to try to discover whether they had been affected.

In March she was back in London in what she referred to as her 'proper place'. She told William not to feel sorry for her.

> Please do not say 'The Grapes are sour'! Beautiful, delightful, noble, memorable, as is the world you and yours frequent – I yet am well content in my shady crevice, which crevice enjoys the unique advantage of being to my certain knowledge the place assigned me. And in my small way I have my small interests and small pleasures![6]

Among these interests was her charity work. Ellen Procter, who later wrote a memoir of Christina, met her at the Factory Girls Club in London Street – a project in which Walter Besant (Annie's brother-in-law) was also involved. It was run primarily for the match girls of Bryant and May, but other factory girls from the East End also came along, 'ropemakers, satchel makers, jam makers.' Apparently Christina got on much better with these teenage girls than she did with children. Christina told Ellen that she would have liked to be more involved with the running of the club, but that her nursing duties wouldn't allow it – her aunts could only be left for short periods.

Christina's enforced isolation increased her shyness and, without her mother to bolster her courage, she found social events more and more trying. She doubted whether friends and family wanted her company. This was particularly so with her sister-in-law. One note reads

> My dear Lucy, William asked me to dine with you next Thursday – shall I come? I know that at times with the kindest goodwill one guest more is one too many, and I shall not doubt your kindness if you frankly tell me it is not convenient.[7]

Unused to visiting alone, Christina found it an ordeal. At one of Lucy's 'at homes' she couldn't bring herself to re-enter the room to say goodbye. She tried to explain to William

> Please give my love to Lucy; and explain that I was on my way to say goodbye when the door at which I was presenting myself shut, and shut me out: I dare say she detects that I am still sufficiently shy to lose heart under such a rebuff. The 'at home' seemed to me very successful, and I only regret not having had a glimpse of your library. What a beautiful stair carpet![8]

Her diffidence and constant need for reassurance must have been irritating for Lucy, and magnified the coolness that existed towards Christina. There were added burdens on William – Christina poured out all her affection on him, relying on his visits in a way that must at times have been onerous.

> Padrone! Questa tua casa!
> You are welcome on the most *cupboard love* terms, always and every way welcome. You shall have a cup of tea, and I will show you a book or two if you care to look at them . . . Why not always come here on Shelley (society) nights?
> Your affectionate old sister[9]

It saddened Christina that though she could share so much with her brother, she could not share the only really important thing – her faith. 'It seems unnatural to love you so much and yet never say one word about matters which colour my life.'[10]

It was with William that she discussed Emily Dickinson's poems which had just been sent to her from America after their publication in 1890. 'She *had* (for she is dead) a wonderfully Blakean gift, but therewithal a startling recklessness of poetic ways and means'.[11] Emily Dickinson's collection suffered, as Christina's would, from the posthumous editing of her relatives and friends. They altered her rhymes, her punctuation and her line arrangements – occasionally inserting different metaphors to 'regularise' Emily's poetry. It was this first, mutilated edition that Christina read and, despite the alterations, its publication was a literary event of great significance. Of Christina's generation Jean Ingelow was still alive, but her *Collected Poems* in 1885 had been received without enthusiasm, and since the death of her favourite brother (to whom she had dedicated all her work) she was so shattered in health that she no longer wrote.

Christina was, despite the many interruptions and hindrances she suffered, at work on another devotional book *The Face of The Deep*, which took her seven years to write. It was a meditation on the Book of Revelation, and the study of its uncompromising and often terrifying vision of the day of judgement seems to have affected Christina's fragile equilibrium. She wrote to William 'Perhaps you do already – but if not and if you would not think it wrong, I wish you would sometimes pray for me that I may not, after having (in a sense) preached to others, be myself a castaway.'[12]

Religious doubt tortured her – what if she had not been good enough, denied herself enough? Past sins and misdemeanours haunted her consciousness. She wrote to William to correct an impression she had given him about the time she spent on morning prayer. It was not half an hour, she told him, but rather less. 'This has justly worried me, as the inaccuracy told in my own favour'. The fires of hell seemed very real to Christina. In *The Face of the Deep* she wrote of her hopes for salvation.

> Even if in this and in much beside I be mistaken, I hope to be held at least in some degree excused. For not (please God) as counting error do I err, but rather as seeing very darkly through my glass.[13]

She hoped through her study of Revelation to find patience, but in the meantime she endured. 'Hourly, momently, there come to me mercies or chastisements', and the picture she gives of her life is bleak.

> I have witnessed tears, death, sorrow, crying, pain. God grant that I may witness the general and particular abolition of all these when Death shall at length be swallowed up in Victory:[14]

The struggle to hold on to her faith was at times almost too much. In this disjointed passage from *The Face of the Deep* nothing has been omitted – the punctuation is Christina's own.

> So long as I live I must, I cannot but, resist, wrestle with somewhat . . . Evil or good, Satan or Christ, I am resisting, I am setting myself against. To fight against Satan is to engage on my side the Stronger than he. To fight against Christ . . . Dear Lord, by Thy mercies, Thy compassions, boundless compassions, mercies innumerable, keep me, keep all from ever knowing what it is to fight against Thee.[15]

Ford Madox Ford observed that 'It has always seemed to me to be a condemnation of Christianity that it should have let such a fate harass such a woman'.[16]

The close of the book is typical of Christina's extreme diffidence towards the end of her life. 'If I have been overbold in attempting such a work as this I beg pardon'.

Aunt Charlotte died in 1890 after being bedridden for more than three years. She left two-thirds of her money to Christina on the understanding that she would continue certain charitable benefactions that Charlotte had been in the habit of making. These included several distant and impecunious Polidori relatives and William disapproved of Christina's continued largesse. After Charlotte's death the lease of the house in Endsleigh Gardens devolved on William and he had the pleasure at last of living in his own house rent-free. However, when Lucy returned from the Mediterranean in 1889 she had made up her mind to move further out of central London to a more elevated position above the winter smog. Although William was very reluctant to move, Lucy's stronger will prevailed and she took the lease of a house next door to her father in Primrose Hill.

Lucy, through the Nineteenth Century Building Society, entered into a novel arrangement whereby after a number of years the lease of the house would become hers. William was put in the position of paying the rent to Lucy, who then paid it to the Society in effect to buy the house for herself. He also had the inconvenience of having to travel twice as far to work. But it was healthier and quieter, and both Lucy and the children enjoyed being so close to Madox Brown. His wife Emma died shortly after they moved in and Lucy was able to oversee both households. Lucy's biography of Mary Wollstonecraft Shelley, which she had struggled to complete despite ill health, finally appeared in 1890.

W.B. Scott died in November, and although Christina mentioned the fact in her letters there is nothing more than regret at the loss of an old friend. She had not heard much from 'the dear old Scotts' for some years.[17] Scott's memoirs in the form of *Autobiographical Notes* were published two years later, considerably edited, and were found to contain several passages about the Rossettis which William found offensive, particularly his attitude to Gabriel. Christina, warned by William, refused to read them, preferring to keep her charitable memories of Scott intact. She is scarcely mentioned in the text apart from a description of Scott's first impression of her at the age of seventeen.

This, and the fact that large parts of his diary were burned, added fuel to L.M. Packer's premise that there had been a love affair between them. However, if Christina had figured very little in Scott's life except as the friend of his wife and sister of Gabriel, there would be little to record about her, and Scott's frank record of his relationships with Alice Boyd and Pauline Trevelyan would have been reason enough to burn his diaries.

That Scott had another secret relationship seems likely. But the tantalising *Poems to Mignon* are quite clearly not written to Christina Rossetti. One of them is entitled 'A Compliment to Mignon Singing' and Mignon's songs are referred to elsewhere. Christina didn't sing, and there is no indication that 'song' could be read as a metaphor for poetry. They are poems written by a man in the city to a woman in the country, (Christina was at that time in London) and they specifically mention Wetherall in the north of England. There is also much word-play on the word 'May' in the poems ('Lady-girl, Mignon, May') suggesting that this could have been her name.

Towards the end of 1891 Christina became aware that her general ill-health had a more specific focus. Consultations with Dr Stewart who had replaced Sir William Jenner as her chief physician revealed that she had cancer of the breast. She was examined by Mr Lawson, a surgeon, who confirmed the diagnosis. Not until the end of May, when an operation to remove the breast had been decided upon, did Christina tell William. She wrote to him on the 20 May, 'At last it seems that something brooding in my health has reached a point demanding sharp treatment'.[18] To Lucy in Bournemouth she was rather more eloquent.

> As to pain, I have felt none worth speaking of, but it seems that it would not be prudent so to trust to this merciful circumstance as to neglect the step now to be taken, and about which I expect to know nothing under the influence of ether ... We are keeping this anxiety from Aunt Eliza ...[19]

Anticipating public curiosity about her condition Christina felt that the best course was to be absolutely frank, and she authorised William to tell the press exactly what was wrong with her.

On 25 May Lawson operated. William was there in the house, where everything was being kept as normal as possible for Aunt Eliza's sake. He recorded in his diary that 'With deep thankfulness I can say that as yet all seems to go on perfectly and even surprisingly well. The future cannot but remain overcast; ... Christina has borne herself like a heroine in this matter.' He called again three days later and saw Christina for twenty minutes – 'She is placid and comparatively comfortable – free from positive pain, allowing for a certain, not quite easy sensation in the left shoulder.'[20] The surgeon hoped that the operation had cured her and told William that the future prognosis was good. For Christina such optimism was misplaced. When Stewart told her that she might well live to be eighty, she wrote to Lucy that she did not 'run up like quicksilver at the announcement'.[21]

At the end of June Dr Stewart sent Christina to Brighton to convalesce, accompanied by William, and she wrote a grateful letter to Lucy thanking her for allowing him to be with her. Christina's health continued to be precarious and in September, back in London, she was still confined to the sofa in the drawing-room. When William called to see her, the maid Harriet Read, who was nursing her, followed him downstairs and confided that the doctor had left a special message for him 'to the effect that the condition of Christina's heart is such as to give cause for grave apprehensions, and one ought to be prepared for whatever may happen.'[22] The painter G.F. Watts wanted to paint Christina's portrait as a gift to the nation but she was not well enough to sit for it.

In the autumn *The Face of the Deep* was published and generally well received. However, a review in *The Rock* suggested that Christina deliberately refrained from making her verses as good as they could be as an exercise in self-denial. She wrote indignantly to William that 'neither as praise nor as blame do I deserve the imputation'.[23] Yet the reviewer was more perceptive than he knew – identifying the conflict between the pursuit of literary excellence and spiritual excellence that lay at the roots of Christina's work. She had, during the second half of her life, consistently put her faith first, and this entailed denying herself, putting herself in second place, sublimating her own wishes and desires to what she believed was the will of God. Her imagination and emotions were restricted and her poetry suffered.

Christina's need to love and be loved in her final years was focused on a young poet called Lisa Wilson. Lisa was still alive in 1932 and told Christina's biographer Mary F. Sandars that she had first written to Christina 'as a very invalidish girl, obliged to lie down a great deal, to thank her for her poems which I had had given to me, and which I loved and admired at once.'

Christina destroyed Lisa's letters to her, as she habitually did all her correspondence, and Christina's letters to Lisa were (according to Helen and Olive Rossetti) burned when Lisa died. M.F. Sandars was however privileged to see some of them. In response to a request to call on Christina to collect a copy of *Time Flies* which she had offered her, Christina wrote 'fetch if it you like, but don't expect me to be as nice as my poems, or you will be disappointed.' Lisa was, on the contrary

immediately attracted to her and later described her as 'my dearest
friend and spiritual mother'.[24]

   Lisa's visits gave Christina considerable pleasure. She nicknamed her
'Fior de Lisa' – the Italian equivalent of the Fleur de Lys and wrote a
poem for her in 1892 connecting both the rose and the lily motifs.

> The Rose is Love's own flower, and Loves no less
> The Lily's tenderness.
> Then half their dignity must Roses yield
> To Lilies of the Field?
> Nay, diverse notes make up true harmony;
> All-fashioned Loves agree;
> Love wears the Lily's whiteness and Love glows
> In the deep-hearted Rose.

She also entertained the young MacKenzie Bell, whom she met through
her parish priest, and he wrote her first biography in 1895. He recalled
her asking him when he first called: 'Perhaps you go into the country in
August to kill something?' and her pleasure when he replied 'I never go
into the country to kill anything'. MacKenzie Bell never forgot his first
impression of Christina. Like Edmund Gosse, he found her formidable.

> . . . demurely attired in a black silk dress she wore no ornaments of any
> sort, and the prevailing sombre tint was only relieved by some simple
> white frilling at the throat and wrists. Her hair, still abundant, had by
> this time a hue which was almost black, and the intermingled grey
> strands, though visible, were not conspicuous. Her cap of some dark
> material, was extremely plain and unobtrusive.
> . . . She gave me the impression of being tall: I thought then, as I do still,
> that none of her portraits sufficiently indicate the commanding breadth
> of her brow. She looked unquestionably a woman of genius.[25]

She was quick to pounce on generalities in conversation. Her nephew
Ford Madox Ford told her that a 'great many people' had told him that
they would like to see her as Poet Laureate after Tennyson's death. She
grilled him thoroughly until he admitted that the actual number who
had mentioned her name could not have been more than eight or nine.
Jean Ingelow's name was also put forward to the Queen as a possible
candidate. Christina was horrified at the suggestion that she herself
might be considered, and told Ford that she would never consent.

   In the spring of 1893 the doctors had to tell Christina that the cancer
had recurred, and this time there was no possibility of an operation. It

spread to the chest wall and then to the lungs and her left arm was swollen with fluid. Christina took the news with fortitude and told William that she was not in any *severe* pain. For William it was particularly sad. Lucy had begun coughing significant quantities of blood in November of the previous year, revealing that the tuberculosis was now in its final stages. On 3 October she left England with her three daughters, Olive, Helen and Mary, for Italy in order to prolong her life as long as possible. William's grief at the prospect of losing the two people closest to him was sharpened by a change in Lucy's attitude to him throughout 1893. He attributed her hostility and aversion – what he called the 'swerve in her feelings' – to her illness.

Aunt Eliza died in June, to the great relief of the family, and once more Christina was a beneficiary. Having never earned more than thirty or forty pounds a year in her life, Christina now possessed a substantial fortune. She made a new will, making William her only heir, apart from a few charitable bequests. In addition she gave William some of the shares left to her by Aunt Eliza, doubling in value his small legacy.

Her new affluence and her charitable disposition made her vulnerable to predators. She was taken in by a man who wrote to her for help. When she responded to his request by sending a letter and a small donation William discovered that he was selling her letters to an autograph dealer. William wrote to ask him to desist, but discovered that his own letter had also been sold. Another supplicant, Mr Gringer, had eventually to be referred to Watts-Dunton, and Christina felt herself unable to help his wife and son, who wrote pitiful letters complaining of his ill-treatment.

In October, shortly after Lucy had left for Italy, Madox Brown – whose health had always been good – suffered a stroke and died suddenly. William and Christina were afraid that the shock of the news would prove fatal to Lucy, who was now very ill at Pallanza on the shores of Lake Maggiore. Letters were written, first telling her that he was ill, then that his condition had worsened, and then finally breaking the news that he was dead. Christina was deeply saddened as she had known Madox Brown since she was in her teens, and she remembered his kindness to her and her family, in particular his support for her brother Gabriel.

After Christmas Lucy's condition became critical. William was unable to leave his post at the Inland Revenue, and Christina, despite her own poor health, offered to travel out with a nurse, or to pay for Lucy's own doctor to be sent. This proved impractical, but Christina did give William expenses for his own journey, which he made in March, in response to a telegram from San Remo, where Lucy was staying. He travelled with his son Arthur and they were afraid that they would be too late. Lucy lingered on, kept alive by her will-power and energy, but eventually died on 12 April.

Christina wrote to William expressing her love for him and her deep regret. Charles Cayley's niece and nephew had called, she told him, to pay their respects, and to bring flowers from Professor Cayley's wife. When Lucy's will was opened it was discovered that all her property, including the house they were living in, had been left to the children. A portrait of herself by Dante Gabriel was the only thing she left to William, and he was in the ignominious position of being a guest in his own home. Christina was angry at Lucy's hurtful action, and wrote to William offering any assistance that he might need, and reminding him that after her death he would be financially secure.

1893 saw the last of Christina's publications. The SPCK brought out a collection of devotional *Verses* – poetry that had previously appeared in her prose works. The effort of copying them out for publication was very tiring, and William felt that she should have allowed the publishers to do it. But she explained that it gave her satisfaction and that, after all, she had nothing else to fill her time. The volume included some of her best poems, the carols 'In the Bleak Midwinter' and 'Love Came Down at Christmas', sonnets including 'Lord grant me Grace to Love Thee in My Pain', earlier poems such as 'The World' and the incomparable 'Passing Away'. Christina offered to dedicate the volume to William, but he pointed out how inappropriate it would be in view of his atheism. When the SPCK sent her the money for the volume and royalties for *The Face of The Deep* Christina returned them as a gesture of protest against the SPCK's publication of a book which appeared to countenance vivisection.

Christina offered to share a house with William, partly to free him from his predicament and partly because she was finding the Torrington Square house much too large for her. She now occupied only the drawing-room floor and she would have liked to exchange its gloomy emptiness for something smaller and more cheerful. However, the doctors told her that she must not consider a move in her present state of health, and the idea was dropped. MacKenzie Bell visited her on a sultry summer afternoon and remarked on the airlessness of the room, despite the windows being thrown open, and the noise of the square with not less than three organ grinders audible – which he found oppressive, though Christina reassured him that she was used to it.

Throughout 1894 she became increasingly ill, and by August could no longer go to church. The Rev. Nash called twice a week to give her communion and talk to her, and William came almost every day. A less welcome visitor was the Rev. Charles Gutch of St Cyprians. William felt that his uncompromising and gloomy view of Christianity, far from comforting Christina, only depressed her and increased her morbid fears for her own salvation.

A bed was moved from the back bedroom to the drawing-room, and from September Christina rarely left it. She took great comfort from the fact that it was the bed her mother had died in. Her cough was very troublesome and at times she was in severe pain – the gripping spasms of advanced cancer – which the increasingly large doses of opiate, prescribed by the doctors, failed to quell entirely. She told MacKenzie Bell 'I have to suffer so *very* much'.

Among the manuscripts at the University of British Columbia is a letter from Christina's neighbour, a young woman with small children trying to earn her living by literature, who complains that she is being disturbed by long sessions of screaming. These are 'particularly distressing' between eight and eleven o'clock in the evening. She adds 'I have a strong suspicion that her screams occur when she is left alone . . . I would have been glad if I could have *helped*; but to sit alone and listen to cries one cannot soothe is distracting'. There was some suggestion by Christina's doctors that the screams were hysterical in origin, but William was indignant at the idea.

Whether Christina's agony was physical or mental, or a combination of both, her sufferings were extreme. William described her state of mind as gloomy and her expectations of salvation almost nil. 'Some of her utterances being deeply painful . . . The fires of hell seemed more realistic than the blessings of heaven.'[26] Christina's sonnet No. 27 from 'Later Life' written more than twelve years earlier was prophetic.

> I have dreamed of Death:- what will it be to die
>   Not in a dream, but in the literal truth,
>   With all Death's adjuncts ghastly and uncouth,
> The pang that is the last and the last sigh?
> Too dulled, it may be, for a last good-bye,
>   Too comfortless for any one to soothe,
>   A helpless charmless spectacle of ruth
> Through long last hours, so long while yet they fly.
> So long to those who hopeless in their fear
>   Watch the slow breath and look for what they dread:
> While I supine with ears that cease to hear,

> With eyes that glaze, with heart-pulse running down
>   (Alas! no saint rejoicing on her bed),
> May miss the goal at last, may miss a crown.

She had hallucinations brought on by the drugs and the brandy ordered by her doctors and brought in – she told William with a smile – 'by the case'. Christina was aware that her mind was not always under control, asking William on one occasion whether the animal she could see on the sheets really was there, or was only an apparition. At other times her mind was crystal clear, and she would talk lucidly to William about old times. She was plagued, as Gabriel had been, by irrational guilt. She begged William's forgiveness for a paint box she had promised him as a child and then not given, and then again because at one point he had told her not to see anyone and she had entertained Charles Cayley to lunch. More than once she talked about Cayley and how much she had loved him 'in terms of almost passionate intensity'.[27]

Almost her last communication was with Frederick Shields, a fervent expression of her affection for him and his wife and how much his friendship had meant for her. His drawing of the Good Shepherd was hung on the wall opposite her bed where she could look at it constantly.

By November she was too weak even to listen to the Bible being read to her. She worried about her cat Muff, a half Persian of tremendous character, who had sat on Christina's desk while she wrote and travelled around the house on her shoulders. William had promised to take one of her kittens, and agreed to take Muff after her death. He asked Christina if she would like to have the cat on her bed, but she was too exhausted for that and acknowledged that she had probably seen her for the last time. For several days she drifted in and out of consciousness, no longer in any pain, too weak to communicate, but apparently able to understand what was said to her. She died at 7.25 on the morning of Saturday 29 December, when only Harriet Read was present. William came immediately to say his own private farewell, and later MacKenzie Bell called and was allowed to see her.

Snow fell on the night before her funeral and the ground at Highgate was white. The service was held at Christ Church, Woburn Square, conducted by the Rev. Nash, and it was very well attended. Musical settings of some of Christina's poems were sung by the choir, and the hymns 'O Rest in the Lord' and 'Abide With Me'. It was a dignified and joyful service. The ceremony at Highgate was strictly private. William and his children, MacKenzie Bell and Lisa Wilson were present together with Harriet Read and other Rossetti servants.

MacKenzie Bell described the scene.

> A sprinkling of snow had remained on the ground, and, as the closing
> words of the burial service were being read by Mr Nash, the winter
> sunshine, gleaming through the leafless branches of some trees to the
> right, revealed in all their delicate tracery, while a robin sang.[28]

The plain stone, angled at the base of the monument erected to her
parents, bore the inscription William felt best suited to celebrate her life,
a verse from her poem 'The Lowest Place'

> Give me the lowest place: or if for me
>   That lowest place too high, make one more low
> Where I may sit and see
>   My God and love Thee so.

A memorial service was held at Christ Church which was packed
with people for whom Christina's poetry had been a living force.
Many had found comfort in her expressions of faith and joy through
suffering. Among her friends, Swinburne felt the loss keenly. He
allowed William to dedicate Christina's posthumous *New Poems* to
him, and wrote a long eulogy on her death, which, despite his
atheism, hints at the possibility of life after death.

> Not here, not here shall the carol of joy grown strong
> Ring rapture now, and uplift us, a spell struck throng,
> From dream to vision of life that the soul may see
> By death's grace only, if death do its trust no wrong.[29]

CHAPTER EIGHTEEN

William wrote in *Some Reminiscences*, 'Christina Rossetti has passed away; personally known to few, understood by still fewer, silent to almost all.' Christina's determination to destroy all personal material, her intense privacy (confiding her feelings to no one), presented contemporaries, and subsequently biographers, with a problem. Even her nieces, Olivia Rossetti Agresti and Helen Rossetti Angeli, admitted that her true nature was 'difficult to get at'. Apart from her surviving letters and poetry the main source of information comes from the recollections of friends, acquaintances and relatives.

Christina's death was followed by a succession of memoirs by those who had known her, and it is difficult to estimate the accuracy of some of these recollections, coloured as they were by personal bias. Christina's own reclusiveness spawned many apocryphal stories. Mrs Virtue Tebbs told of an 'at home' where her poetry was under discussion. At a particular point in the conversation a small woman dressed in black stepped forward into the middle of the room and said 'I am Christina Rossetti', before sitting down again. The story was told at second hand by a friend of Mrs Tebbs and is so out of character that it must be treated with caution. Perhaps more reliable is the story recounted by Katharine Tynan that Christina would pick up pieces of paper in the street in case they had the name of Jesus printed on them.

The general tone of the memoirs and articles printed immediately after Christina's death was one of reverence. She became 'Saint Christina'. The *Daily News* in its obituary made the comment that 'Her noblest books were those books without words that she lived'. Like most women writers of the period she suffered from the conflation of her life and her poetry. Watts-Dunton in his article for the *Athenaeum* wrote that 'It was the beauty of her life that made her personal influence so great, and upon no one was that influence exercised with more strength than upon her illustrious brother Gabriel'. In all her obituaries her submission and self-sacrifice, her denial of 'the egoism of the artist' was approved, because it fitted so well with Victorian ideals of womanhood.

An article on Jean Ingelow after her death states that 'it is impossible for the thoughtful to overlook the lesson that the lives of women like Jean Ingelow and Mrs Oliphant and Christina Rossetti ought to impress upon women of today.' It goes on to talk about 'the simplicity, the refinement, the purity' of their work, and commends them because they 'claimed no "rights", stirred up the muddy depths of no turbulent passions and emotions, struck no keynotes, sounded no discords, avoided all forms of advertisement'. It also made it difficult for women seeking to break the mould to look on them as literary precedents. The critical assessment constrained Christina and Jean Ingelow within the mould and tried to constrain critical thought in a similar manner, often substituting the moral value of their work for its literary value. Had their work been as flaccid as the critic suggested, it would not have survived, nor would it have deserved to.

The image of Saint Christina, the ideal daughter and sister, caring for her parents and brothers, shedding light upon their lives, blots out the passionate angry woman whose self-sacrifice was achieved only through great suffering and the denial of her sexuality. MacKenzie Bell's reverential biography published in 1898 scarcely mentions James Collinson or Charles Cayley. Christina exists only in the context of her family and her work. But, however interesting Christina's 'life poem' may be to subsequent curious generations, it is in the end the poetry that matters, standing apart, by itself, telling its own story. The importance of this 'other story' was stressed by Dora Greenwell in her essay 'Our Single Women'. 'It is surely singular that woman, bound ... to a certain suppression in all that relates to personal feeling, should attain in print, to the fearless, uncompromising sincerity she misses in real life'.

William, as the only surviving member of the Rossetti family, took it upon himself to edit Christina's letters and poetry, as he had previously done for Gabriel, and he wrote a short memoir to accompany the collected edition of her poems. Although usually honest in what he says, William does not always tell the whole truth – he was after all, writing within the constraints of the time. He regarded the 'true and rightful principles in biography', as sympathy and truth. 'The portrait presented should be a consciously favourable one ... as far as candour will allow'[2] and this has to be borne in mind when reading his account of Christina's life.

In 1896, surprised by the quantity of unpublished work he found after her death, William published a volume of 233 *New Poems*. This attracted the adverse criticism that he had 'raked together all that (he) could find, however indifferent in several instances and presented all to the public, who would gladly have dispensed with many'.[3] The standard of *New Poems* is variable, and it includes poems which Christina had judged not up to her usual standard as well as many which were too personal to publish. Among the best belonging to the latter category were 'A Pause', 'Long Looked For', 'Introspective', 'The Heart Knoweth Its Own Bitterness', 'Today and Tomorrow' and 'By Way of Remembrance'. The others are interesting because they show her development as a poet and the directions that her mind took from time to time.

William published a *Collected Edition* of her poetry in 1904 prefaced by a memoir and, though this does not include all her poems, it is still the most comprehensive edition of her work available to the general public. (A complete edition is under preparation in the USA.) It includes her juvenilia and all but seventy of her manuscript poems. Much of the typography is William's own, his preference being 'for a fully applied system of indenting', although he admits that his own system is difficult to apply to Christina's poetry because of her variation of metre and line length. William had reluctantly to abandon its 'fully uniform application' in many instances where the poem's rhyme schemes would not conform to his plan. Even in this small way Christina's poetry refuses to conform to the constraints and limitations of others. But, more significantly, William also felt free to alter words in some of the poems – passion in one case becomes pathos – to tone down the sensuality which is one of the strongest characteristics of her poetry, but which seemed inappropriate to her brother. Similar problems beset both Emily Brontë and Emily Dickinson, whose work was subjected to posthumous editing by their families. Charlotte even admitted to destroying some of Emily Brontë's pieces, and inserted two stanzas into 'The Prisoner' in the 1850 edition of Emily's poetry.

Most of the criticism of *New Poems* was directed at William as editor, for resurrecting what Christina had deemed unfit for publication. For Christina herself there was what MacKenzie Bell described as an 'outburst of eulogy', which was, nevertheless qualified by gender. Andrew Lang in the *Cosmopolitan Magazine* wrote that 'There can be little doubt that we are now deprived of the greatest English poet of the sex which is made to inspire poetry rather than create it'.[4] The powerful and disturbing effect her poetry had on the reader gave rise to extravagant claims for her genius. Sir Walter Raleigh thought her the greatest poet of his time. Of her inspiration, Watts-Dunton wrote in the *Athenaeum*, 'It seemed to me to come from a power which my soul remembered in some ante-natal existence and had not even yet wholly forgotten'.

Other critics were more restrained. Arthur Benson in the *National Review* identified the element of dream-thought in her poetry – the vivid internal landscapes she delineates with an artist's eye.

> Some writers have the power of creating a species of aerial landscape in the minds of their readers, often vague and shadowy, not obtruding itself strongly upon the consciousness, but forming a quiet background, like a scenery of portraits, in which the action of the lyric, or the sonnet seems to lie. I am not now speaking of pictorial writing, which definitely aims at producing, with more or less vividness, a house, a park, a valley, but of lyrics and poems of pure thought and feeling, which have none the less a haunting sense of locality, in which the mood dreams itself out.[5]

William Rossetti thought that Christina was unrivalled in her ability to fuse 'the thought into the image, and the image into the thought.' Another critic identified 'sincerity as the servant of a finely touched and exceptionally *seeing* nature,' while others commented on her 'stern philosophy of life'.[6]

It was inevitable that there should be a backlash. Some was personal – a reaction to Saint Christina. Violet Hunt (who was Ford Madox Ford's mistress) described her as uncongenial and sharp-tongued, focusing on her reclusive last years and her astringency. From a literary point of view a new generation of poets was emerging, headed by Yeats and Eliot. T.S. Eliot's definition of Modernism distinguished personal emotion from literary emotion, the former being of little interest to the reader, and this new view excluded women like Christina and Elizabeth Barrett Browning for the very emotional directness which is one of the strengths of their work. Christina was criticised (in common with other women writers) for narrowness of range, and the monotony of a single emotional key. Ford Madox Ford, himself an established literary figure by the time he wrote about his aunt, defended her, writing that she was the poet of suffering, and 'suffering is a thing of all ages'.

But to identify Christina only as the poet of suffering neglects the many other poems she wrote in a mood of ecstasy, and which form a large part of her work. Her poetry covers the whole range of human emotion and much of it is universal and timeless. Charles Sisson remarks, in his preface to her *Selected Poems* in 1984, that 'human emotions persist through all the changes of circumstance and ideology'. He describes her work as 'controlled and passionate', and grants her 'complete mastery' within the parameters she set for herself. The qualities which, above all others, have enabled her poetry to live are her simplicity and directness. There is no veil of metaphor between the poet and the reader, and her language is strong and uncluttered – the thought never obscured by unnecessary adjectives or adverbs or by an excess of emotion. Unlike Dora Greenwell, Jean Ingelow and – often – Elizabeth Barrett Browning, the 'I' of the poem is usually the poet herself. Jean Ingelow writes in the third person, or hides behind a masculine 'I', even when she writes the telling verse

> O, let me be myself! But where, O where,
> Under this heap of precedent, this mound
> Of Customs, modes, and maxims, cumbrance rare,
> Shall the Myself be found?[7]

she is writing in the person of a male poet/scholar in search of success. Christina's 'presence' in her poetry, her direct address to the mind of the reader, is what marks her poetry out from that of her contemporaries.

Although Christina has also been admired by poets such as Basil Bunting, Philip Larkin and Elizabeth Jennings, her work has not found favour with twentieth-century academic critics. Her influence on Swinburne and Hopkins, acknowledged at the time, has been largely ignored. The *Pelican Guide to English Literature*, widely used in literary studies, contains an essay on Pre-Raphaelite poetry which discusses Dante Gabriel and Christina Rossetti, and William Morris. The 'chief critical attention' is given to Dante Gabriel, though his poetry is apparently, when compared to Christina's, over-sophisticated, artificial, lush and mannered. Christina's poetry 'never' has these defects, but

It is significant that one finds oneself appraising her work in these negative terms. For negation, denial, deprivation are the characteristic notes of Christina's religious poetry: and it must be admitted that an extensive reading of it is depressing. The sadness, often morbidity, which is felt even in her delightful poetry for children, even in *Goblin Market*, certainly in *The Prince's Progress*; the felt absence of any outlet for aggressive impulses, deepening into depression or resignation; the compensating yearning for death imagined as an anodyne, an eternal anaesthetic – these are familiar to every reader of her poetry. And it is difficult to find many poems in which she either transcends them or turns them into the conditions for major creation.[8]

W. Robson does go as far as to admit 'a certain community of temperament' between Christina's 'Spring Quiet' and Gerard Manley Hopkins 'Heaven-Haven'. The only poems considered in the essay are 'A Pause', praised for 'simplicity and naturalness' and 'exquisite good taste and spiritual good manners', and the 'Sonnet' – 'Remember me when I am gone away' which is unfavourably compared to Shakespeare's 71st sonnet. Christina's exhibits 'shy reserve, tenderness and wistfulness', lacks argument and seems 'if not mawkish, a little *mièvre*'. He goes on to observe that 'the comparison with Shakespeare's sonnet leads us to call the other sonnet, with a limiting intention "feminine": in the absence of the verve and chargedness there is felt to be a thinness, a lack of substance'.

However, Christina is commended because her poetry lacks the 'sonorous and vatic manner, at one and the same time declamatory and embarrassingly intimate' which W. Robson suggests mars the work of Elizabeth Barrett Browning. There are echoes of the Jean Ingelow article in Robson's comment that, despite the fact that Christina's poetry is 'deprived, depressed and monotonous' it is redeemed by the fact that she can be called 'a lady' and that 'this will be understood to have no implications of snobbery'.[9]

This analysis explains why Christina's reputation grew after her death, at the expense of Elizabeth Barrett Browning's. The latter's work was seen as active and vigorous, having an intellectual muscularity which strove to be masculine in character – what Dante Gabriel had referred to as 'falsetto muscularity'. Christina's was seen as essentially feminine, i.e. passive and non-intellectual and therefore better because it did not seek to stray outside the territory allotted to women. Female poets were caught in a double bind: if they were 'feminine' they were praised, but this quality excluded them from comparison with their male counterparts on an equal footing; if they were seen as 'unfeminine', like Elizabeth Barrett Browning, they were condemned for unsuccessfully trying to imitate men. In either case, because of this gendering, their work 'failed' when the male critical standard was applied to it. It is only in the second half of the twentieth century, with the emergence of feminist literary criticism and new critical theories from France, that the work of women like Christina Rossetti has been rediscovered.

It was Christina's lyricism that attracted Virginia Woolf, whose keen ear for the music of words delighted in poems such as 'When I am Dead My Dearest' and 'A Birthday', which induced in her a sense of abandonment and rapture. The same quality led composers such as Gustav Holst, Vaughan Williams and Delius to set her poetry to music.

Virginia Woolf predicted that we would still be singing 'My heart is like a singing bird' when Torrington Square was 'a reef of coral, perhaps, and the fishes shoot in and out' of Christina's bedroom window.[10]

The American writer Willa Cather was in general very critical of other women. In an essay published in the *Nebraska State Journal* in 1895 she assessed Christina's poetry as being neither 'vital nor potent enough to greatly influence or guide the poets of the future, nor fervid and impassioned enough to claim immortality'. She thought that Christina had not been given the 'divine fire' in large enough measure, 'only a spark which wasted the body and burnt out the soul', ignoring the fact that it is an uncontrolled blaze which consumes – the spark merely singes. Paradoxically, like other Americans, she was enthusiastic about Christina's religious poetry, admitting that 'she wrote with the mystic enraptured faith of Cassandra, which is a sort of spiritual ecstasy, and which is to the soul what passion is to the heart.'[11]

Whatever her public opinion of Christina's poetry, Willa Cather was irresistibly drawn to 'Goblin Market', its ambiguity perhaps mirroring her own, and a quotation from the poem is used as an epigraph for her volume of short stories called *The Troll Garden*, where the dominant theme is the enjoyment of forbidden fruit which often proves fatal. The heroine of 'Death in the Desert' wastes away and dies, like Jeanie – here there is no possible redemption. The characters live in that wild country inhabited by Goblins that exists beyond the walls of well-ordered Victorian gardens. Nothing is safe. Beauty corrupts, and art is dangerous. For those who wish to enjoy the troll garden there are considerable risks and a price to be paid for freedom.

Modern feminist scholarship has placed Christina's poetry firmly within the 'aesthetics of renunciation', to quote Gilbert and Gubar in *The Madwoman in the Attic*, and has focused on the subversive elements in 'Goblin Market' and in her earlier poetry where her articulation of the struggle for a voice within a creed which consistently denied it to her, and a self-hood which at the same time must be self-less, articulates the central conflict of the woman writer in the nineteenth century. This conflict was intensified for Christina by her faith. Dora Greenwell stated that her own aim was to 'bring her external existence into harmony with her inner life'.[12] In Christina's case this was achieved at the expense of her inner life; it was the external existence of religious ritual, conformity and submission that won. Germaine Greer in a 1975 edition of *Goblin Market*, asserted that Christina was 'appalled by the uncontrollable violence of her own nature' and suppressed her emotions, using her 'piety as a metaphor for her own frustrated sexuality'.[13]

In her poem 'The Lowest Room', which Gabriel Rossetti thought too like Elizabeth Barrett Browning in style, one sister questions a woman's lot, after reading Homer.

> Too short a century of dreams
> One day of work sufficient length;
> Why should not you, why should not I,
> Attain heroic strength?
>
> Our life is given us as a blank;
> Ourselves must make it blest or curst:
> Who dooms me I shall only be
> The second, not the first?

She is rebuked by her younger sister, who reminds her that their lives are ruled by Christ and not the classical values of Homer. Like Christina the 'I' of the poem finds the resignation of all ambition hard to achieve.

> Not to be first: how hard to learn
> That lifelong lesson of the past,
> Line graven on line and stroke on stroke
> But thank God learned at last.

Worldly ambition has been denied for heavenly reward, for after death 'the last shall be first'. It was Christina's final hope.

> Yea, sometimes still I lift my heart
> To the Archangelic trumpet-burst,
> When all deep secrets shall be shown,
> And many last be first.

She saw herself as a broken bowl to be remade in the heavenly fire into a golden chalice – 'A royal cup for Him, my King'. Even her art had to be refashioned to meet what she thought was the will of God. Joy, passion, sensuality, despair and stoical resolve give way to devotion, strained patience and resignation. There is nothing in her later poetry to equal the passionate vision of mystical union with Christ portrayed in 'Passing Away'. The last poem she wrote, shortly before she died and found by William Rossetti among her papers, views death, not as a triumph, but as a release.

Sleeping at last, the trouble and tumult over,
Sleeping at last, the struggle and horror past,
Cold and white, out of sight of friend and of lover,
Sleeping at last.

No more a tired heart downcast or overcast,
No more pangs that wring or shifting fears that hover,
Sleeping at last in a dreamless sleep locked fast.

Fast asleep. Singing birds in their leafy cover
Cannot wake her, nor shake her the gusty blast.
Under the purple thyme and the purple clover
Sleeping at last.

REFERENCES

CHAPTER ONE

1. Willa Cather *Nebraska State Journal* 13.1.1895
2. Theodore Watts-Dunton *Athenaeum* 5.1.1895 pp 16–18
3. William M. Rossetti *Some Reminiscences* London 1906
4. Ibid
5. *Poetical Works of Christina Rossetti* with Memoir ed. William M. Rossetti Macmillan, 1904
6. Edmund Gosse *Critical Kit-Kats* London 1896
7. *Some Reminiscences*
8. *Critical Kit-Kats*
9. *Poetical Works*

CHAPTER TWO

1. C.R. *Poetical Works* Enrica
2. C.R. *Verses* 1847
3. Elizabeth Barrett Browning *Aurora Leigh* Book I p. 379
4. Ibid p. 389
5. C.R. *Poetical Works* A Royal Princess
6. Alice Meynell *The Colour of Life and Other Essays* London 1896
7. C.R. *Poetical Works* The Convent Threshold
8. Mrs Gaskell *Wives and Daughters* Ch. 11, 1906 edition
9. *Dante Gabriel Rossetti: Family Letters* with Memoir ed. William M. Rossetti
10. C.R. *Poetical Works*
11. Quoted in *Christina Rossetti* by MacKenzie Bell 1897
12. Bodleian MSS Notebook No. 1.
13. Caroline Norton (1808–1877) was the granddaughter of the playwright Richard Brinsley Sheridan. She made an early disastrous marriage to the Hon. George Norton which ended in separation after violent episodes. Her husband kidnapped the children and she did not see them again for some years. She supported herself by writing poetry, novels and articles for literary journals, and was rumoured to have had affairs with Lord Melbourne and Sidney Herbert. She used her political influence to secure reform of the marriage laws and the laws of child custody. She

was at the centre of a major political scandal and George Meredith used her story for his novel *Diana of the Crossways*.

14. For a fuller discussion of hysteria see Elaine Showalter, *The Female Malady* Virago 1987

15. Ashley MSS British Library 1386

16. C.R. *Verses* 1847

17. *Family Letters of Christina Rossetti* ed. William M. Rossetti 1908

CHAPTER THREE

1. W.B. Scott *Autobiographical Notes* ed. W. Minto London 1892
2. Holman Hunt *Pre-Raphaelitism and the Pre-Raphaelite Brotherhood* London 1905
3. Ibid
4. Ibid
5. Ibid
6. D.G.R. *Family Letters*
7. Holman Hunt *Pre-Raphaelitism* etc
8. C.R. *Poetical Works*
9. Leslie Parris, *Pre-Raphaelite Papers* p. 64 London 1984
10. C.R. *Family Letters* 23.11.1848

CHAPTER FOUR

1. C.R. *Maude* London 1897
2. *Christina Rossetti: Selected Poems* ed. C.H. Sisson, Carcanet 1984
3. C.R. *Poetical Works*
4. C.R. *Family Letters* August 1849
5. Ibid 31.8.1849
6. Ibid 19.9.1849
7. Ibid 26.9.1849
8. C.R. *Poetical Works*
9. Ibid

CHAPTER FIVE

1. C.R. *Family Letters* 8.8.1850
2. Ibid 14.8.1850
3. Ibid 3.9.1850
4. D.G.R. *Family Letters*
5. Ibid
6. C.R. *Family Letters* July 1851
7. Ibid 4.8.1852
8. Ibid 28.4.1853
9. D.G.R. *Family Letters*
10. Watts-Dunton *Athenaeum* 5.1.1895 p. 16
11. D.G.R. *Family Letters*

CHAPTER SIX

1. D.G.R. *Family Letters* 28.3.1854
2. C.R. *Poetical Works*
3. Ibid

4. Emily Brontë *How Long will you Remain . . .*
5. *Poetical Works* – notes by W.M.R.
6. D.G.R. *Family Letters:* E. Gosse *A.C. Swinburne*
7. C.R. *Time Flies* 22 August 1885 SPCK
8. *Some Reminiscences*
9. *Family Letters* C.R. 13.11.1854

CHAPTER SEVEN

1. Edmund Gosse *Critical Kit-Kats*
2. Dora Greenwell *North British Review* February 1862
3. W.M.R. Notes to *Poetical Works of Christina Rossetti*
4. L.E. Landon *Stanzas on the Death of Mrs Hemans*
5. W.M.R. *Poetical Works of Christina Rossetti*
6. Ibid Notes to p. 335
7. Family Letters p. 98
8. Max Beerbohm *Rossetti and His Circle* London 1922
9. D.G.R. *Family Letters* with Memoir
10. W. Dorling *Dora Greenwell: A Memoir* London 1885
11. W.B. Scott *Autobiographical Notes*
12. Alice Meynell *The New Review* February 1895
13. Gerard Manley Hopkins
14. D.G.R. *Family Letters* with Memoir
15. Alice Meynell *The New Review*

CHAPTER EIGHT

1. W.M.R. Notes to *The Poetical Works of Christina Rossetti*
2. C.M. Bowra *The Romantic Imagination*
3. Edmund Gosse *The Life of A.G. Swinburne*
4. Edmund Gosse *Critical Kit-Kats*
5. Maureen Duffy *The Erotic World of Faery* London 1972
6. St John's Gospel Ch.6, v.54
7. MacKenzie Bell *Christina Rossetti* p. 207
8. W.M.R. *Poetical Works of C.R.* Notes to p. 375

CHAPTER NINE

1. C.R. *Time Flies* London 1885
2. D.G. R. *Family Letters* with Memoir
3. T. Hall Caine *Recollections of D.G.R.* London 1882
4. W.M.R. *Some Reminiscences*
5. British Columbia MSS 30.11.1860 C.R. to W.M.R.
6. Edmund Gosse *The Life of A.G. Swinburne*
7. C.R. *Family Letters*
8. Ashley MSS British Library
9. Ford Madox Ford *Ancient Lights* London 1911
10. C.R. *Family Letters*
11. *Rossetti-Macmillan Letters*
12. A. Cayley to C.R. *Family Letters*
13. C.R. *Family Letters*

14. Helen Rossetti Angeli, *Rossetti: His Friends and His Enemies* London 1949
15. T. Hall Caine *Recollections of D.G.R.*
16. Ibid
17. D.G.R. *Family Letters* with Memoir
18. H. Gilchrist *Anne Gilchrist: Her Life and Writings* London 1887
19. Edmund Gosse *Life of A.C. Swinburne*
20. Trevelyan MSS University of Newcastle upon Tyne
21. C.R. *Family Letters. British Quarterly*, July 1862
22. *Emily Dickinson: The Complete Poems* ed. T.H. Johnson, Faber & Faber London 1970. Nos. 430, 512, 646.

CHAPTER TEN

1. Edmund Gosse *Critical Kit-Kats*
2. C.R. *Poetical Works* p. 58
3. W. Dorling *Dora Greenwell: A Memoir*
4. C.R. *The House of D.G.R.* Literary Opinion 1892
5. D.G.R. *Family Letters* with Memoir
6. C.R. *Family Letters*
7. Grace Gilchrist *Good Words* December 1896
8. C.R. *Family Letters*
9. Edmund Gosse *Critical Kit-Kats*
10. W.M.R. *Rossetti Papers* see also the *Troxell Letters*
11. *The Times* 22 August 1863
12. Ashley MSS British Library
13. C.R. *Family Letters* British Columbia MSS
14. *Athenaeum* 7.8.1897
15. Alice Meynell *Jean Ingelow*
16. H. Gilchrist *Anne Gilchrist: Her Life and Writings*
17. *Athenaeum* 7.8.1897
18. Elizabeth Barrett Browning *Aurora Leigh* Book I
19. *Fraser's Magazine* 18.8.1864
20. C.R. *Family Letters*
21. Ibid
22. British Columbia MSS

CHAPTER ELEVEN

1. C.R. *Family Letters*
2. Ibid
3. Ibid
4. Ibid
5. W.M.R. *Rossetti Papers*
6. British Columbia MSS
7. C.R. *Poetical Works Later Life*, No. 22
8. C.R. *Time Flies* 14 June
9. W.M.R. *Some Reminiscences*
10. C.R. *Poetical Works Later Life* No. 21
11. C.R. *Time Flies*
12. W.M.R. *Some Reminiscences*

13. MacKenzie Bell *Christina Rossetti*
14. *C.R. Family Letters*
15. *Rossetti–Macmillan Letters*
16. H. Gilchrist *Anne Gilchrist: Her Life and Writings*
17. *C.R. Poetical Works* Notes
18. British Columbia MSS 1869
19. Ibid
20. MacKenzie Bell *Christina Rossetti*
21. *C.R. Poetical Works* Song, p. 382
22. *C.R. Seek and Find* 1879 pp. 32/3
23. *C.R. Family Letters* 11.9.1866
24. British Columbia MSS
25. *C.R. Poetical Works* Monna Innominata No. 11
26. British Columbia MSS

CHAPTER TWELVE

1. *The Diary of William Allingham* London 1907
2. W. Dorling *Dora Greenwell: A Memoir*
3. Edmund Gosse *Critical Kit-Kats*
4. Max Beerbohm *Rossetti and His Circle*
5. *Critical Kit-Kats*
6. *C.R. Letter and Spirit* 1883
7. *Critical Kit-Kats*
8. *W.M.R. Some Reminiscences.* Walt Whitman's *Poems Selected and Edited by W.M. Rossetti* (based on the 1856 and 1860 editions) was published in London in 1868.
9. H. Gilchrist *Anne Gilchrist: Her Life and Writings.* Letters from Anne Gilchrist to William Rossetti were published in 1870 as *A Woman's Estimate of Walt Whitman.*
10. Ashley MSS British Library
11. W.B. Scott *Autobiographical Notes* Vol. II p. 200
12. Ashley MSS British Library
13. British Columbia MSS
14. *Blackwood's Magazine* August 1871
15. Ford Madox Ford *Ancient Lights* London 1911
16. *Anne Gilchrist: Her Life and Writings*
17. *C.R. Family Letters*
18. British Library Ashley MSS
19. D.G.R. *Family Letters* with Memoir Oct. 1871
20. W.M.R. Diary – from C.R. *Family Letters*
21. *C.R. Family Letters*
22 D.G.R. *Family Letters* with Memoir
23. Ibid
24. *C.R. Family Letters*

CHAPTER THIRTEEN

1. *Women Reading Women's Writing* ed. Sue Roe Harvester 1987
2. *The Pelican Guide to English Literature* Vol. 6 1958
3. *Athenaeum* 7.8.1897 'A Poetic Trio'
4. Theodore Watts-Dunton, *Athenaeum* 5.1.1895

5. W.M.R. *Some Reminiscences* Vol. II
6. C.R. *Family Letters* 10.7.1873
7. Ibid. July 1873
8. Ibid. 5.11.1873
9. *Rossetti–Macmillan Letters*
10. C.R. *Letter and Spirit* p. 101
11. *Rossetti–Macmillan Letters*
12. D.G.R. *Family Letters* with Memoir
13. W.M.R. *Some Reminiscences*
14. Ibid. Vol. II, pp. 432/3
15. W. Dorling *Dora Greenwell: A Memoir*
16. *The Academy* 6.12.1875
17. *Athenaeum* 27.12.1874
18. C.R. *Family Letters*
19. Ibid. August 1874
20. Ibid. 14.12.1875
21. Ibid. 22.12.1875
22. Ibid. July 1876
23. Ibid. July 1876
24. Ibid. September 1876
25. C.R. *Time Flies* 7 November

CHAPTER FOURTEEN

1. C.R. *Family Letters*
2. Ibid. ?12.3.1877
3. C.R. *The Face of The Deep* 1892 p. 536
4. C.R *Family Letters* 6.8.1877
5. Ibid. 5.8.1877
6. MacKenzie Bell *Christina Rossetti*
7. C.R. *Family Letters* 30.8.1877
8. Ibid. 1877
9. Ibid. 11.10.1877
10. W.M.R. Memoir from *The Poetical Works of C.G.R.*
11. C.R. *Family Letters* June 1878
12. Ibid. 17.12.1879
13. Ibid. 25.7.1879
14. British Library Additional MSS
15. C.G.R. *Family Letters* 21.10.79
16. Ibid. 20.7.1880
17. Ibid. February 1878
18. Ibid. September 1880
19. Ibid. 6.9.1880
20. *Troxell Letters* 1878
21. MacKenzie Bell *Christina Rossetti* p. 105

CHAPTER FIFTEEN

1. C.R. *Family Letters* 1.1.1881
2. C.R. *Called to Be Saints* 1881 pp. 148/9

3. Ibid. *All Saints*
4. *Rossetti–Macmillan Letters*
5. C.R. *Family Letters* 26.7.1881
6. Ibid. 4.8.1881
7. *Athenaeum* 10.9.1881
8. C.R. *Family Letters* 5.9.1881
9. MacKenzie Bell *Christina Rossetti* p. 92
10. C.R. *Family Letters* 9.8.1881
11. Charlotte Yonge *Womankind* London 1876
12. MacKenzie Bell *Christina Rossetti* p. 111/2
13. H. Gilchrist *Anne Gilchrist: Her Life and Writings*
14. MacKenzie Bell *Christina Rossetti* p. 112
15. C.R. *Family Letters* 2.12.1881
16. Ibid. 21.12.1881
17. Ibid. 8.3.1882
18. Ibid. 14.3.1881
19. MacKenzie Bell *Christina Rossetti* p. 89
20. Ibid.

CHAPTER SIXTEEN

1. MacKenzie Bell *Christina Rossetti* p. 98
2. C.R. *Family Letters* 1883
3. Ibid. 26.2.1883
4. MacKenzie Bell *Christina Rossetti* p. 90
5. Ibid. p. 91
6. Ibid.
7. Ibid. p. 92
8. Ibid. p. 88
9. C.R. *Time Flies* 27 January
10. Ashley MSS British Library 1386 7 1886
11. C.R. *Letter and Spirit* 1883 p. 27
12. C.R. *Called to be Saints* 1881 p. 435
13. C.G.R. *Family Letters*
14. A. Mary F. Robinson *Emily Brontë* W.H. Allen 1883
15. C.R. *Family Letters* 24.8.1883
16. W.M.R. *Some Reminiscences* Vol. II
17. C.R. *Family Letters* 7.12.1883
18. Ibid.
19. W. Dorling *Dora Greenwell: A Memoir*
20. C.R. *Family Letters* 15.12.1883
21. Ibid. 17.11.1884
22. Ashley MSS British Library 1386
23. C.R. *Family Letters* 18.2.1892
24. Harry Ransom Humanities Research Center University of Texas at Austin MSS
25. C.R. *Family Letters* 10.6.1885
26. *The Bookman* February 1895
27. HRHRC University of Texas MSS
28. *The Bookman* February 1895

29. *The Bookman* 'Santa Christina' January 1912
30. C.R. *Family Letters* 19.1.1886
31. MacKenzie Bell *Christina Rossetti*
32. Diary of Frances Rossetti from C.R. *Family Letters*

CHAPTER SEVENTEEN

 1. W.M.R. *Some Reminiscences* Vol. II
 2. C.R. *Family Letters* 21.4.1886
 3. Ashley MSS British Library 1386
 4. Ford Madox Ford *Ancient Lights*
 5. C.R. *Family Letters*
 6. Ibid. 10.12.1888
 7. British Columbia MSS
 8. C.R. *Family Letters* 23.4.1891
 9. MacKenzie Bell *Christina Rossetti* p. 129
10. C.R. *Family Letters* 8.5.1888
11. Ibid. 6.12.1990
12. Ibid. 8.5.1888
13. C.R. *The Face of the Deep* p. 528
14. Ibid. p. 495
15. Ibid. p. 490
16. Ford Madox Ford *Ancient Lights*
17. C.R. *Family Letters* November 1889
18. Ibid. 20.5.1892
19. Ibid. 23.5.1892
20. W.M.R. Diary from C.R. *Family Letters*
21. C.R. *Family Letters* 20.3.92
22. W.M.R. Diary 5.9.92, from C.R. *Family Letters*
23. C.R. *Family Letters* 9.11.1892
24. M.F. Sandars *The Life of Christina Rossetti* London 1930
25. MacKenzie Bell *Christina Rossetti* p. 137
26. W.M.R. *Some Reminiscences*
27. Ibid.
28. MacKenzie Bell *Christina Rossetti* p. 182
29. Ashley MSS British Library 4994

CHAPTER EIGHTEEN

 1. *Some Recollections of Jean Ingelow by her Early Friends* London 1901
 2. W.M.R. *Some Reminiscences*
 3. C.R. *Poetical Works* (Preface)
 4. *Cosmopolitan Magazine* June 1895
 5. *The National Review* February 1895
 6. MacKenzie Bell *Christina Rossetti* Ch.10
 7. Jean Ingelow *Poems* Honour 1863
 8. *The Pelican Guide to English Literature* Vol. 6.
 9. Ibid.
10. V. Woolf *The Nation and Athenaeum* 6.12.1930 and *The Common Reader*
11. Willa Cather, *Nebraska State Journal*, 13.1.1895

12. Dora Greenwell *Our Single Women* from *Essays*
13. Germaine Greer *Goblin Market* Stonehill Pub. Co. New York 1975

SELECT BIBLIOGRAPHY

MANUSCRIPTS

The University of Texas at Austin, Harry Ransom Humanities Research Center

The University of British Columbia (which now holds the Helen Rossetti–Angeli-Imogen Dennis collection previously at the Bodleian Library)

The British Library, London (the Ashley Library MSS which include seven of Christina's notebooks)

The Bodleian Library Collection, Oxford (Includes nine of Christina's notebooks and photocopies of the British Columbia MSS deposited by Georgina Battiscombe)

Material relating to W.B. Scott and the Trevelyan family is held by the University of Newcastle upon Tyne

BOOKS AND PERIODICALS

Acland, Alice *Caroline Norton* Constable 1948

Allingham, William *The Diary of William Allingham* London 1907

Angeli, Helen Rossetti *Rossetti: His Friends and His Enemies* London 1949

Athenaeum 7 August 1897 'A Poetic Trio'

Battiscombe, Georgina *Christina Rossetti: A Divided Life* London 1981

Bell, MacKenzie *Christina Rossetti* London 1898

Beerbohm, Max *Rossetti and His Circle* London 1922

Bornand, Odette *Diary of W.M. Rossetti 1870–73* Oxford 1977

Bowra, C.M. *The Romantic Imagination* London 1949

Browning, Elizabeth Barrett   *Aurora Leigh* London 1856
                                        Poetical Works Oxford 1916

Burne-Jones, Georgina *Memorials of Edward Burne-Jones* London 1904

Caine, T. Hall *Recollections of Dante Gabriel Rossetti* London 1882 and 1922

Cather, Willa   *Nebraska State Journal* 13.1.1895
                        The Troll Garden New York 1905

Charles, E.K. *Christina Rossetti: Critical Perspectives* London 1988

Chitham, Edward *Emily Brontë* London 1984

Contemporary Review, The 'The Fleshly School of Poetry' October 1871

Cook, Eliza *Poetical Works* London 1869

Crump, R.W. *Christina Rossetti: A Reference Guide* Boston 1976

D'Amico, Diane *Victorian Poetry* Vol. 27 No. 1 1989. 'A New Reading of Christina
    Rossetti's "From Sunset to Star Rise"'

Dickinson, Emily *The Complete Poems* ed. T.H. Johnson Faber & Faber London 1970

Dorling, William *Dora Greenwell: A Memoir* London 1885

Doughty, O. and Wahl, J. *Letters of Dante Gabriel Rossetti* Oxford 1965

Duffy, Maureen *The Erotic World of Faery* London 1972

Evans, B. Ifor 'The Sources of Christina Rossetti's Goblin Market' *The Modern Language
    Review* April 1933

Rowton, Frederick ed. *Female Poets of Great Britain* London 1848

Ford, Ford Madox   *Ancient Lights* London 1911
                    The Pre-Raphaelite Brotherhood London 1907

Forster, Margaret *Elizabeth Barrett Browning* Chatto & Windus 1988

Freud and Breuer *Studies on Hysteria* Penguin Books 1974

Gaskell, Elizabeth *Wives and Daughters* London 1906

Gaunt, William *The Pre-Raphaelite Tragedy* London 1942

Gérin, Winifred *Emily Brontë* London 1971

Germ, The January, February, April, May 1850

Gilbert, Sandra M. and Gubar, Susan *The Madwoman in the Attic* Yale University Press
    1979

Gilchrist, Grace 'Christina Rossetti' *Good Words* December 1896

Gilchrist, H. *Anne Gilchrist: Her Life and Writings* London 1887

Gosse, Edmund   *Critical Kit-Kats* London 1896
                 Algernon Charles Swinburne London 1917

Greenwell, Dora   *Poems* 1848
                   Essays 1866
                   'Our Single Women' *North British Review* February 1862
                   Two Friends 1867
                   Carmina Crucis 1869
                   See also William Dorling

Greer, Germaine Introduction to *Goblin Market* Stonehill Publishing Company, New
    York 1975

Hake, Thomas *Memoirs of Eighty Years* London 1892

Hatton, Gwynneth *An Edition of the Unpublished Poems of Christina Rossetti* (Oxford Thesis)
    1965

Hemans, Felicia *The Poetical Works of Felicia Hemans* ed. W.B. Rossetti with Memoir
    London 1879

Hill, G.B. ed. *Letters of D.G.R. to William Allingham 1854-70* London 1897

Hinkson, Katharine Tynan   'Christina Rossetti' *The Bookman* February 1895
                            'Santa Christina' *The Bookman* January 1912

Hopkins, Gerard Manley   *Notebooks and Papers* ed. H. House Oxford 1939
                          Poems ed. Robert Bridges London 1918 and 1930

Hunt, Holman *Pre-Raphaelitism and the Pre-Raphaelite Brotherhood* London 1905 2 Vols

Hunt, Violet *The Wife of Rossetti* London 1932

Ingelow, Jean *Poems* London 1863

Some Recollections of Jean Ingelow by Her Early Friends London 1901

Landon, Laetitia Elizabeth   *The Improvatrice* London 1824
                              The Troubadour London 1825
                              The Golden Violet London 1827

The Venetian Bracelet London 1829

Poetical Works London 1850

Life and Literary Remains ed. L. Blanchard London 1841

Leighton, Angela 'The Fallen Woman and The Woman Poet' *Victorian Poetry* Vol. 27, No. 2, 1989

Lurie, Alison 'Witches and Fairies' *New York Review of Books* 2.12.1971

Macmillan, G. ed. *The Letters of Alexander Macmillan* London 1908

Marsh, Jan   *Pre-Raphaelite Women* Weidenfield & Nicolson 1987

Elizabeth Siddal London 1989

McNeil, Helen *Emily Dickinson* Virago Pioneers 1986

Meynell, Alice   'Christina Rossetti' *The New Review* February 1895

The Colour of Life and Other Essays London 1896

Mills, Ernestine *Life and Letters of Frederick Shields* Longman Green 1912

Moers, Ellen *Literary Women* London 1976

Norton, Caroline 'Goblin Market and Other Poems' *Macmillans Magazine* September 1863

Packer, L.M.   *Christina Rossetti* Cambridge University Press 1963

ed. *The Rossetti–Macmillan Letters* University of California Press 1963

Parris, Leslie ed. *Pre-Raphaelite Papers* London 1984

Patterson, Rebecca *The Riddle of Emily Dickinson* London 1978

Pelican Guide to English Literature, The Vol. 6 London 1958

Proctor, Ellen A. *A Brief Memoir of C.G. Rossetti* London 1895

Robinson, A. Mary F. *Emily Brontë* London 1883

Roe, Sue ed. *Women Reading Women's Writing* Harvester 1987

Rossetti, Christina Georgina (in order of publication)

Verses G. Polidori 1847

Goblin Market and Other Poems Macmillan 1862

The Prince's Progress and Other Poems Macmillan 1866

Poems Robert Bros. Boston 1866

'Dante: An English Classic' *Churchman's Shilling Magazine* May 1867

Commonplace and Other Stories F.S. Ellis 1870

Sing-Song Routledge and Sons 1872

Annus Domini 1874 James Parker & Co.

Speaking Likenesses Macmillan 1874

Goblin Market, The Prince's Progress and Other Poems Macmillan 1875

Seek and Find SPCK 1879

A Pageant and Other Poems Macmillan 1881

Called to be Saints SPCK 1881

Letter and Spirit SPCK 1883

'Dante: The Poet Illustrated out of the Poem' *Century Magazine* 1884

Time Flies SPCK 1885

Poems Macmillans 1890

The Face of the Deep SPCK 1892

'The House of D.G.R.' *Literary Opinion* 1892

Verses SPCK 1893

                           New Poems ed. W.M. Rossetti Macmillan 1896

                           Maude James Bowden 1897

                           Poetical Works with Memoir ed. W.M. Rossetti 1904

Rossetti, Dante Gabriel   *The Poetical Works of D.G. Rossetti* ed. W.M. Rossetti London 1900

                           The Collected Works of D.G. Rossetti ed. W.M. Rossetti London 1886

                           Letters of D.G.R. to William Allingham ed. G.B. Hill London 1897

Rossetti, William Michael   *D.G. Rossetti: Family Letters* with Memoir 2 Vols London 1895

                           Pre-Raphaelite Diaries and Letters London 1900

                           The Rossetti Papers 1862-70 London 1903

                           Some Reminiscences 2 Vols London 1906

                           The Family Letters of Christina Rossetti 1908

Rowton, Frederick ed. *Female Poets of Great Britain* London 1848

Ruskin, John   *Sesame and Lilies* 1871

             Of Queens' Gardens 1902

Sandars, Mary F. *The Life of Christina Rossetti* London 1930

Scott, William Bell   *The Year of the World* London 1846

                    Poems London 1854

                    Autobiographical Notes ed. W. Minto London 1892

Sharp, William 'Some Reminiscences of Christina Rossetti' *The Atlantic Monthly* June 1895

Showalter, Elaine *The Female Malady* Virago 1987

Sisson, Charles H. ed. *Christina Rossetti: Selected Poems* Carcanet 1984

Spark, Muriel and Stanford D. *Emily Brontë: Her Life and Work* London 1966

Stevenson, L. *The Pre-Raphaelite Poets* University of California 1972

Swinburne, A.C.   *A Century of Roundels* London 1883

                     A Midsummer Holiday and Other Poems London 1884

Tilt, Edward J. *On the Preservation of the Health of Women* London 1851

Trevelyan, Raleigh *A Pre-Raphaelite Circle* Hamish Hamilton 1975

Troxell, Janet C. *Three Rossettis: Unpublished Letters* Harvard University Press 1937

Vicinus, Martha, *Suffer and be Still* London 1972

Watts-Dunton, Theodore 'Christina Rossetti' *Athenaeum* 5.1.1895

Webster, Augusta   *Portraits* London 1870

                 Mothers and Daughters 1895

Weintraub, Stanley *Four Rossettis* London 1976

Woolf, Virginia   *The Second Common Reader* 1932

              Women and Writing Women's Press 1979

Yonge, Charlotte M. *Womankind* London 1876

INDEX

OXFORD

MORE OXFORD PAPERBACKS

Details of a selection of other Oxford Paperbacks follow. A complete list of Oxford Paperbacks, including The World's Classics, Twentieth-Century Classics, OPUS, Past Masters, Oxford Authors, Oxford Shakespeare, and Oxford Paperback Reference, is available in the UK from the General Publicity Department, Oxford University Press (RS), Walton Street, Oxford, OX2 6DP.

In the USA, complete lists are available from the Paperbacks Marketing Manager, Oxford University Press, 200 Madison Avenue, New York, NY 10016.

Oxford Paperbacks are available from all good bookshops. In case of difficulty, customers in the UK can order direct from Oxford University Press Bookshop, 116 High Street, Oxford, Freepost, OX1 4BR, enclosing full payment. Please add 10 per cent of the published price for postage and packing.

WOMEN'S STUDIES FROM
OXFORD PAPERBACKS

Ranging from the *A–Z of Women's Health* to *Wayward Women: A Guide to Women Travellers*, Oxford Paperbacks cover a wide variety of social, medical, historical, and literary topics of particular interest to women.

DESTINED TO BE WIVES

The Sisters of Beatrice Webb

Barbara Caine

Drawing on their letters and diaries, Barbara Caine's fascinating account of the lives of Beatrice Webb and her sisters, the Potters, presents a vivid picture of the extraordinary conflicts and tragedies taking place behind the respectable façade which has traditionally characterized Victorian and Edwardian family life.

The tensions and pressures of family life, particularly for women; the suicide of one sister; the death of another, probably as a result of taking cocaine after a family breakdown; the shock felt by the older sisters at the promiscuity of their younger sister after the death of her husband are all vividly recounted. In all the crises they faced, the sisters formed the main network of support for each other, recognizing that the 'sisterhood' provided the only security in a society which made women subordinate to men, socially, legally, and economically.

Other women's studies titles:

A–Z of Women's Health   Derek Llewellyn-Jones
'Victorian Sex Goddess': Lady Colin Campbell and the Sensational Divorce Case of 1886   G. H. Fleming
Wayward Women: A Guide to Women Travellers
Jane Robinson
Catherine the Great: Life and Legend   John T. Alexander

OXFORD LIVES

Based on original research and written in each case by acknowledged experts on their subject, the authoritative accounts included in the Oxford Lives series are the best biographies available.

RODIN

Frederic Grunfeld

Until the publication of this book, Auguste Rodin, the greatest sculptor of the nineteenth century, had been notoriously ill-served by his biographers. 'All the stuff written about him' commented George Bernard Shaw 'is ludicrous cackle and piffle.'

Frederic Grunfeld's original and exhaustive research has enabled him to penetrate the legends perpetrated by Rodin's earlier hagiographers and detractors. For the first time a clear picture of Rodin's life emerges: his impoverished youth, his many love-affairs, his friendships and enmities, his public life, and above all his devotion to art and the life-long struggle to achieve official recognition without compromise.

The age in which Rodin lived is also vividly conveyed. After his early successes Rodin was surrounded by the wealthy and famous. Zola, Balzac, Rilke, R. L. Stevenson, Edith Wharton, Debussy, Oscar Wilde, Edward VII, Clemenceau, and Kaiser Wilhelm II are just some of Rodin's famous contemporaries who figure in his life story, and without whom the story would not be complete.

'Frederic Grunfeld has written a biography which by any normal standards must be called definitive. It is deliciously crammed with information . . . Rodin's erotic obsessions are explored with a degree of tact rare among modern block-buster biographies.' *Sunday Telegraph*

Also in Oxford Lives:

Clara Schumann: The Artist and the Woman   Nancy B. Reich
Gladstone 1809–1874   H. C. G. Matthew
Nikolai Gogol   Vladimir Nabokov
James Joyce   Richard Ellmann

OXFORD POETS

Oxford Paperbacks has one of the finest lists of contemporary poetry. It includes well-established and highly regarded names, as well as exciting newcomers from Britain, America, Europe, and the Commonwealth.

Winner of the 1989 Whitbread Prize for Poetry

SHIBBOLETH

Michael Donaghy

This is Michael Donaghy's first full-length collection. His work has a wit and grace reminiscent of the metaphysical poets, and his subjects range widely, responding in unexpected ways to his curiosity and inventiveness. Among the varied pieces collected here are a number of love poems remarkable for their blend of tenderness and irony; a terse 'news item'; playful 'translations' of a mythical Welsh poet; and an 'interview' with Marcel Duchamp.

As the American critic Alfred Corn says:
'Michael Donaghy's poems have the fine-tuned precision of a ten-speed bike, the wit of a streetwise don, a polyphonic inventiveness . . . Poems so original, wry, and philosophical as these are hard to come by. Don't think of passing them up.'

Also in Oxford Poets:

Blood and Family   Thomas Kinsella
Selected Poems   Fleur Adcock
On Ballycastle Beach   Medbh McGuckian
Adventures with My Horse   Penelope Shuttle